FOUNDATIONS OF THE TEMPLE

A Witchcraft Tradition of Love, Will & Wisdom

by
Christopher Penczak

COPPER CAULDRON
PUBLISHING

Credits

Editing: Raye Snover (lead editor) with Michael Cantone, Antonella Erconlani, Justin Gaudet, Silver Lyons
Cover Art: Terra Nova Creative • *terranovacreative.com*
Interior Art: Mark Bilokur, Derek O'Sullivan, Christopher Penczak
Cover Design: Terra Nova Creative • *terranovacreative.com*
Layout & Publishing: Steve Kenson

Acknowledgements

Special thanks to all the members of the Temple, particularly our Board of Directors, Council Leaders, Ministers, Deputies, Volunteers, and Legal and Business Advisors who brought the vision of the Temple into physical and communal reality. In particular, we are appreciative of those who started this venture together, including Alix Wright, Cami Wright, Jocelyn VanBokkelen, Mary Hurley, Bonnie Boulanger, Michael Cantone, Matooka Moonbear MacGowan, Wrentek Kerne MacGowan, Silver Lyons, Wesley Lyons, Nimue Lyons, Derek O'Sullivan, Mark Bilokur, Frater C, Nicole Dupré, Christopher Giroux, Elsa Elliott, Bonnie Kraft, Rama Danu, Stevie Grant, Lisa Kulis, Deb Brown, Krista Carmichael, Carolyn Kepes, Steve Kenson, and Adam Sartwell.

Disclaimer

This book and all included spells, rituals, formulas, and advice in it are not substitutes for professional medical advice. Please confer with a medical professional before using any herbs, remedies, or teas in any manner. Unless specifically indicated, formulas are not intended to be consumed or ingested. The publisher and author are not responsible for the misuse of this material.

Copper Cauldron Publishing does not endorse any suppliers or resources mentioned by contributors.

Copyright ©2014 Temple of Witchcraft, All Rights Reserved. Foundations of the Temple of Witchcraft is a trademark of the Temple of Witchcraft, in the United States and/or other countries. No part of this work may be reproduced, stored in a retrieval system, or transmitted in any form or by any means, without the prior permission in writing of the Copyright Owner, nor be otherwise circulated in any form other than that in which it is published.

For more information visit:

www.templeofwitchcraft.org

www.coppercauldronpublishing.com

ISBN 978-1-940755-01-4, First Printing

Printed in the U.S.A.

Our goal is the initiation of consciousness

in alignment with Love, Will, and Wisdom

to perform the Great Work.

• • •

We seek the

restoration, sustainment, and evolution

of humanity

to the Garden of the Gods

• • •

We partner with the holy races

of Angels, Faeries and Creatures

with the Stars, with Nature, and with the Ancestors,

to be at One with the Heart, Mind, and Will of the Divine

Other Temple of Witchcraft Related Books

Copper Cauldron Publishing
The Three Rays of Witchcraft by Christopher Penczak
Tastes from the Temple by Dawn Hunt and the Temple of Witchcraft Community
The Plant Spirit Familiar by Christopher Penczak
The Green Lovers edited by Christopher Penczak
The Mighty Dead by Christopher Penczak
Ancestors of the Craft edited by Christopher Penczak
The Waters and Fires of Avalon by Christopher Penczak and the Temple of Witchcraft Community

Llewellyn Publications
The Inner Temple of Witchcraft by Christopher Penczak
The Inner Temple of Witchcraft CD Companion by Christopher Penczak
The Outer Temple of Witchcraft by Christopher Penczak
The Outer Temple of Witchcraft CD Companion by Christopher Penczak
The Temple of Shamanic Witchcraft by Christopher Penczak
The Temple of Shamanic Witchcraft CD Companion by Christopher Penczak
The Temple of High Witchcraft by Christopher Penczak
The Temple of High Witchcraft CD Companion by Christopher Penczak
The Living Temple of Witchcraft Vol. I by Christopher Penczak
The Living Temple of Witchcraft Vol. I CD Companion by Christopher Penczak
The Living Temple of Witchcraft Vol. II by Christopher Penczak
The Living Temple of Witchcraft Vol. II CD Companion by Christopher Penczak

TABLE OF CONTENTS

Introduction 1
Chapter One: The History of the Temple 5
   Coven of the New Dawn Seal 10
Chapter Two: Why Witchcraft? 15
Chapter Three: Structure: Spiritual and Terrestrial 25
  The Body of the Temple 25
   Dodecagram with the Zodiac Signs 28
  The Leadership of the Temple 31
   Temple Organizational Chart 34
  Membership Levels 35
  A Magickal Order 39
Chapter Four: Beliefs of the Temple 47
  Divinity 48
   The Pentacle of Divinity 49
  Cosmology 57
   Elemental Wheel 58
   Three Orientations of the Elements 59
   Septagram with Principles 60
   The Three Rays 62
  Magick 62
   Triune Soul Model 64
  Nature & Occult Tradition 68
Chapter Five:
Allies in the Temple 72
  The Temple Egregore 73
   Morrighan T-shirt Design by Derek O'Sullivan 76
Chapter Six: The Temple Sigil and Symbols 89
   The Temple Sigil 89
   Pentagram with the Elements 90
   Tree of Life 91
   Hexagram with the Planets 93
   Temple Ministry Sigils 95
   TAllAT Sigil 95
Chapter Seven: The Teachings of the Temple 97
  The Great Work 108
  The Garden of the Gods 110
  Formula for Temple Initiation 115
   Elemental Initiation Circle 124
  Spiritual Concepts within the Temple 125
Chapter Eight: Core Practices 135
   Symbols of Balance 142

Chapter Nine: Holy Days and Rituals **162**
Founders' Rituals 218
TempleFest 219
   TempleFest 2014 design by Mark Bilokur..220
Chapter Ten: Witchcraft Culture **221**
Modernity and Tradition 221
We Are the Other People 225
Muggles, Cowans & the Garden of the Gods...................228
Wisdom Sayings 230
Spiritual Virtues 236
   Belenus by Derek O'Sullivan...243
Customs and Views 250
Appendix One: Birth Chart of the Temple **267**
   Birth Chart of the Temple of Witchcraft..267
Appendix Two: Articles of Incorporation............................**270**
Appendix Three: Temple By-Laws **275**
Appendix Four: Temple Policies **291**
Appendix Five: Frequently Asked Questions.......................**293**
Appendix Six: Glossary of Terms..**297**

Introduction

At a Temple of Witchcraft leadership retreat, someone asked a question about the founding of the Temple. I answered, and that lead to another question about the structure of the Temple. Following that was a question on the spiritual powers involved in the Temple's rituals. It soon became clear to me that while we had all the answers to these questions in various places, there was not one resource where they could be answered at once, not only for leadership, but for members and other interested parties.

Though relatively new in terms of public work in the NeoPagan movement, the undercurrents of the Temple of Witchcraft have been around for many years in the New England area. As we have grown, everyone has different parts of the story, depending on their level of training, and when they joined us in the story. Some parts are more likely to be forgotten, and others emphasized. Some are lost in the necessary evil of legal language when forming Articles of Incorporation and By-Laws.

At the third annual gathering of the Temple in a festival we host, TempleFest 2012, I was asked to give a workshop on all things in the Temple of Witchcraft tradition. We had most of the lead ministers in attendance along with a lot of brand new people, and those who had been members, students, and guests over the years. People got a chance to hear more about the history and structure and ask questions. They encouraged me to get more of this information out to those interested, as we have a unique perspective on a lot of ideas for community, magickal training, and mysticism. While in the era of modern media, I felt I should also fall back on my own passion, writing books. Even in this age of websites, social media, and online videos, sometimes the simplest answer is a book where a foundation can be laid. So you have in your hands the results of all these questions and encouragement: an overview of the Temple of Witchcraft for beginners and community members alike.

The Temple of Witchcraft considers itself a modern meritocracy of magick and spiritual evolution. Our guiding principle as described in our founding legal documents is:

The mission and purpose of the Organization shall be to aid the training of practitioners and clergy in the religious and spiritual traditions of Witchcraft, Wicca, Paganism, Heathenism, and other Earth-based traditions. We shall encourage, publish and teach these traditions and the arts associated with them. Further our organization shall provide a place where both public and private events may occur in accordance with our mission. Such events that will be included in our mission shall be educational workshops, classes, seasonal and astrological celebrations, rites of passage, spiritual guidance, interfaith outreach and community building events. Our focus shall be on the Spiritual Arts and Sciences, along with the personal and community development that occurs through such arts and sciences. The study of the aforementioned traditions includes; the study of mythology, culture, healing, and mysticism.

We shall provide these services through our organization and from time to time with other spiritually based organizations that share our similar philosophies. Our aim is the regeneration and advancement of the rich cultural, philosophical and religious heritage drawn from the related traditions of Witchcraft and Earth-based spiritual paths. We will also strive to provide to the public and the media accurate and concise information about Witchcraft and related Earth-based traditions.

While this gives us a wide range of goals and flexibility to work with in terms of a legal structure, our Members Handbook gives our purpose a little more poetic color:

The purpose of the Temple is to provide religious support to the Witchcraft, Pagan, and Magickal communities. Our work is twofold, being both otherworldly and terrestrial. We seek to provide experiences, teachings, and models to bring a closer connection between spirit and matter, through individual and community projects.

On an individual level, our goal is to awaken the potential of the human soul to its natural gifts of psychic awareness, communion with nature and the spirits and the ability to perform magick. Each individual seeks to live a magickal life and we help provide the support to understand and experience the mysteries of our tradition, and through it, the magick in every moment. Through these spiritual awakenings, we seek to expand the initiate's consciousness through the alignment of our souls with Love, Will, and Wisdom to complete what is known among magicians as "the Great Work." It is the fulfillment of your souls' purpose in this lifetime and the possibility to move to the next level of awareness beyond the Wheel of Fate.

Beyond the individual level, when we hold our vision of the world, we seek the restoration, sustainment, and evolution of humanity to the Garden of the Gods, the cooperative consciousness where all things are in harmony and community. Our ancient Pagan myths define this state of awareness as the First Garden, known as Avalon, Hesperides, Zep Tepi, Shamballa, Lemuria, Mu, the Blessed Isles, and even Eden from Judeo-Christian mythology. We manifest this vision through both our inner workings and service to the greater community. By these actions, we plant the seeds and tend the garden of Witchcraft culture, art, tradition, and community.

In essence we seek to be both a school and community for the evolution of the soul through the art, science, and religion of Witchcraft. Through the use of magickal spirituality, we seek to advance and evolve our understanding within the world. We provide education in both outer forms, explaining what is Witchcraft and magick, and the basic life skills that the arts and sciences can provide. We provide an opportunity to those willing to do deeper work in the spirit of the ancient mystery schools, set in the context of our modern life, including taking advantage of the rise of technology and communication. Ultimately this deeper education is at the heart of our mission. We furthermore provide the structure for a greater community to grow, whereby people can offer their own unique gifts to the community, as well as ask for and receive help. The more someone is able to operate in training and community in an effective and healthy manner, the more potential responsibility one is given to be a part of the organization and leadership.

Through this book we hope to share our own philosophies and systems to provide those seeking to know more about the Temple of Witchcraft a better understanding of not only the structure, but the underlying magickal thought behind the structure.

This book is a fundraiser for the Temple of Witchcraft. One hundred percent of the profits, or all money collected beyond the production, publication, and shipping of this book goes to the Temple of Witchcraft, which is a federally recognized 501(c)(3) religious organization/church. It draws from leadership retreat sessions, articles from our newsletter, *The Temple Bell,* our website, *templeofwitchcraft.org,* our membership and ministerial manuals and original information put down in print for the public for the first time.

I hope you enjoy it and find inspiration within it, whether your own path crosses that of the Temple and goes its own way, or flows along with ours for a time.

Blessed be,
Christopher Penczak
Co-Founder
July 2012 Full Moon

CHAPTER ONE: THE HISTORY OF THE TEMPLE

While one could argue that the formation of the Temple of Witchcraft was through a series of fortunate coincidences, in retrospect, I feel that everybody involved was guided through a slow and organic progression of tradition and community building. Even when I look back on the teachings, seemingly eclectic and scattershot at the start, a general cohesiveness in thought, philosophy, terminology, and ethos has developed that staggers my imagination. I know I did not have it in mind, so I can only assume I was part of a greater pattern and purpose.

The Temple teachings really began with my own journey into Witchcraft. I'm often asked if I came into the Craft through a Witchcraft family, as my mother was also a practitioner, but I actually started as a skeptic. A family friend and mentor revealed to me that she was a Witch when she saw my own troubled search for meaning after graduating Catholic High School. I was certain I was not Catholic, but not sure of what I would be. I looked into eastern philosophy—Taoism, Buddhism, Hinduism—though I found it interesting, I didn't find anything that clicked on anything more than an intellectual level. I had an earlier appreciation for alchemy and herbalism, but cast that in the area of childhood play, a desire to "make potions" and not any deep spirituality. Most of the histories on alchemy at the time end with "and alchemy turned out not to be real, but paved the way for modern chemistry." I almost became a chemical engineer because of that, but at the last possible moment in my high school career I veered into music and ended up going to college for a degree in music performance. The mix of scientific interest and artistic expression was exactly what I needed to later appreciate Witchcraft.

My initial interest was to pull my older mentor out of the obvious cult she had joined. It seemed crazy to me. How does a rational, successful woman, whom I admired greatly, raising two children as a single mom and running her own business, get confused enough to think she is a Witch and can cast spells? I wanted to understand so I could reason with her. The more I learned, the more I liked what she had to say. She didn't tell me until I was eighteen, as Witches don't believe in proselytizing. This was in the days before we even thought about Pagan and Witchcraft families and households, or equal civil rights. Witchcraft in her mind would always be on the fringe. She explained that while there were groups and organizations, covens and orders, there was no one way for everyone, and no one Witch "Pope" though quite a few people acted as if they were the Pope of All Witches. Soon I was attending her coven's open Moon rituals, or esbats, and she was tutoring me in meditation, tarot and the basics of the altar and tools.

After some pretty amazing experiences, she felt she had taught me as much as she could and sent me to her own teacher, Laurie Cabot, the Official Witch of Salem, Massachusetts. At the time Laurie was focused on teaching Witchcraft independently in three degrees. The Cabot Tradition would later go on to form its own non-profit organization, the Cabot-Kent Hermetic Temple. The first degree is Witchcraft as a Science, dedicated to the study of alpha trance, psychic development, meditation, and understanding the principles behind magick and meditation. The second degree is Witchcraft as an Art and Science, covering more familiar Witchcraft concepts of the magick circle, spell-casting, and formulation. One is considered a Priest or Priestess after the second degree. The third degree, which I did not take at the time, is Witchcraft as a Religion. It was training for clergy to be High Priestesses and High Priests.

In my own classes for the first and second degree was my mother and one of our best family friends, someone I consider a sister. When we graduated in 1993, the three of us began practicing as a study circle and eventually called ourselves a coven. At first I was really excited to share what I had learned with some close friends. Unfortunately these were close friends from my Catholic School days who were more religious than I realized and I lost many of them. I decided to be a little more discreet about what I shared and with whom. Still people at the music college of my university noticed a shift in me. I was more happy, more confident, more in tune. Many asked me what I was doing. I slowly shared with a few people, and it didn't hurt that my spirit sister in my coven was attending the same school to get the word around that we were Witches. I found myself with a group of people interested in learning more.

Initially I wanted to send them to my mentor, but she was not "out of the broom closet" and didn't want the attention. She later opened her own Witchcraft store, but at the time she didn't want to be public. I then sent them to Salem, Massachusetts, and Laurie Cabot, but Laurie was taking a bit of a sabbatical from her usually heavy teaching schedule. She stopped teaching at Crow Haven Corner, a store her daughter Jody owned and was looking for a new "home base." She had many false starts and it wouldn't be until years later that she would again open her own shop on Pickering Wharf. So soon I was leading a once a month meditation group, sharing little bits of what I knew and felt confident sharing. We did meditations, past-life regression, and some healing work.

In 1995 I met my partner Steve Kenson and, along with beginning a romance, he shared with me a wide range of magickal practices I was not familiar with, including Core Shamanism, Hermetic Qabalah, and Chaos Magick. I had also begun studies in metaphysics outside of more traditional Witchcraft and Wicca, which would eventually lead me into holistic health paradigms, yoga, Theosophy, and Celtic Reconstructionism. I also graduated from college just before, and began my career in the Boston music industry.

Through the urgings of the people around us, our once a month study group expanded into a coven, as well as a spiritual book club, and eventually classes. While Laurie wasn't teaching, I was asked to teach what I knew in a formal Witchcraft class. I resisted for a long while.

Along with the urgings from people, I started having visions in my meditations of my matron goddess, Macha, an Irish Crow and Horse Goddess. While I find her loving, I do agree with the Celtic lore that she is also forceful. She would appear, nose to nose with me, telling me "You need to teach more." I would be startled, and eventually outright refuse. Anytime I did not agree, the meditation vision would end and I would snap back to waking consciousness. My personal practice began to suffer and I relied on it pretty thoroughly to navigate my job at Fort Apache, a local Boston recording studio turned record label and artist management company. After several weeks, I agreed in frustration. She smiled, promised I would never have to worry about money and would be taken care of, and disappeared. The blocks in my personal practice dissolved. My job also dissolved in three days, as I received a lay-off notice.

Try as I might, I could not get an office job, temporary or otherwise, in the area. As a Sun sign Taurus, I needed to know when my next pay check was coming. I applied and was accepted for eight temporary jobs. Each suddenly filled the position with someone permanent either before I got there or a day or two into the job. None lasted more than three days and the last employer's office burned down the night before I began! I decided with the urging of all my loved ones to take it as a sign and began writing some ideas I'd had, that would later become my first book, *City Magick*. I also began putting up two sets of flyers: Meditation Classes and Witchcraft Classes. I got much more interest in the Witchcraft Classes. I started with my monthly study group.

I altered and expanded a bit of what I learned from Witchcraft I and created a seven week class. When it was done, I was asked for more, so I did the same with Witchcraft II. The group was still anxious for more information, so I took the experiences and ideas of my personal practice and began forming the foundations of what would eventually become Witchcraft III, IV and V in the Temple of

Witchcraft. As friends and family noticed the beneficial changes in these first students from the coven, they too, sought out classes. Between word of mouth and what little flyer advertising I had done, the classes expanded.

Many of those involved in the first class also became involved in a quarterly newsletter I began with Steve, called *The Second Road*. My contacts at the local metaphysical and occult stores where we distributed the newsletter led to some invitations to teach, starting with the prestigious Unicorn Books in Arlington, MA, where I first took over their Wheel of the Year celebrations and then their Witchcraft classes, until their eventual closing in 2006 and the follow up community group Lap of the Goddess until 2009.

Along with members of the Unicorn Books community, as well as some that would be future members of the Temple of Witchcraft, we coordinated and performed a global spell for marriage equality rights for all gay, lesbian, bisexual, and transgender people. It was planned to occur on the first full Moon after the 35th anniversary of the New York Stonewall Riots. We performed it on Thursday, July 1. 2004 at Unicorn Books. It was part of an effort with *magickalactivism.com*, a short lived web based movement. The current shifts of marriage rights for GLBT people could be pointed at as the initial success and work of the spell.

My mother and I also held a semi-public Samhain celebration at her home in conjunction with the coven for thirteen years and the coven held various semi-public rituals, including some at America's Stonehenge. The coven itself went through a few iterations before finding stability in the identity of the Coven of the New Dawn.

By the end of 1998, I was teaching five nights a week, making a full-time living and coordinating a system of teaching that became known as The Temple of Witchcraft. Small packets of class notes were expanded again and again until they were made into a book format and the first, *The Inner Temple of Witchcraft*, was published by Llewellyn Publications in 2002, along with a CD companion of all the meditations and exercises. Subsequent books followed, generating six books and CD sets for the five level teaching system, and the concept traveled across the world, wherever Llewellyn books were distributed.

Coven of the New Dawn Seal

In 2005, Steve and I met Adam Sartwell, a natural Witch and psychic from Vermont who was already familiar with the *Temple of Witchcraft* books and incorporated aspects of them into his own practice. He was also greatly influenced by rural traditions of folk magick, Hawaiian Huna, and The Silva Mind Control Method. His own understanding and traditions influenced me in the writing of the remaining books in the series and subsequent classes. Particularly, he influenced the development and importance of the Three Soul model in the Temple, naming the three souls the Watcher, Namer, and Shaper. His devotion to the Greek goddess of Witchcraft, Hecate, as well as our mutual experiences with Hecate in the Between the Worlds festival community, led to our ninth "Sabbat," the Feast of Hecate, which we celebrate annually in the Temple on August 13th. Steve's own later experiences and studies brought ecstatic magick, trance possession, and New Orleans style Neo-Voodoo, or "Voodoo Nouveau," to the mix as well as a healthy love of Chaos Magick. Looking at *The Charge of the Goddess*, whereby "All acts of love and pleasure are my rituals" the three of us entered into a romantic triad relationship. This provided an additional platform for the eventual Temple to embrace a wide range of sexual and romantic expressions.

The self-identified archetypes of the relationship—Sorcerer, Knight, and Faery Prince—became seeds for the eventual evolution of the *Three Rays of Witchcraft*, material that became central to the evolution and advancement of the Temple beyond the publicly available books published by Llewellyn. The public archetypes became Sorcerer, Sovereign, and Seer. The three of us eventually founded Copper Cauldron Publishing, LLC, to create and distribute more advanced materials and products. Originally we created Copper Cauldron as a cooperative effort to help financially support the Temple but at the request of the federal government, the publishing work was separated from the Temple itself.

With the public classes and rituals, and availability of the material, the system soon began forming a community of those who identified with the Temple teachings. Many were seeking greater identity and belonging in the Neopagan community. Other Witches had clear names to identify shared history, beliefs and rituals. People identified as Gardnerian, Alexandrian, Anderson Feri, Reclaiming, Blue Star Wicca, or Cabot. No such label or organization existed for those involved with what would be known as the Temple teachings.

The original impetus was tools and techniques, not community, but community and the interactions of community often are a technique in the evolution of the soul. Many did not seek to become teachers "hiving off" from a parent coven to create a new coven. That can be good, as not everyone is called to be a teacher, and those who do teach and are not truly called to teach often do not do well in the long term for themselves or students. Guilt should not be the motivating force of a teacher. Many graduates sought to serve as ministers, but not teachers and were at a loss as to how to go about such service in the Pagan or mainstream community. Some got legally ordained through other organizations. Many went on to other traditions and some just languished, not knowing what comes next.

After a very brief period where some students, seeking this, identified themselves, sometimes in jest and sometimes seriously, as either "Christopherians" or "Penczakians," I decided to take action.

While the traditions named after their founders serve a wonderful purpose in the evolution of Witchcraft, I feel there does not need to be any more of them, and if we were to use a name, the name should reflect the changing energies of the new aeon and be beyond any one person or personality if it is to survive and thrive.

The teaching system that led to the community eventually led to the formation of a formal tradition administered by a legal body. I had spent eight years traveling around the country as a guest in many communities, festivals, and gatherings, and had the chance to observe and speak to many elders of our Pagan community, those who created the foundational organizations that began the recognition of our traditions. I got a chance to see what worked and what didn't, what ideas I liked and which I didn't. On some level I knew a greater shift of organization was coming, though at the time I wasn't planning on it being solely focused around the Temple teachings.

When that became clearer, I began the necessary vision work to deepen my own contacts with the spirits. First came Macha, and through her, the trinity of the Morrighan. Other deities made themselves known, most often those we called upon in public ritual and my personal practice. My own work in Theosophy deepened my understanding of what Witches call The Mighty Dead, the enlightened ancestors. I asked for those who would support this work and got inspired contact from these ancestors of Witchdom. Particular allies from the animal spirits and angelic realms made themselves known in the vision workings with myself, Steve, Adam and other key graduates and friends of the program. For me, it peaked in a vision of the Three Rays of Witchcraft which became the guiding paradigm of the Temple.

Soon the trio of Founders began forming the structure of the Temple, consulting with legal advisors on how to best incorporate in the state of New Hampshire and attain Federal recognition. The key was to create a legally recognizable structure for those in the government to understand, yet stay true to the organic and occult values of the modern Witchcraft movement. We developed a "meritocracy" similar to other occult fraternities. While consensus is an Aquarian ideal, we opted for a more will driven cooperation. The image of the web with many lines in and out of the center, yet many rings supporting the entire structure was used to guide, with twelve main "strands" to be the foundation, based upon the Zodiac.

We began gathering these leaders, looking to see who wanted to do what in community, and including them in the vision workings. From those gatherings a core group of leaders that would become the Board of Directors was formed, including our first other "official" Temple teacher, Alix Wright, and our business advisors Isis MacDare and Mary Hurley. Around the core formed a council of advisors, each focused upon a specific work within the Temple, through the proposed structure of twelve ministries supporting a Mystery School and Seminary. Many leaders and volunteers were drawn from the Coven of a New Dawn, as well as regular guests to the coven, until it was decided, due to personal shifts, goals, and careers to put the coven on indefinite hiatus and focus upon the Temple.

Some brought specific practices to the blend in forming the Temple. My own travels brought me into greater communication with esoteric authors with similar and complimentary teachings, including Orion Foxwood, T. Thorn Coyle, Michelle Belanger, and Raven Grimassi. My own work deepened through both study of alternative and "New Age" modalities of healing and further study and time with my first teacher, Laurie Cabot. Aries Lead Minister Michael Cantone brought an emphasis of martial arts and eastern mysteries. Scorpio Lead Minister Chris Giroux brought ancestor traditions from African traditions such as Ifa. Wrentek MacGown brought a strong Norse and Celtic influence, while Matooka Moonbear MacGown oversaw the Women's Mysteries in the Cancer Ministry along with her deputy Silver Lyons, and they connected us to the other Goddess traditions and the Red Tent Movement. Several students associated with the teachings of R.J. Stewart, John and Caitlin Matthews, Dion Fortune, and other Western occultist influenced our practices, as well as students involved in Tibetan Buddhism. We received enormous support from Kimberly Sherman-Cook, author and co-founder of the Pagan Education Network of Massachusetts, who guided us through the legal procedures. We incorporated in New Hampshire in 2009 and later applied for and received our 501(c)3 nonprofit federal status in 2010.

What formed was a modern structure to hold older ideas and traditions. Education was paramount, and the core system remained the same. Opportunities for community and service were created on a variety of levels, so no one person held the responsibility for ministering. Advanced education and cooperative projects were created. The temple continues its work in New England and has ministers and volunteers doing our work in locations around the United States, and through our online programs, members and students across the world.

The Temple really grew from continually asking the questions "Is there more?" and "What's next?" The teachings incorporate many view points looking for that world wisdom found everywhere in many different expressions. After every single training, there was a burning desire to find more to learn and incorporate. That ethos has been embodied in the idea that no one system or tradition, including the Temple, can have all the answers or even ask all the right questions. Asking "What's next?" includes both the personal practice and what is next in our way to serve the divine and the community, a modern take on the "Whom does the grail serve?" question of the Arthurian mysteries.

CHAPTER TWO: WHY WITCHCRAFT?

In the First Age, there was no need for Witches,
For everyone was like a witch.
Everyone knew they were magickal, a part of the Web.
Everyone drew life from one source, one well.
Everyone knew their Witch-soul.
When we forgot, we needed those to remind us.
When we fell asleep, we needed those to awaken us.
When we were in the dark, we needed those to keep the Spark of Magick alive.

Why would someone in this modern day and age, someone of sound mind and body, go around calling themselves a "Witch?" Why would you use that word? Witches are evil old women out to steal children, eat babies, and cause all manner of illness and strife, right? That is the image many have of the Witch, the green skinned, hooked nose, hagged face woman with a pointed hat riding around on a broom, brought to us most clearly by modern Halloween decorations. Those were exactly my thoughts fifteen years ago, when my first teacher used the "W" word with me. Little did I know then that I would later so strongly identify with the word Witch, find it so empowering for me and the people in my community, that I would use it to describe myself, too. In fact I found it so important to my spiritual practice, I co-founded an organization called the Temple of Witchcraft!

Since founding our tradition, I've realized how difficult it can be to operate in the mainstream world with the word "Witchcraft" in your name. It can be tough when listing religious services in newspapers, working with hospitals and prisons, and yet, as a legal church, that is a part of our ministry and outreach. I've had several people, whom I love, admire, and respect working on the fringes of traditional healing—yoga teachers, Reiki masters and homeopaths—ask: Why not use another word? Why not call it something else? You'd get more people interested in all the good work you do if you just changed the word. Have you thought about that?

We did. Truly. For a short time, we were going to call ourselves the Temple of Wisdom, as that name also embodied our principles. We look at Witchcraft as a wisdom tradition. Yet, if we, in this modern and "enlightened" age, don't take a stand and call ourselves what we really are, who will? It's much like asking a Christian organization, if Christianity were not so mainstream, to remove "Christ" from their name and teachings and just talk about love. While love is the heart of the Christian teachings, for a good Christian, such wisdom comes through the figure of Christ. For a Christian to deny him would be akin to following in the footsteps of the Apostle Peter, who denied Christ on the night he was betrayed. Christians grew as a tradition by living their faith with courage. Can we do any less?

I am a Witch. What I learned from my teachers is Witchcraft. They referred to themselves as Witches, and their teachers before them also called themselves Witches. While we imagine long dynasties of Witch traditions and families stretching through the centuries, popular scholarship now discourages that idea, but the name and identity had to come from somewhere. As modern Witchcraft was just coming out of the shadows, a new vocabulary was growing, and we used it to help introduce ourselves to our family, friends, and the world in a more gentle manner.

If someone asked us what we practiced religiously, we would start with the words "Earth Religion." If they asked questions or expressed an openness, perhaps we would describe our practices similar to

Native American traditions honoring the Earth, Sky, and the four directions, as we also do. Somehow once we passed the 1960s, Native American practices gained the perception of nobility and true spirituality, as well as being safe, to mainstream America, when prior they were unknown or seen as savage.

If our querent passed the Earth Religion test, we would use the word Pagan. Pagan is now a catch-all term for Earth traditions based upon mostly European cultures. It's a Latin word and used to refer to the people in the rural areas who had not quite converted to Christianity, so they were still Pagan. Some Pagans adopt the term in the Christian sense, meaning non-Judeo-Christian-Islamic, and adopt all other cultures into their paganism, including Asian, African, and South American cultures.

If the word Pagan didn't cause a stir, we would then use the word Wicca. Wicca is the modern, first legally-recognized term for our practices in the United States. For a long time, it was synonymous in our communities with the religion of Witchcraft, as there was not much variety. Wicca was a less scary word for people outside of our communities, when compared to Witchcraft. Today, Wicca refers to two complimentary, but different, streams of teachings. The first is British Traditional Wicca, specifically referring to the traditions known as Gardnerian and Alexandrian Wicca, and their immediate offshoots. Interestingly enough, the founders of those traditions usually spelled it "Wica," but it was fairly synonymous with Witchcraft. To be in those traditions, you must be trained and initiated by a qualified teacher or coven who has the authority to initiate. Mostly due to the independent streak of America, Solitary Wicca or Eclectic Wicca grew out of those teachings, but one had no formal training, and anyone could self-declare or self-initiate without the blessings of a group or teacher. Information was shared in books, online, and through simple, non-hierarchical circles.

If the person we were speaking to was not frightened by the word Wicca, then we said we were a Witch, and what we practiced was Witchcraft. We had laid sufficient groundwork to have a dialogue. Today, we are much more out of the shadows, with wider legal recognition, federally-recognized religious organizations, and even guidelines for military chaplains ministering to Wiccan and Pagan enlisted personnel. While such previous conversations were helpful, we must move forward to have ourselves recognized in our communities without apology. We are always happy to speak, to educate, and to work with people, but no other religion has to, or should, apologize for its name. We realize our traditions, theology, and history are very different from the majority of mainstream traditions currently recognized and run the risk of conforming too much to other organizations to be better recognized by the public, losing what makes Witchcraft so valuable and special for us in the first place. We don't worship in vast congregations or have the same ecclesiastical hierarchies. We don't see the world in the same way. We must preserve, develop, and share our particular viewpoint, and we can't do that if we are not true to ourselves.

The word Witchcraft is important to me. While we might not be practicing what our spiritual ancestors did three thousand or even three hundred years ago, the same can be said about many other religions that have grown and developed. The identity of the Witch throughout many times and cultures is a part of our ancestral inheritance. We are reverent of the Earth and our ancestors, and without a solid foundation in who, what, and where we have been, we cannot hope to forge a future. To divorce ourselves from our past is to lose valuable lessons in areas of religion, society, and power. Without our roots, we'd wither. We've managed to survive and regenerate due to the strong roots we have.

To understand the word helps us untangle misconceptions from the past and create a new future within the evolving global society, rather than completely outside it. There will always be something fringe to our tradition, for it is a mystery religion that is not for everyone. We do not profess to have the single answer for everyone. We simply hold open one of many gates into deeper wisdom.

Wicca is actually an old term for a male Witch and *wicce* for female, and forms the root of our word Witchcraft. While in our mythic view of our tradition many have translated Wicca as related to the words for wise, the most current etymological understanding is that is relates to terms meaning "to bend or shape" referring to our magick and healing. A *wiccan* simply means "to practice witchcraft" in Old English. As we trace the etymology back, we enter into trickier waters, as words with such a strong cultural bias as Witchcraft has, can be distorted. This is the etymology I learned, though admittedly it was from a Witch, so her interest was in furthering a positive image of the Old Religion, as she called it. Such a lineage does help those on the outside to understand how Witches see themselves, even if scholarship proves it to be more mythic than factual. The Middle High German *wicken* means "to bewitch or divine the future." It is traced to the Old German *wih*, meaning "holy." The Old Norman word *ve* is most likely related, and it means "temple." That is one of the reasons why we consider ourselves a temple tradition, and use the name Temple of Witchcraft, even though our temples are just as likely to be roofed by the sky and stars as they are to be physical buildings.

So with that perspective, you can see why restoring the understanding of our religion as "holy" is so important to me. That is why I used the word Witch to describe myself, and to connect to my long line of spiritual ancestors. That is why I use the name Witchcraft proudly to describe my path. Those who are drawn to our path resonate with the word. It is a beacon that gathers us. When I've taught the same material under the banner of Earth Spirituality, it drew fewer and less magickally inclined individuals. If everyone who identifies with the word were to use it, and be able to speak about it both personally and historically, we'd do well in evolving our culture's understanding of our path. That is a big part of our mission in the Temple of Witchcraft.

Why a "Temple" of Witchcraft?

One might ask that if Witches were traditionally on the fringe, at the edge of society, often alone, why do we need a public temple under the umbrella of a non-profit religious organization? It's a fair question, and before our establishment, one many of us struggled to answer.

While at one time our ancestors needed to work in the shadows to survive and thrive, and there will always be an element of shadow to our work, we are entering a time of light. We're not only opening up the doors to the Witch's Hut at the edge of the village, but many of us are setting up shop in the heart of the village, next to every other spiritual institution. There was a time when it was enough for people to quest for us, to seek the magick when in dire need on an individual basis. Now, in a time of great global change, it is not enough to let people seek us out. When the collective needs magick, we must go to the village, and be visible and available as a possibility.

Many say the next aeon is an Age of Light, and in this age, what some describe as the Age of Aquarius balancing the needs of the unique individual with the greater community, no one path has all the answers. The pluralistic, council view where wisdom and perspective is shared, is what will guide us. We believe wholeheartedly that the absence of many of the Witch's wisdoms in our modern worldview is what is killing the world, or at least our society upon it. It will only be with the addition of our perspective, along with many other Earth honoring, nature reverent traditions, that we will find our collective way. The ability to hold science and religion in either hand, in balance, is a necessary step in our evolution as a species. The ability to see the material as sacred as well as the intangible is another key to the current crisis to change our perspective. Most important is to look at the entire system of not only the planet, but the universe, as interconnected and alive, and rather than fighting amongst ourselves, looking at cooperative models, like systems within one body, for the good of all involved, a missing lens to view our current situation.

But to claim our seat as an equal at the table of world wisdom, we must be visible. We must be transparent. We must do all that we can to dispel the fear and propaganda around us. While there will always be fear of magick, and of those who can easily go into the dark, let the fear be for real reasons, and not misunderstandings and superstitions. Then it can be understood and transformed into mutual respect.

In ancient times, the Pagan temples were a part of society, paid taxes, collected money, and offered services of rites, rituals, healing, and education. They were part of the weft and weave of their communities. We have not had that for a very long time. To restore and evolve our worldview to serve the greater good, we must be a part of society in some way again. We must interact through intra- and inter-faith gatherings and be available again to those who seek magick and the old gods, but might not seek to be Witches.

If we feel there is a lack of our values and worldview in the overarching culture and leadership and want our worldview and voice heard, we can't always be the religion people come to from a previous religion, with no support structure to educate people and create culture. Otherwise, we will never grow beyond the stage of gathering people who feel disenfranchised, abused, or victimized. Many people come to Witchcraft and Paganism today with a persecution complex. The archetype of the Witch can be attractive, and hopefully ultimately healing, for many who experience that sense of persecution, but as both individuals and as a community, we must grow beyond that being a primary expression of our path. As more Pagans of various types raise children and those children go out into the world, whether or not they practice as ministers and high priests and high priestesses matters less than modeling our spirituality and understanding to others. To do that, we have to change the model in which we are working in and in some ways, become a greater part of our society.

Temples of the ancient world dealt with the issues of their people at the time, from the religious to the social. They were places of gathering and worship, but also places of healing, education, and community. As Wicca and Witchcraft shifts from being solely an exclusive mystery cult of clergy, of priestesses and priests, for only clergy, we need to not only look to ancient Pagan temples, but think about how they have served, and how they must be transformed.

The fear of institution in the general Pagan-Wiccan-Witchcraft culture means that almost nothing we create lasts beyond the lifetime of the creator. If we want sacred sites dedicated and accessible to us in our community, we need to allow new institutional structures to hold them for posterity. Our temples need to deal with the issues of our current community. We start with people who have had spiritual disconnection or wounding, who are seeking knowledge, community, and healing. We face issues of harm to the environment, our food supplies, and the specter of nuclear and biological warfare. Fundamental rights to life that are now called into question have become part of the social justice movements, along with advancing social rights for all. Modern Witchcraft, despite its ancient roots, is still a child in the family of religions, lacking deep cultural practices, traditions, and cohesive mythology and theology. We work together to develop culture, paradigms and world-views that are inclusive, yet do not water down the mystery and magick.

When the modern magickal movements started, some would say as early as the 18th Century with the advent of the Spiritualist Church or the 19th Century with Theosophy, the Craft was much more esoteric and hidden. There were no open circles, no festivals, and no "how to" books. People talked in riddles and you had to know someone who knew someone to get a foot in the door to these groups. It would be quite exclusionary. Not everyone was welcome. There was no "Paganism" in the way we know it today until the late 1960s. There was Pagan philosophy, but little community. It was quite literally "occult," hidden from view, and only a quaint and kitschy thing as mainstream media reported it. Despite the rural quaintness of Gerald Gardner's Wicca, few involved were of any lower social class. Gardner himself, like Aleister Crowley before him, came from a wealthy family. Social institutions were not needed or wanted in those days.

Soon what we call Wicca today became entwined with counterculture movements and "-isms" including the counterculture movement of the 1960's and the growing movements of environmentalism, feminism, and other social justice movements. This opened it up to appeal to many beyond the "occult" movement and those simply interested in an alternative spirituality, a new way to think, feel, and operate in the world. Not everyone wanted to join a coven or lodge, and if they did, it didn't quite mean the same thing. People looked for the community found in a church, with different shared values and methods of operating. Earth Religions, Paganism, Wicca, and Witchcraft all developed together with blurry lines separating them. Many practitioners identified with all these labels and none of them. This continued to develop in the counterculture circuit until it started to filter first into the urban environments with an occult community, and then outward into the suburbs, getting popularized by modern media, movies and television in the late 1980s and '90s.

One can only go so far as a counter to something more orthodox before presenting a sustainable, viable alternative as a new way of doing things, even if the new way was based on some ancient ideas. It was at these same times that deeper thoughts and plans on community developed, though the seeds were planted long before by figures such as Oberon Zell Ravenheart with his Church of All Worlds, Selena Fox and her Circle Sanctuary, the Aquarian Tabernacle Church, the controversial Church and School of Wicca, and the Temple of Nine Wells. Rather than a place that tended to draw only the reactionary and rebellious, which has been a necessary stage, Witchcraft, Wicca and Paganism began to draw a wider and hopefully even deeper range of practitioners, creating many layers to the community.

We face the challenge of a Temple in a transition from an industrial society to one balancing the paradox of global information and communication with local community and ecology. We are rooted in mythos of an agrarian world, but are disconnected from that reality in most of our day-to-day experience. Like the shifts of tradition from the Hunter-Gatherer cultures to the Agrarian, we create new structures, but in the age of global information, we harken back to not only the agrarian, but the tribal in our magick, as if in this new age, all the ages are occurring on some level concurrently. How do we weave all of these strands together to create something new for us all? That is the challenge of our current society, and the task of magickal practitioners, organizations and communities.

Today, churches are often tax-exempt, and work in a different framework within society. They have certain expectations to operate within a community as a productive part, doing various forms of ministry for their own congregation and beyond. To be part of a greater society, even though it can be quite hard, we must begin to work within those models. Part of the model is the government recognition on both a state and federal level through the 501(c)3 tax exempt status, granting recognition as a legal religion. Donations are tax exempt, just like other mainstream religions. We can more easily hold land and property, and maintain places to gather. Many of our gathering places held in private hands disappear when that individual passes, their own finances become troubled or there is a personal rift in the community. For a "land-based" or "Earth-based" tradition, we have precious little land we can call our own, where we can practice easily in groups unmolested, where power can build and grow. We have few places were our dead are buried according to our rites.

A basic understanding of geomantic practices shows how Christianity took over the sacred lands of the European Pagans, and imprinted their rituals, culture, and symbols upon these vortices, which were in turn disseminated across the globe. If we want to add our voice to the global dialogue, as a land based path, we must establish our sacred sites again, and let them sing out across the world.

Resources controlled by a more transparent institution can prevent such losses. With greater resources, this gives us an ability to operate on equal footing with larger, and more long standing religious institutions. 501(c)3 status grants our ministers legal rights (or "equal rites") for weddings, funerals, hospital visits, and prison visits. The avenues of recognizable service become more open to us. Then we can slowly add our own expectations and view of what it means to be a priest/ess and minister, and what it means to serve, expanding the definition to include not only human service, but the land, spirits, planet, and cosmos.

Those who have gathered at the crossroads since antiquity have been considered practitioners of an illicit religion. That still holds true today. Many of our greatest practitioners are rebels, peasants, poets, artists, black sheep, and horned goats making their own way, and yet still find support in like minded fellows sharing similar goals. We will not simply be invited to sit at the table of world religions, for we have been a shadow to all the world religions. Sometimes maligned openly, other times subversively, as unwanted but necessary. Like the fairy godmothers and wicked witch queens of the fairytales, we need to invite ourselves and just show up. Sometimes we bring blessings and seemingly grant wishes. Other times what we say is not what they want to hear, but it's necessary anyway.

Chapter Three: Structure: Spiritual and Terrestrial

Unlike other institutions, magickal or otherwise, that seek to emulate what has come before, when we founded the Temple of Witchcraft, we sought to parallel our spiritual ideals in the structure of the organization, applying the old occult adage, "As above, so below. As within, so without." While its been difficult to explain at times, and we've had to conform to some legal expectations when dealing with the government, it has been well worth it.

The Body of the Temple

The body of the Temple is fairly simple. It's divided into three basic circles or groups. We can look at the body of the Temple as concentric rings, rather than a hierarchical model. The leadership of the Temple is like a network spread through the three rings. These three rings are the Ministerial Church, the Mystery School, and the Seminary.

What might be considered the Outer Ring of the Temple is the Ministerial Church. It is outer simply because it deals with the public more than any other part of the Temple. The Ministerial Church is generally open to the public and consists mostly of General Members, those who have attended at least three Temple of

Witchcraft official events and wish to be recognized as General Members by receiving a consecration at a public Temple ritual. The Ministerial Church provides service and support in many areas of interest for the community.

Like the outer ring of the Zodiac in an astrological chart, the Ministerial Church is also divided into twelve segments, each based on the themes and symbols of the twelve zodiac signs. Each of the twelve has three components to their work in the community. The first deals with some aspect of the outer world, service and outreach to not only members, but to those who are curious or have a need Witches can help with to improve our community and our world. The second is specifically for those on the path of the Pagan, Witch, Magician, or Practitioner of magickal spirituality. They are usually more ritualistic and focused. The third aspect is often unseen and more magickal, working behind the scenes for the good of the Temple and greater community.

The twelve ministries are:

- **Aries:** The Ministry of Aries is based upon the archetype of the Warrior and maintained and designed to serve those who identify as the Warrior. Aries ministry is involved in military outreach and support, self-defense in both the physical and psychic sense, and responsible for the overall warding and protection of the Temple.
- **Taurus:** The Ministry of Taurus is based upon the image of the Steward. It involves those who are devoted to the planet Earth, the environment, and animals. Taurus provides environmental education and action, provides support to animals in an animal ministry and conducts Earth healing rituals.
- **Gemini:** The Ministry of Gemini is based upon the Trickster. Those with strong thinking, communication, or computer skills are drawn to this work. Gemini oversees media outreach, online and technical support, and questioning assumptions about the Temple through the use of humor. Gemini also oversees the Gay Lesbian Bisexual Transgendered

Queer/Questioning (GLBTQ) spiritual ministry, or "Queer Spirit" ministry.

- **Cancer:** The Ministry of Cancer is founded upon the image of the Mother Goddess. Cancer is focused upon support and caregiving, including social services such as food drives, organizing the kitchen at sabbats, offering children's ministry, and primarily facilitating the Divine Feminine Mysteries.
- **Leo:** The Ministry of Leo uses the image of the Artisan as its guide. Artwork, creativity, and performance are the keys to Leo's work. This ministry group oversees the community involvement in art, music, and theater, ranging from drum circles and ritual music to art work from worship and promotional purposes, such as T-shirts. The Leo ministry oversees the crafting of tools and the rituals for the general success of the Temple.
- **Virgo:** The Ministry of Virgo is based upon the dual image of the Servant and the Healer. Virgo ministry works to support the Temple in a variety of ways, including apothecary services in the Temple store, organizational skills, and healing rituals and magick.
- **Libra:** The Ministry of Libra focuses upon the work of the Judge. Strong skills of communication, education, and discernment are needed to work in Libra. Libra provides services for the Temple in terms of public relations, higher education opportunities for professional ministers, and most importantly, conflict mediation.
- **Scorpio:** The Ministry of Scorpio guards the threshold of the gates of life and death as the Guardian. Scorpio ministry deals with care and support for the dying and grieving and communion with the ancestors. Rituals to help those cross over and help those who are left behind in grief. Scorpio also oversees the education and training in sacred sexuality in the traditions of Witchcraft.
- **Sagittarius:** The Ministry of Sagittarius is one of education, embodied by the Teacher. Sagittarius ministry oversees the publication of public documents and educational texts, the administration of the Mystery School and Seminary, and

communion with the inner teachers, the Mighty Dead of our Timeless Tradition.

✦ **Capricorn:** The Ministry of Capricorn is embodied by the Father and leadership by example. Capricorn guides the Temple's prison ministry, both in person and via correspondence. Capricorn is also the guide to rites of passage and the Divine Masculine Mysteries.

✦ **Aquarius** – The Ministry of Aquarius is embodied by the Rebel, the paradox of both individuality and community found in its sign. As the sign of sudden upheaval, Aquarius ministry coordinates disaster relief efforts. Aquarius builds community through festivals, parties, and events—including TempleFest—and Aquarius is responsible for bringing unorthodox and unusual ideas to the Temple for consideration.

✦ **Pisces** – The Ministry of Pisces is that of the Ecstatic, finding bliss in movement and ritual. The duties of Pisces are offering ritual and liturgy to the public, including sabbats, esbats and other ritual events. Pisces ministry oversees trained ministers in counseling, particularly in forms of divination. Lastly, the inner ministry oversees Temple divination, offering guidance and prophecy in times of need.

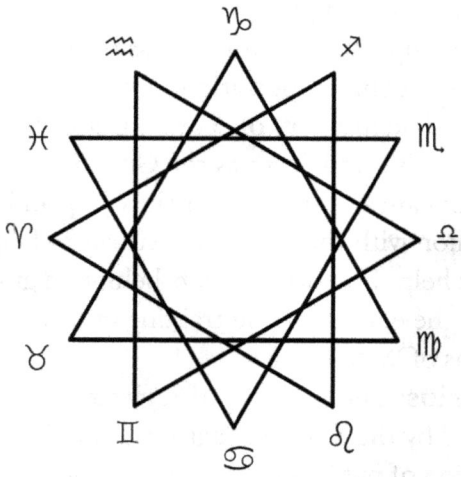

Dodecagram with the Zodiac Signs

The second ring is the Mystery School. The Mystery School is a set of teachings applied by Ministers in the Sagittarius Ministry to help develop magickal skills and personal evolution. There are four levels to the Mystery School, based upon the four elements of fire, earth, water, and air. Each level is complete unto itself, and usually requires the successful completions of the previous level. In total, they provide thorough intellectual and practical education in the Western Mystery Tradition and occultism as seen through the eyes of a modern Witch. Usually general members seeking to go deeper will commit to the Mystery School, starting with *The Inner Temple of Witchcraft*, and progress or take breaks from training as needed.

The third and last ring in the structure is the Seminary. "Seminary" is a difficult word because, as of this writing, we by no means think we are conferring the equivalent of a Masters of Divinity. Though accreditation in academic standards is an eventual goal, the prime purpose of the Seminary is to train graduates of the Mystery School as High Priestesses and High Priests. Graduates of the Seminary can then choose to volunteer in the Ministerial Church and eventually become ordained through the Temple, and even serve in the leadership. So the outer ring leads to the inner ring and the inner ring sends you right back to the outer ring in the role of service, one of the great mysteries for those of us following the ways of the Cunning Man and Cunning Woman.

Our three rings of the Temple embody the three basic definitions of a Witch and the practice of Witchcraft. They are 1.) the Vocation of the Craft; 2.) the School of the Soul, and 3.) The Secret Society. All three aspects have a history in our Craft, and are needed in the world today.

The Ministerial Church provides a place in the modern world to ply our Craft as Cunning Women and Cunning Men. Witchcraft is a vocation. Oftentimes those who are not Witches (*cowans* in Wiccan teachings, or now, due to the rise of popularity of the *Harry Potter* series of books, "muggles") seek magick and healing. In days past they were an established part of a village, along with the blacksmith or baker, and often worked as a "white witch" begrudgingly aside the local priest. While the village folk practiced folk traditions, they were often Christian, not religiously Pagan. In the most ancient of times, those we call Witches today fulfilled the function of the "shaman" in other cultures, the medicine person and religious authority. Today, many Witches fulfill this role by working in an occult or metaphysical shop, or professionally building a practice either overtly as a Witch practicing divination and healing, or covertly in a more holistic practice. Through the Ministerial Church, we can clearly be Witches, offering magick for society in a variety of ways appropriate for the modern era. Our magick can be in ceremony and ritual, divination and healing, as well as our perspective to community, the environment, and problem-solving.

The Mystery School embodies the second definition of the Witch. Many see our illustrious tradition as a school for the soul. We harken back to the ancient mystery schools of Egypt and Greece, and in particular the traditions of Orpheus, Dionysus, and the famous Eleusinian Mysteries echo a resonance of Witchcraft for the modern Witch. Many of our festivals seek to reenact or reinvent these ancient mysteries, and our covens and traditions work in the same way on the deeper mysteries and long term training of the soul for personal evolution and enlightenment. Like these traditions we go beyond the fear of death by facing death in our mystery.

Like it or not in this coming Age of Light, Witchcraft has always been considered some sort of initiatory secret society. This is a tough piece to integrate and express in the modern era of public institutions. In many ways, it is the not-so-secret society, but a society, a sorority and fraternity of bonded members nonetheless. While we in the Temple see kinship with all who identify and function as Witches (and who is a Witch is between them and the gods) one can feel peer-ship with those who are living as Witches actively operating in a magickal life. Just as there are other professional peer groups, and membership takes an actual successful act or accomplishment in that group, Witchcraft is the same. Far less regulated today, perhaps, but we know our own when we see them. The Temple's seminary allows peers to gather and gain support and mentorship in this changing age. Perhaps we no longer have the secret words and handshakes of a Masonic order, but those with eyes to see can see their own regardless of the tradition or stripe. We are welcoming to those who found themselves living as Witches through different means even if they are not a part of our Temple. The secret is in the way of life, something unseen by others, rather than strict oath-bound details not to be shared. We believe the best way to preserve the mysteries is to show them in plain sight. Those with the eyes to see and ears to hear will find them, and all others will pass by them unaware.

THE LEADERSHIP OF THE TEMPLE

While the boundaries and space of the Temple are held by the three rings of its structure, the Leadership starts at the center and radiates outward towards the edges, to extend the strands of connection and communication through all parts of the organization.

In the center are the three founders, Christopher Penczak, Steve Kenson, and Adam Sartwell. While not holding a legal distinction other than lifetime membership, the founders hold the three principles the Temple was built upon: Will, Love, and Wisdom. The material of *The Three Rays of Witchcraft,* looking at the principles of Will and Power, Love and Trust, and Wisdom and Knowledge as the foundations for the evolution of the Witch, and the realms they are connected to—Angelic, Faery and Ancestral respectively—became key ingredients in the work of the Temple of Witchcraft. At each Ostara, the three founders switch the ray they are devoted to for the year, and the special rituals and responsibilities change in their duty for the health and well being of the Temple. Each ray and office is associated with a particular magickal archetype. The Red Ray is the Sovereign. The Blue Ray is the Seer, and the Yellow Ray is the Sorcerer. The triad is also known as the King/Queen, Prophet, and Priest. While the Temple is not legally authorized for independent charters, future "satellites" of the Temple, known as Branches, would require three ordained ministers to hold these three energies in that satellite location. Those in such a special role would be designated as Keystone Bearers.

The legal leadership of the Temple is its Board of Directors. The offices found in most non-profit corporations can be found in our own structure, including President, Vice-President, Treasurer, and Secretary. Yet they are aligned esoterically with the four elements, and a fifth element and office is added to complete our pentagram formation.

Office	Element	Role	Responsibility
President	Fire	Leadership	Aries, Leo, Sagittarius
Vice-President	Water	Support	Cancer, Scorpio, Pisces
Secretary	Air	Information	Gemini, Libra, Aquarius
Treasurer	Earth	Resources	Taurus, Virgo, Capricorn
Advisor	Spirit	Objectivity	All Ministries, Volunteer Coordinator, Outreach and Interfaith

The board is the pentagram, or pentacle, if the symbol of the star is inscribed in a circle. In occult teachings, this has become a symbol of the practice and religion of Witchcraft, standing for the five senses and the sixth psychic sense, as well as the elements of earth, air, fire, water, and spirit exemplified in the board of directors. The pentacle is also an image of divinity, seeing three points for the Triple Goddess and two points for the Dual God. The pentacle has long been a symbol of the gateway to the mysteries, the five-petalled rose of the Goddess and the incarnation of humanity with two arms, two legs and a head. It is both protective from all harm and enhances our spiritual awareness. The board's mission is to both preserve the mysteries and guide the Temple to success while protecting it from harm.

Each of the officers oversees that aspect of the Temple, with the fifth office being a "Director at Large" able to trouble shoot, problem solve, and give an outside perspective on situations. Each director in turn oversees three of the twelve ministries in the Ministerial Church, and the Lead Minister of each ministry reports directly to that board member.

The board is aided by a Council, consisting of twelve members, each a Lead Minister for one of the twelve ministries based upon the Zodiac. Ministers have a certain freedom to build their ministry as they see fit within the proposed guidelines of the Temple, and work with their board member for support and problem solving. The council advises the Board when necessary, and the Lead Ministers of the Council are encouraged to be involved in Board meetings and discussions.

The Zodiac itself is esoterically divided in what astrologers call *decans*, each thirty degree sign is subdivided into three ten degree decans, and associated with various constellations. Each Lead Minister is authorized to appoint three deputies, like the decans, and work with them as they see fit. Some ministry deputies are focused upon one of the three specific areas of the ministry. Others work cooperatively on all three ministries simultaneously. The tone and structure is set by the Lead Minister's vision for the Ministry.

From time to time, the Board of Directors can, often at a Lead Ministers request, create special positions and committees that do not fall under the twelve ministries. Supervision is given to the person most appropriate on a case by case basis.

Ministers can hold multiple roles in the Temple leadership structure. One minister can simultaneously hold the role of Founder, President, Sagittarius Lead Ministry and be a deputy in another ministry. Regardless of numbers of roles, only the members of the Board of Directors have a legally binding vote and only one vote is given per person.

Members are encouraged to be engaged and volunteer, taking smaller leadership roles and growing their service and leadership skills along with their magickal training, to take on greater roles and responsibility as they so feel moved.

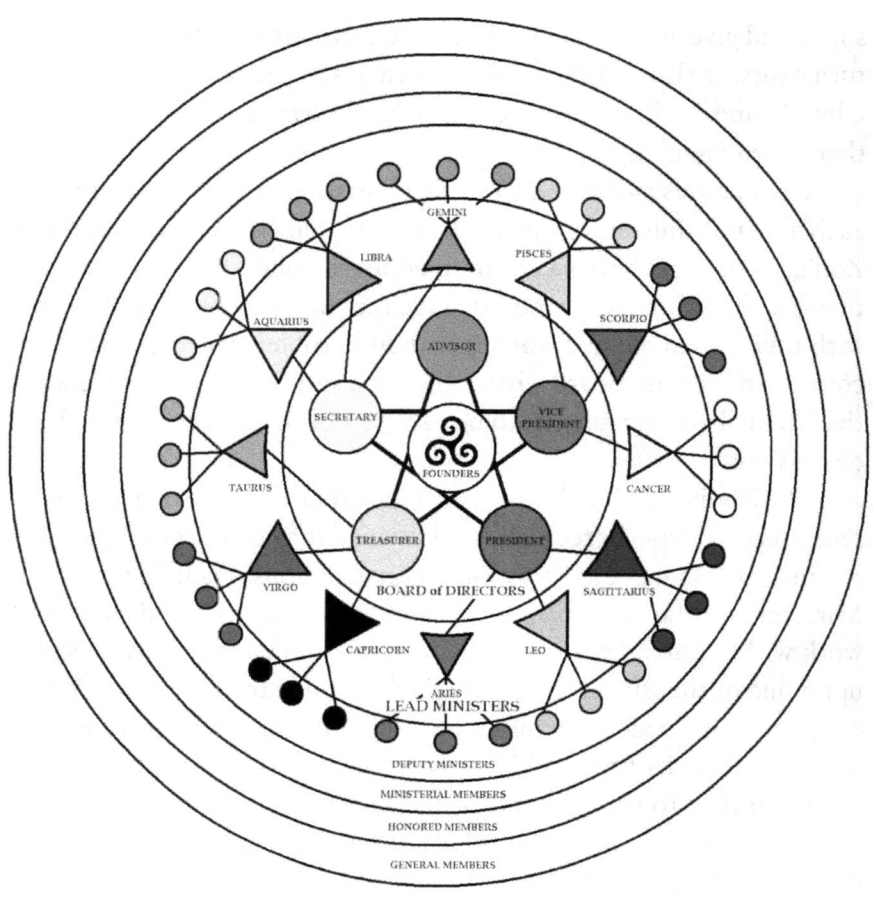

Temple Organizational Chart

As a cooperative "meritocracy" we tend to only consider people who have gone through a certain level of personal and magickal training for positions of leadership or authority, usually starting small and, as trust is earned, moving onto more complex projects or responsibility. Rather than working with a larger number of potentially qualified people outside of our structure, which past experiences in other organizations has shown often leads to misunderstandings, assumptions, and greater conflicts and power struggles, the shared cultural experience of similar training brings people together and grants a base level vocabulary, ethos, goals, and a shared tool box of accepted personal and interpersonal skills, both magickal and mundane, to solve problems. With that foundation and understanding, members can bring their diverse outside experiences in other traditions and organizations to enrich the Work. This greatly facilitates the cooperative model, with each "strand of the web" working to support the whole. The shared foundation creates an understanding that all involved have a deep willingness to seek their own spirituality in the model of community as outlined in the Temple, an assumption that cannot always be made in other organizations or projects. In times of difficulty, we look back to the principles of Love, Will, and Wisdom to guide us, and the mission of restoring a time of enchantment, the Garden of the Gods, to the world.

As part of our organizational understanding, our cooperative meritocracy, we know that we are all working on teams within teams, and many members of our team are not corporeal. The cooperative element extends to the unseen allies we have agreements with, who aid our work as inner world contacts. None of us is expected to carry more than we can, with the work in both the outer and inner worlds divided amongst our teams. The Temple acts as a bridging organization, manifest partially in the material world, and partially between and beyond, in the temples and holy groves of the inner planes of Witchdom.

Membership Levels

While many of the Temple's events are open to the general public, like any religious organization, it is a Mystery Tradition, with deepening levels of membership that come with different benefits and responsibilities. The membership levels deal with the various concentric rings of structure of the Temple itself.

Level	Body	Requirements	Ritual
General Membership	Ministerial Church	Three or more official functions	Consecration

Honored Membership	Mystery School	Attend Mystery School	Initiation
Ministerial Membership	Seminary	Complete Witchcraft Five	Elevation, Ordination
	Council	Ordination	Admission to the Council
	Board of Directors	Ordination	Majority Vote
Founding Membership	Core Leadership	Limited to three Founders	(Keystone Bearer)

General Membership is offered to anyone who attends three or more official Temple events. At the next public ritual (even if its the third event) a potential general member can be consecrated before the community as a member. Through a ritual involving the consecration of the palms of the hands with Temple Oil, and a formal welcoming with the words "May there always be peace between us" the new member is welcomed into the overall body of the Temple. Some see this as similar to dedication, but it is not a requirement to go forward. Many like to be a part of the community without having to promise to go onto further study or work. This is the ideal place to belong, but on your own terms, attending the public events hosted by the Ministerial Church and being involved in the services provided by the twelve ministries.

Honored Membership is established when one commits to the Mystery School by enrolling in the Witchcraft One program and being accepted, or testing out of Witchcraft One and/or Witchcraft Two, and getting accepted. Successful completion of the course results in an initiation ritual appropriate for that level. For in-person courses, the initiation is usually facilitated by the course instructor. For online students, the ritual for initiation is provided for direct contact from the spirits of the Temple of Witchcraft in a solitary setting. This is quite different for most from what is considered self-initiation. Many distant students will receive in-person blessings upon their initiation, a subsequent consecration by their teacher or another leader in the Temple. These "seals" to that level of work are usually given at larger community gatherings where many from across the country attend, such as TempleFest (see **Chapter Eight**). Honored members are encouraged to be involved in the Temple through volunteering and community building, and generally deputies for the twelve ministerial branches are from honored members.

Ministerial Membership occurs when one successfully completes the Seminary Program of Witchcraft Five. Initiation—often called elevation when one is already an initiate within a tradition—is given in a similar manner to honored members, either through direct ritual with the instructor, or through initiatory formula for the distant students with the possibility of formal recognition through a consecration seal ritual at a larger gathering of Temple members. Ministerial Members are encouraged to perform their own work in the community and can hold a Lead Minister position within the Temple, heading up one of the twelve ministries. While Lead Minister positions are not technically a membership category, they are one of the deepest levels of service within the Temple. Ministerial Members are welcome to seek official ministerial credentials with the Temple by applying for ordination.

Ordination gives the legal benefits of a religious organization to the ordained minister, including the legal recognition to perform handfastings (weddings), funerals, unsupervised (by the Temple) prison visits, as well as spiritual counsel and care, healing, and teaching. Only ordained ministers can teach in the Mystery School or Seminary, though other members can teach short term workshops for Sagittarius Ministry. Lead Ministers are generally also ordained. Ordination qualifications must be renewed periodically, with continuing education responsibilities.

Founding Membership is a legal and spiritual distinction for those who founded the legal body of the Temple or will carry on the spiritual responsibilities of those founders. Founding members embody the three principles of Will, Love, and Wisdom in the teachings of *The Three Ray of Witchcraft,* a pivotal document for the Temple. The three Founders are Christopher Penczak, Stephen Kenson, and Adam Sartwell. Founding membership cannot be revoked, but it can be resigned. While the status confers lifetime membership and spiritual responsibility, the legal, decision-making power of the Temple still is found in the hands of the Board of Directors. Upon resignation or death, Founders can name their successor for their position, or without such naming, the Board of Directors can vote upon the appropriate replacement. Each is responsible for not only leading the Temple by their particular principle for the year, but for rituals to embody those principles in the Temple. The rituals are known as the King Stone Rite, the Cauldron of Peace, and the Congress of the Bones, respectively.

While not the same in terms of membership designation as a Founder, a position in harmony with the Founders is that of Keystone Bearer. Those who are parts of duly authorized satellite or branch Temples of the main body of the Temple in a different area would hold a similar spiritual and leadership responsibility. Three Keystone Bearers are needed in the establishment of such a satellite, and such bearers must be ordained members in good standing.

Beyond these legal definitions of membership, we honor and recognize elders of our tradition, both in lifetime chronology and in terms of years within the Craft as a whole and/or years within the Temple of Witchcraft community.

The Temple does not proselytize or seek to convert others to increase our membership. We believe magickal teachings and experiences should be open and accessible to seekers of the mysteries, but ours is not not a path of conversion. Since the goal of the serious practitioner is to be clergy, a priestess or priest in some capacity, we realize our ways are not for all and would not presume that our beliefs are superior to others. There are many paths to the center, and ours—both Witchcraft, Wicca and Paganism as a whole, and the Temple specifically—are simply one path.

Although the three founders of the Temple are gay men, the Temple is not a gay, queer, or GLBTQ, tradition. It welcomes all orientations and gender identities, going beyond the traditional heteronormative view of older occult traditions, but does not restrict itself in terms of sexual orientation, or identity.

A Magickal Order

Modern Witches seeking community use a lot of words to find and define that sense of community and belonging. The coven structure is sometimes described as a family, with the High Priestess and High Priest as surrogate parents and the various students as siblings. While that model can work, it can also foster the dysfunctional family dynamics many of us come to Paganism and Witchcraft to escape and heal. Many don't wish to "grow up to be parents" in the model of "hiving off" and starting our own covens. Our ministry takes us elsewhere. While members of the Temple of Witchcraft are welcome to have covens on their own, we are not a coven-based system. The Temple assumes adult relationships and discourages parental, and other projections upon peers, mentors and teachers. Covens are traditionally limited to thirteen members and require a much greater personal commitment than the Temple does. Many covens do not allow you to learn from other teachers/sources, while the Temple encourages it.

Another popular word, used loosely in a larger context is "tribe." Some feel tribe denotes Native American tribal tradition and prefer the term "clan." In either case, these are powerful words. Tribe and clan denote a genetic link or, if not genetic, adopted through formal ritual. While many of us are in our "chosen family," tribal traditions take that bond in a more serious way. It implies a personal responsibility for the welfare of the other beyond what many of us might consider reasonable or acceptable in our own culture. Tribe and clan denote a shared cultural experience, and while we are all in the culture of the nation of "Witchdom" we are often coming from different cultural backgrounds, both in the endless variety of America and, when working in an international organization, the world. If someone lost their job, do you, or the Temple in general, have the means of supporting such a person until finding a new job? While we can offer support, it is difficult to offer such levels of support to all members across the world.

Clans and tribes require oaths and loyalties, much like an adoption process that is difficult to break. Commitment is lifelong. The breaking of such ties implies something has gone wrong. While in a magickal order, one can usually resign if paths no longer converge, with no hard feelings. Your commitment to magick can be lifelong, to spirit lifelong, but if you wish to leave the group, you are free to go as you please. Some groups identified with clan or tribe all live together, sharing personal expenses along with a magickal path. The bond is much more personal and the commitment is far beyond that of an in-person class, even if it's part of a larger body of training in a tradition.

The Temple of Witchcraft is more of an esoteric order. The term "order" can sound cold to some, and I agree, but it also implies a certain level of detachment that those seeking mystical evolution need to cultivate. We need to operate both in the personal and the transpersonal worlds, but identify with the highest self, going beyond the ego. The Greek Mystery schools, specifically the Orphic, have a saying, "I am a child of the Earth and the starry heavens, but my race is of the heavens alone."

While esoteric or occult orders can be friendly and foster good personal relationships, ultimately it is about the Work, and being called an order that maintains a temple reminds us of the Work. People in the Craft often get personal relationships mixed up in the efforts of the Work, and confuse personal love with Perfect Love, and substitute friendship/love for the Work, where, in an ideal world, such friendship and love support the Work. When peers, teachers, and mentors hold one to the standard of the Work, and a student is confused about the personal relationship, they take that to mean they are not loved or supported. Suddenly seemingly implied obligations are perceived as betrayals on the part of the one who has confused the personal and the transpersonal. Some of that can't be avoided, as it's human nature, but if the structure is clearly spelled out, much of it can.

In many ways, the Work is not meant to be warm and fuzzy, and the most Loving thing you can do at times is to be stern and disciplined, and not indulge in sentiment. Many can use sentiment to not fulfill obligations to the Work. Other times, warm and fuzzy is called for, and when a new level is met, the sternness can be released for a simple peer to peer understanding. At times we have to discourage, or even bar, those whom we feel a personal warmth towards, from going onward. It has not reflection of our personal feelings, but is necessary as they are not ready for the next stage of the Work. If the overall tone is warm and fuzzy, and then you are no longer friendly in a moment when setting a boundary, it can be confusing for the person on the receiving end, even when it's necessary. Sometimes one must be cruel to be kind in the long run. An order in a temple implies the Work is first and foremost, and personal relationships can develop, but are not the basis of the Work.

In some ways, I find the bonds of an order stronger, as it means everyone there has chosen to be there in every moment, and also has a way of reaching across to other groups. An order is more universally welcoming. Anyone appropriate to the work can join the order from different cultural backgrounds. Clan/tribe can separate and divide, even if that is not their intention, stating "this is us" and "that is not us" while order is an expression of the Timeless Tradition. The Temple of Witchcraft as an order is one expression of it. I see a different expression of many of the same principles in the Gardnerians, Thelemites, and even the Rosicrucians to name a few. We're simply newer, and have more work ahead of us. The flavor of this expression speaks to my soul more than the others. So that's why I'm in this expression of the Timeless Tradition. The expression of an order is a particular way of creating group identity and consciousness that can be quite different from tribe/clan. It was purposely chosen by the founders and leaders of the Temple when we became more public beyond the small groups studying the system of the Temple.

A helpful way for me to think of it, and perhaps for some of you, is more like the Jedi Order from *Star Wars*. Though philosophically flawed a bit due to the dualistic nature of light/dark as good/evil that is not found in Witchcraft, in the movies exists a body of adepts in their magickal arts. They have a common bond of training. They find kinship in common experiences and goals. They are different from the mainstream due to their abilities and experiences, and bond through it. They have faced similar ordeals. They support each other and their community. Through hard work one can rise through the ranks of experience and eventually have a voice in leadership. A higher spiritual purpose is the shared vision. Everyone is personally sovereign and have no true obligation beyond the Work, and doing your True Will. If that takes you away from the order, we wish you well. If it brings you back to the order, we will welcome you. All of these things are part of an order.

Different orders express it differently. Some are friendlier than others. Some are purposely impersonal at every step of the way. Some can be more tribal in their feel, even if they are not a tribe. Ultimately an order is a mystery school and the community that supports it and is supported by it, and that is the ultimate purpose of the Temple, a school for the soul. The only true commitment you are making is to the Work and your part in the Work, to the level of your ability. If you choose to teach others in the long term, great. If you find really great friends in the order, even better. Some of you might find that you don't click with people around you and don't feel instant bonds of friendship. That doesn't mean you are any less connected to the order or the body of the Work. Either those feelings will be a part of your work, or not. I know myself, in my first and second degree training, I can't say I really enjoyed too many people on a personal level. I found friendship in Paganism later, but it was not mandatory to do the Work.

We can be a friendly order. We can be a social order. We can be a loving order and be supportive of each other. That can be our expression of it. We can call it whatever we want as individuals, as long as we realize those are the parameters and not inadvertently make assumptions beyond it. Each class and group sets a different tone and should be free to do so.

An order is a way of expressing a group of mystics and initiates, an expression of the universal sisterhood/brotherhood, without the use of a gender term that would be exclusionary. Fraternity or sorority could also be used. If only there was another word that implied both without gender, but there isn't to my knowledge. Perhaps a new word that has yet to be coined is more appropriate, but for now, we prefer the term order as it is more specific to what has been created in the Temple of Witchcraft. Order also implies the group of initiates who have taken education in the Mystery School and Seminary, helping serve the overall body of the Temple, where the members are less unified by the Work.

Extensions of the Order

While the nucleus of the Temple of Witchcraft as a legal structure is rooted within the land of New Hampshire, we anticipate its slow growth throughout America and the world. We have several different ways to extend the work and community beyond the original Ministerial Church, Mystery School, and Seminary.

- **Committees** – Lead Ministers and the Board of Directors can organize committees, and nominate committee chairs to head such groups. Each committee will focus on a particular area of business within the Temple and report to the appropriate Lead Minister or Board Member.
- **Guilds** – Lead Ministers can create and organize guilds in the area of their ministry, or the Board of Directors can authorize guilds for any activity within the mission of the Temple but outside of the parameters of any of the twelve ministries. They are smaller bodies within the organization dedicated to a specific area. They are less business oriented than a committee, and able to function longer term in both magickal and mundane areas.
- **Ordained Ministries** – Ordained Members of the Temple can operate a professional ministry within the Temple of Witchcraft in their own location. Such ministers simply coordinate their events and efforts with the appropriate ministry when doing "official" Temple events, and have freedom to operate their own unofficial, non-Temple events and teachings as they see fit.
- **Training Coven** – While the Temple is not coven-based, an ordained minister can create a training coven, a long term working group specifically designed for the minister to take students through the five degrees in the Temple. One need not create a training coven to teach the five levels. An ordained minister can coordinate their public class efforts through the Sagittarius Ministry.
- **Modern Coven** – Graduates can organize a coven structure of past graduates of the Mystery School and Seminary, gathered together in an Aquarian cycle of rotating leadership and roles without a formal hierarchy.

- **Circle** – A less formal organization meeting regularly to study and grow, often based upon a specific theme, topic or area of ministry.
- **Branch Temples** – A Branch Temple, also often called a Satellite Temple, is an extension of the Temple's main activities in a different location, and can possibly include a physical location where the Branch operates. It must have at least three ordained members in good standing to be Keystone Bearers of the Three Rays, and operate a Mystery School, Seminary, and Ministerial Church in this new location. Branch Temples are not fully independent and do not have a charter from the main Temple, but are overseen by the main Temple with the same roles and responsibilities. One does not, and most likely will not, have to be in an established branch to do some of the Temple's work in a new location. Such ministers would do it as part of their own independent Ordained Ministry.

Ceremonial magician John Parsons' "We Are the Witchcraft," in his book, *Freedom is a Two Edged Sword,* acknowledges a universal connection amongst all Witches in function everywhere, as the "oldest organization in the world", yet "when there is too much organization we depart."

We in the Temple try to precariously balance between freedom and enough organization to help support people in the Will, on their quest with Love and Wisdom. We as an organization and community cannot be all things to all people, and know that Witchcraft is not a path for all. For some it's a brief stop, for others, never seen. Like the mycelium beneath the forest floor, we can provide a hidden undercurrent of support to all, but most will not be aware that we are present. By being a public organization, we provide points of ingress to this work for those who wish to join us.

There are times in our Work where it serves to work independently and alone, or in very small groups. Our educational structure provides support and mentoring, and can flower into longer student-mentor relationships, small circles, loose-knit guilds and even covens. There are times when the goals of our Work require branching out into larger areas, or more structured and coordinated efforts the solitaires and circles cannot arrange. The hub of wheels within wheels, webs touching webs, provides the flexibility and adaptability for both scenarios.

Ultimately our balance is between the will and direction of the individual and the cooperative effort of the community. We create a model that embodies that paradox of individual/community found in the Age of Aquarius, and ways to manifest both simultaneously through a cooperative ministry model that does not sacrifice the magickal path and the work, and worth, of the individual. Dealing with this paradox is a challenge facing all spiritual seekers in the coming age.

The two seemingly conflicting currents are one, like the two strands of a DNA chain, or the twin serpents of the caduceus. Our training and work embodies the twin currents of not only the individual and community, but the seemingly paradoxical pairs of spirit and matter, or the esoteric and practical. We are both planting seeds for long term, seemingly intangible changes in consciousness and culture, while also looking to produce tangible results in the lives of individuals and communities here and now.

To better manifest these goals, we see our training as encompassing the roles of both priest/ess and minister. While the minister is actively working for the community, serving both humans in a traditional ministerial role and the greater world through the environment, social justice, and cooperative organization with others, the priest/ess is actively working esoterically, serving the needs of the spirits, gods, land beings, planet, and creator. Many of the acts of magick and ritual, in partnership and service, mediate power in unknown and unseen ways, but are just as important.

The skill sets required for both jobs are different, and many struggle trying to embody both, not realizing they are in effect, two separate functions. While they are complimentary, and it is ideal to have skills in both sets, we know that the Will of many Witches guides them more to one path or the other, or even somewhere in between, using magick in the arts and other forms of bridging between the worlds and currents of life and power. We support and train in both, and make a distinction between the High Priest/ess and Minister, and require all ordained ministers to have the training of the High Priest/ess, if not always the calling, but many can choose to serve the gods and spirits without engaging as ministers to the greater community.

In times past, Witchcraft covens had no real ministerial role, as the Cult of the Witch did not serve the greater community, or interact with it beyond occasionally offering help to individuals who asked. Perhaps we did in ancient times, when our spiritual ancestors ran the official sacred temples of the gods in the city-states and long gone civilizations. There were always those ancestors who practiced the illicit religions at the crossroads and in the far away places, alone or in small groups. The practice of both are the inspiration for much of our Witchcraft movement today, starting with the coven structures of Traditional Wicca and the clans of Traditional Craft.

While High Priestesses and High Priests act as clergy to their coven, who were also their students and in many ways a surrogate family, they did not develop the professional skills of clergy in other denominations. There was no greater Pagan, New Age, or metaphysical community to serve, and the rest of the population was not looking for ministry from Witches. As we've grown into the role of a religion, albeit a mystery tradition, the greater community is looking for the same support, services, and skills from our own clergy, and we are adapting our models to fit the new needs of the world. Like the wild weeds, we grow into the spaces available to us and flourish under difficult conditions.

Chapter Four: Beliefs of the Temple

A magickal order is not based upon dogma, but mutual experience. No one is required to believe anything, but there are often symbols, principles, and ideas common to the magickal order. This collective knowledge helps facilitate certain experiences in consciousness, and gives a mythic and cultural framework in understanding them. There is an old folk saying: "Witches don't believe, we know." It's not so much that we feel we know what is best for everyone, we simply know our own experience. Belief is not required, just an open mind and a willingness to follow a technique to experience a deeper understanding of spirit.

As a religious nonprofit recognized by the United States government, we are asked as a part of this process to share our theological and spiritual beliefs. They are considered "statements of belief" though the tradition is one of experience, not blind faith. While belief in the following concepts is in no way mandatory, they inform our understanding of divinity and expression of a spiritual practice. These points can help a seeker understand the similarities of the Temple of Witchcraft with other traditions, as well as the differences as we seek the Mysteries.

DIVINITY

We experience divinity as *panentheistic*, meaning the divine expresses itself through the paradox of being both immanent, or manifest in the world through the body of the universe, and transcendent, or beyond the material world. Humanity, nature, and the entire cosmos, seen and unseen, are expressions of divinity and not separate from it. The entire cosmos seen and unseen is the body of the divine.

The divine has many expressions. It can express itself as a single consciousness, the Great Spirit. While often seen beyond gender or form, if a default gender pronoun is used, the feminine form, to honor the Goddess as the creative source and body of all things, is usually the expression. The Great Spirit can express dualistically, in what we call "The Two Who Move as One in the love of the Great Spirit" or Goddess and God. In Temple theology, our particular view of the Two are as the Weaver and the Singer.

The Goddess is the Weaver of Fate, and the Web of Fate itself, woven from her body. She is triple in nature, as heaven, earth and underworld, or maiden, mother and crone, expressions of past, present and future. The God is the Singer and the Song, known as the *Logos,* the Word, or the *Oran Mor,* the Great Song. His song reverberates through the web. His heartbeat keeps time to the song. He manifests dualistically as a God of Light and Life and a God of Death and Darkness. This is the Green Man and Sun God on one side, with the Horned Hunter and Hunted God and God of Death on the other. Their interplay keeps the song going. He holds open the gates of Matter and Spirit, allowing the Goddess to express herself as both manifest and unmanifest.

In the realm of the planets, the two manifest as the Moon Goddess and Sun God, the Lady of Silver and the Lord of Gold. In the terrestrial realm, they become the Goddess of the Earth, known as Gaea or Ge in ancient Greece, but known by many names all over the world, and the God of the sky, the sky father, Ouranus to the Greeks.

The Child from the union of the Goddess and God is often seen as the Serpent, both male and female, the god of desire, ecstasy, and death, who is the consciousness that rises and falls in the universe.

The Pentacle of Divinity

Beyond the most common expressions of divinity as Goddess and God, the universe can be seen as three primary forces that are also reflected in the individual self. The three forces are known as the Divine Will, Divine Heart, and Divine Mind. Together, these three powers collectively comprise the Great Spirit. Drawing from older mythology, we call the Divine Will the *Dryghten*. The Divine Heart is known as *Celi Ced* and the Divine Mind as *Cruthear*.

The Power of the Father and the Mother
The Power of the Great Above and the Great Below
Gave rise to all the worlds and powers we know today.
From the Father rose the worlds of Fire and Air
Of Atziluth and Yetzirah
From the Mother rose the worlds of Water and Earth.
Of Briah and Assiah
From these primal powers, these first four primal worlds
Came the rise of the first three powers,
The first three essentials
Rising like drops out of the primal void
as the cracked shell of the mirrored egg became the first cauldron
The first three rays of life
Extending out from the three first drops of creation
Born out of the first light and primal sound.
The three came forward as Severity, Mercy and Mildness
Of the alchemist's Sulfur, Mercury and Salt,
Of the Red, Blue and Yellow,
Of the Divine Will, Divine Love and Divine Wisdom.
Of Dryghten, Celi and Ceugant.
From that point forwards, all things shall be seen truly in three.
The one, its opposite and the force that connects the two.
The Mother, The Goddess, The Great Weaver
Gathered together the threads of creation.
She, like creation, is many faceted, containing her own beginning, middle and end.
She, like creation, is three faced, three formed.
One weaves the thread.
One measures the thread.
One cuts the threads and begins again.
Across time she appears as a maiden, as a mother and as a crone
Across time she appears as the past, the present and the future
Across time she weaves threads of what was, what is and what will be.
One for each of her fingers, one for each of her worlds, for the ten realms of creation
Each of the ten threads emanating from the other, emanating from her own body.

Each of ten threads became more dense, more solid and more thick than the other,
Each of the ten threads, reflecting the light of the Secret Fire
Creating worlds of different textures and colors.
She wove a thread of pure spirit, closest to her and the Father, like a Crown
She wove a thread of starlight and a thread of space,
Threads called Wisdom and Understanding
She wove a thread of amethyst and a thread of blood,
Threads called Mercy and Severity
She wove a thread of gold and a thread of green,
Threads called Beauty and Victory
She wove a thread of silver and a thread of quicksilver,
Threads called Foundation and Splendor
She wove a thread of matter, the thread of shape and form, to start the Garden
And She wove a secret thread of shadow, of Knowledge, ultraviolet and invisible,
for the Serpent Child, slipping it between all the others threads,
unseen and uncounted by most.
With the threads She created the sacred patterns, the Manred,
And She wove all of creation into being.
Webs within webs were woven, until there was a beautiful tapestry of many threads
And there the many-eyed Goddess, in view of everything,
Waited in the Center of Creation like a spider in her web
As the one who is three who is one.
The Father, The God, turned the great Loom of Time and Space for the Lady.
The turning of the wheel echoed the first sound, just as the web reflected the first light.
His energy, his fire, fueled the turning of the Wheel upon which she wove.
He stokes the fire of the Cosmic Forge of his body.
His energy, generated from his dual nature of light and darkness, life and death
He is two faced, looking forward and backward, up and down
But his true heart is found between the two sides.
His true mystery, like the Serpent, is found in the space between.
While He turns the Wheel, She weaves the Web.
While She sits in the center, He sings a song.
His song shakes all the threads of the tapestry, like the strings of a harp.

He sings the song of the universe for those who have the ears to hear.
He keeps time by striking the anvil with his hammer, keeping the beat of the Clock of Eternity,
The Heartbeat of the Universe.
He is two who are one who are three.
He is the Father and Son, Brother and Lover
Singing the Song of Creation, the Oran Mor, the Great Song.
Together, Lady and Lord, Mother and Father, Goddess and God
Are the Two Who Move as One within the Love of the Great Spirit
The Weaver and the Singer, the Web and the Loom
Together in love and partnership, they make the Web and the Wheel of Wyrd.
Together in love and partnership, they made the Way of Wyrd.
The last of the worlds, of the threads, was the world of the Garden
The Garden is where things take shape and form.
The Garden is where things manifest.
The Garden was needed to connect the heavens and the depths.
Only a tree in the garden could reach up to the heavens and draw down the light.
Only a tree in the garden could shield the depths, and provide cool darkness
So the hidden things could grow.
The web stretched far and wide, and the Goddess desired to grow something,
Something that would connect all the worlds and show her the full measure of her web.
She reached into the fertile garden, which was already a part of her own body, and planted a seed, an acorn in the caldera,
the first cauldron of the cosmos,
the center of the cosmos, the dark eye.
The Lady and Lord nurtured the acorn.
She watered it with her love.
He shone his light on it.
Soon, their love made something new.

Divinity has many more expressions in the Temple beyond the One, Two, Three, and Five aspects of the All. We see the seven wandering stars, the seven "planets" of the ancients as gods. They include the Sun, Moon, Mercury, Venus, Mars, Jupiter, and Saturn. While we also honor and include the outer planets, asteroids or planetoids as expressions of deity within the solar system, the seven planets of the ancient world have special significance. They are associated with a variety of angels, spirits, intelligences, corresponding to the seven days of the week, chakras and alchemical operations. We also consider their "shadows" the guardians of the gates in the descent to the underworld.

In the mythos of the eight-spoked wheel of the year, we see clearly the transition of life force, of the God, upon and within the matrix of creation, the Goddess. One expression of the god's divinity is in the eightfold manifestations. Four gods for the four aspects of agriculture, named Jacks, and four for the aspects of the Horned God, spread out through the year. They are:

Yule	Goat-Horned God
Imbolc	Jack of the Frost
Ostara	Ram-Horned God
Beltane	Jack of the Green
Litha	Bull-Horned God
Lammas	Jack of the Corn
Mabon	Stag-Horned God
Samhain	Jack of the Lantern

Lastly we look at divinity via the journey of the heavens through the twelve gates of the Zodiac. Each represents a lesson our High Priestesses and High Priests experience, much like the twelve labors of Hercules. While many deities from the various pantheons can fulfill the role of each of the twelve, we have specific manifestations of the divinities in our own work in the Temple of Witchcraft, with names and images. They include:

No.	God Name	Sign	Title	Card	Letter
1	Heyan	Aries	Warrior	Emperor	E - Heh - Window
2	Varrest	Taurus	Steward	Hierophant	V/F - Vav - Nail
3	Zazaz	Gemini	Trickster	Lovers	Z - Zain - Sword
4	Tarama	Cancer	Mother	Chariot	H - Cheth - Fence
5	Chutal	Leo	Artisan	Strength	T - Teth - Serpent
6	Yokutu	Virgo	Healer	The Hermit	I/Y - Yod - Hand/ Seed
7	Laramunth	Libra	Judge	Adjustment	L - Lamed - Oxgoad
8	Nantur	Scorpio	Guardian	Death	N - Nun - Fish
9	Sikaro	Sagittarius	Teacher	Alchemy	S - Samekh - Prop
10	Ayeohpanay	Capricorn	Father	Devil	O - Ayin - Eye
11	Zarbata	Aquarius	Rebel	Star	Tz - Tzaddi - Fishhook
12	Qaylan	Pisces	Ecstatic	The Moon	Q - Qoph - Back of the Head

No.	Element	Elemental Color	Planet	Planetary Color	Zodiac Color	Gems
1	Fire	Red	Mars	Red	Red	Ruby, Garnet, Diamond
2	Earth	Green	Venus	Green, Pink	Red-Orange	Emerald, Rose Quartz

Foundations of the Temple

3	Air	Yellow	Mercury	Orange, Multicolor	Orange	Agate, Carnelian
4	Water	Blue	Moon	Silver, Lavender	Yellow-Orange	Moonstone, Pearl, Beryl
5	Fire	Red	Sun	Gold, Yellow	Yellow	Citrine, Topaz, Diamond, Amber
6	Earth	Green	Mercury	Orange, Brown	Yellow-Green	Agate, Sapphire
7	Air	Yellow	Venus	Green, Pink, Pastel	Green	Peridot, Jade
8	Water	Blue	Pluto	Black, Scarlet	Blue-Green	Diamond, Obsidian, Jet
9	Fire	Red	Jupiter	Blue, Purple	Blue	Sapphire, Lapis, Turquoise
10	Earth	Green	Saturn	Black, Wine	Blue-Violet	Onyx, Garnet, Jet
11	Air	Yellow	Uranus	White, Electric Blue	Violet	Opal, Aquamarine
12	Water	Blue	Neptune	Sea Green, Blue	Red-Violet	Amethyst, Aquamarine

Polytheism

Panentheism is considered "soft polytheism" by some. In days past, all Pagan, Neopagan, Wiccan, and Witchcraft traditions were considered polytheistic, meaning a belief in many (*poly-*) different gods (*-theism*). As theological language has become more precise, some would use the word Dualism to denote the beliefs of many British Traditional Wiccan groups that focus solely on a concept of The Goddess and The God. Those who believe all gods are essentially manifestations of one source, and ultimately all things are a part of that manifestation are considered *monists*, which are explicitly different from *monotheists*, who believe in only one god, but that god is often considered separate and distinct from creation. The Temple of Witchcraft can be considered monists, due to our teaching of the

Principle of Mentalism (See **Cosmology** below) though all Hermetic traditions would also likely be considered monists as well. Monotheists often consider "untrue" religions to all be polytheists, because they are worshipping "false" gods. For some, like the Catholic Church, this equates to heresy.

Polytheism was soon divided into what is considered "soft" polytheism and "hard" polytheism. Hard polytheists see all of the gods as absolutely separate and distinct entities. There is no concept of all gods are one god and all goddesses are one goddess. Each has their own energy, identity, and agenda. Soft polytheists believe in multiple gods as expressions of a greater creative and sustaining spirit, and that many of the gods of one culture are the same as another, wearing different "masks" and names to be recognized by that cultural lens. There is only one Moon goddess, the expression of the Moon, but she has many names across the cultures. This soft polytheism is expressed in "The Charge of the Goddess," an essential part of Wiccan/Witchcraft prose and liturgy, as reworked by Craft mother Doreen Valiente.

The Charge of the Goddess

Listen to the words of the Great Mother, Who of old was called Artemis, Astarte, Dione, Melusine, Aphrodite, Ceridwen, Diana, Arianrhod, Brigid and by many other names:

"Whenever you have need of anything, once in the month and better it be when the moon is full, you shall assemble in some secret place and adore the spirit of Me Who is Queen of all the Wise. You shall be free from slavery, and as a sign that you be free you shall be naked in your rites. Sing, feast, dance, make music and love, all in My presence, for Mine is the ecstasy of the spirit and Mine also is joy on earth. For my law is love unto all beings. Mine is the secret that opens upon the door of youth and Mine is the cup of wine of life that is the cauldron of Ceridwen that is the holy grail of immortality. I give the knowledge of the spirit eternal and beyond death I give peace and freedom and reunion with those that have gone on before. Nor do I demand aught of sacrifice, for behold, I am the mother of all things and My love is poured out upon the Earth."

Hear also the words of the Star Goddess, the dust of Whose feet are the hosts of heaven, Whose body encircles the universe:

"I Who am the beauty of the green earth and the white moon among the stars and the mysteries of the waters, I call upon your soul to arise and come unto Me. For I am the soul of nature that gives life to the universe. From Me all things proceed and unto Me they must return. Let My worship be in the heart that rejoices, for behold – all acts of love and pleasure are My rituals. Let there be beauty and strength, power and compassion, honor and humility, mirth and reverence within you. And you who seek to know Me, know that your seeking and yearning will avail you not, unless you know the Mystery: for if that which you seek, you find not within yourself, you will never find it without. For behold, I have been with you from the beginning, and I am that which is attained at the end of desire."

I once spoke to a friend who is a conservative hard polytheist. I did say that I thought all the gods were individual entities with their own desires and agendas, just like people. He said, "Ha! I knew it! I knew you were a hard polytheist." He had a difficult time understanding my next statement, that I did not think people were as separate and distinct as he did, so giving gods the same level of separation did not give me the same worldview. Just as people are like cells within the body of the Earth Mother. She is an organ in the body of the solar system. Our Sun is like a cell within the body of the galaxy. The gods are like cells within the unseen etheric and astral bodies of these beings, part of a greater collective whole. Nothing is truly separate. Everything is part of the greater body of creation, the living web of the Weaver.

While a lot of other words can be used to describe beliefs of divinity in the Temple of Witchcraft, including animist, pantheist, polytheist, we prefer the word panentheistic, as it best sums up the mystery of the paradox we seek to resolve in our experience of the divine, beyond any words and titles.

COSMOLOGY

While no human map can adequately describe the nature of the spirit worlds, we use several "maps" that tradition has left us to better navigate those experiences with context and understanding. We can see the cosmos simply divided into manifest and unmanifest, or physical and non-physical, separated by a veil. Just as the physical world has many manifestations across the cosmos, so too does the non-physical. We see through the shamanic lens, an upper world of the heavens and a lower world of the depths, connected by the middle world associated with the realm of nature, time, space, and humanity. Just as the physical world in the middle is populated by humans, animals and plants, so too are the other worlds populated by spirits, gods and ancestors. The spirit worlds can be further divided into seven layers, each more subtle than the next, or the realms associated with the Qabalistic Tree of Life, becoming ten (some say eleven) realms in total.

The model of the four elements as the foundational building blocks of the universe is a powerful ally in our work. Our ceremonies call upon the four elements in four directions to anchor our ritual space. The elements are commonly called Earth, Air, Fire, and Water and represented by the associated physical phenomena, but they are beyond manifestation. They are archetypal forces influencing all of creation. They are generated from a mysterious fifth element, known as Spirit, Akasha, or Ether, and they return to it. The four directions, seasons and elemental tools of the magician are linked with them, and we believe various entities guide, govern, and direct their actions. Such spirits are known as *elementals*.

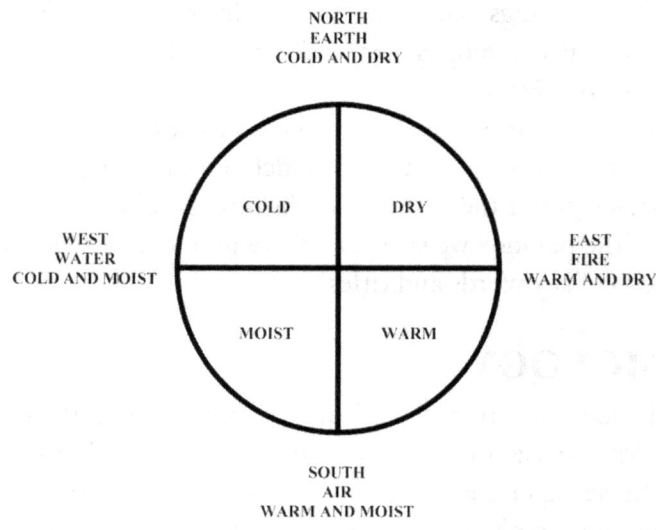

Elemental Wheel

- **Earth:** Earth is the manifestation of material reality and the principle of sovereignty. Earth corresponds with North, Winter, and the Stone. Alchemically earth is cold and dry. In the body we equate it with bone.
- **Water:** Water is the manifestation of emotional reality, also known as the astral plane or collective unconsciousness and the principle of compassion. Water corresponds with the West, Autumn, and the Cup. Alchemically water is cold and wet. In the body we equate it with blood.
- **Air:** Air is the manifestation of mental reality and the principle of Truth. Air corresponds with the South, Spring, and the Sword. Alchemically air is warm and wet. In the body we equate it with breath.
- **Fire:** Fire is the manifestation of energetic reality and the principle of Victory. Fire corresponds with the East, Summer, and the Wand. Alchemically fire is warm and dry. In the body we equate it with flesh.

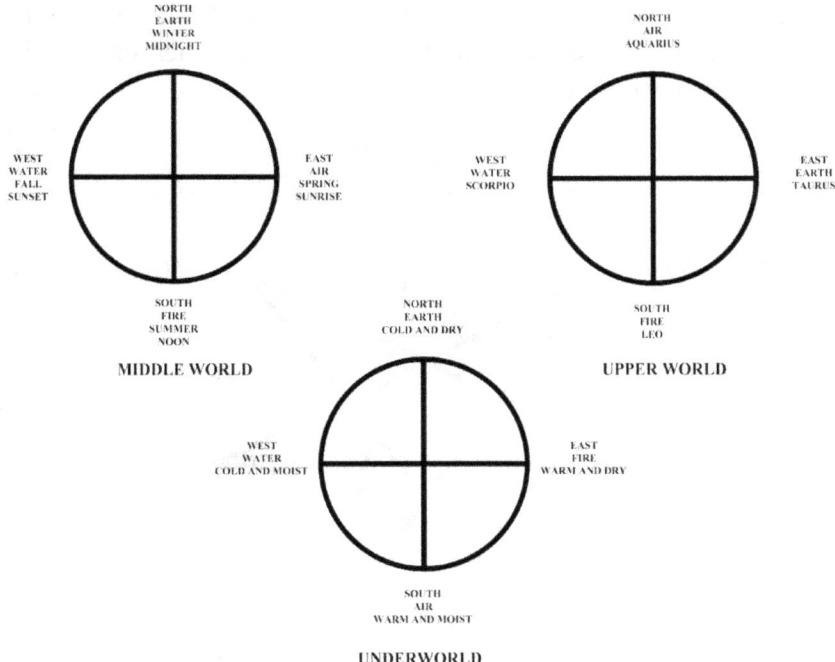

Three Orientations of the Elements

Foundations of the Temple

Some rituals switch the directions associated with the elements depending upon the purpose of the ritual and the style of the ritualist. We have elemental orientations for the lower world, upper world, and middle world, and continue to experiment with them.

Along with the four elemental powers, our cosmology is governed by seven seeming "laws" or principles, codified in Hermeticism as the Seven Hermetic Principles. The modern understanding of these principles is best described in a text known as *The Kybalion*, a philosophical explanation of the laws governing the function of the universe and humanity's relationship with it.

1. *The Principle of Mentalism* – We are all thoughts in the Divine Mind.
2. *The Principle of Correspondence* – As above, so below; As below, so above.
3. *The Principle of Vibration* – All things vibrate, all things move.
4. *The Principle of Polarity* – All things have their opposites.
5. *The Principle of Gender* – All things are male and female.
6. *The Principle of Rhythm* – All things have their cycles and seasons.
7. *The Principle of Cause and Effect* – All causes have their effect, all effects have their cause.

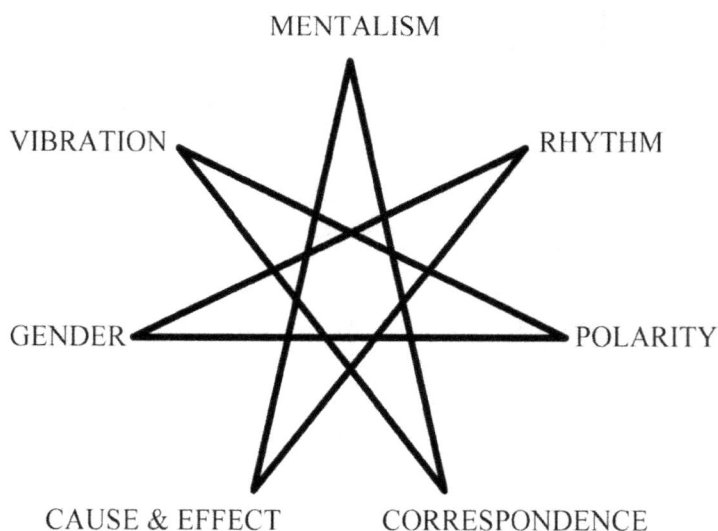

Septagram with Principles

While each of the seven principles adds to our understanding of the cosmos from a metaphysical perspective, central to our cosmology is the relationship between the World, or Microcosm, with the Universe, or Macrocosm, best illustrated today through the art and science of astrology. It is the Principle of Correspondence in action. We believe there is correspondence between events on Earth and events in the heavens, but one does not cause the other. The Microcosm and Macrocosm are intimately linked, and each reflects the other.

Extended from the triune godhead of the Divine Will, Divine Mind, and Divine Heart flow three powers. From them, three "rays" of light emanate outward through creation, poetically known as the Red Ray, Blue Ray, and Yellow Ray, or quality, as the Straight Line, the Bent Line, and the Crooked Line. Only through a union of Power, Love, and Wisdom within an individual can true magickal enlightenment occur.

Red Ray – Straight Line – Divine Will – Also known as the magickal will, True Will, mystic will, or dharma, it is the divine purpose of your soul. This magickal will governs, guides, and directs all magickal, ethical, and spiritual actions and goals. The discovery of the magickal will and its application is the process of exploring the mysteries. Through alignment with the Will, we gather Power.

Blue Ray – Bent Line – Divine Heart – Also known as Perfect Love and Perfect Trust, Divine Compassion, or Unconditional Love, it is the loving nature of your soul. This divine love is not personal, and grants us the ability to feel the interconnectedness between us and all things, material and spiritual, for our magick and spiritual evolution. Through alignment with the Heart, we gather true Compassion.

Yellow Ray – Crooked Line – Divine Mind – Also know as the Genius or True Knowing, it is the divine knowledge and awareness of the soul, beyond the bounds of space and time. This divine knowledge is not learned, memorized, or studied, but the inherent knowledge and wisdom found within, reflecting the creative knowledge of the universe. Through alignment with Divine Mind, we gather Wisdom and Cunning.

Foundations of the Temple

The Three Rays

MAGICK

Witchcraft can be described as a "magickal spirituality." To paraphrase a classic definition, magick is the art, science, and spirituality of causing change in conformity with one's will. Every thought, word, and deed is a potential act of magick, and shapes our reality. Many in the Temple of Witchcraft prefer Aleister Crowley's spelling of the word, with a "k," to differentiate it from stage show illusion. Affectionately known as "Uncle Al" to some, his definition of magick is paraphrased above as one of the most influential twentieth century occultists.

Magick works through an understanding of the divine connection. As we are expressions of divinity, through that divinity we are connected to all things. Magick is a technology for communing with the divine, be it specific spirits, deities, or powers, or the universe as a whole, through the use of meditation, ritual, prayer, and visionary trance. Our workings can be for wisdom, guidance, and healing, or to manifest changes that we desire. Each of us is responsible for shaping our reality through the practice of magick. Magick can occur through concentration, ritual, charm, art, dance, prayer, and communion with the spirits and divine.

Magick is fueled through life force, called *prana* or *chi* in certain circles. This life force sustains and animates all things, including all humans, plants, fungus, and minerals. We can divide the currents of life force into masculine and feminine, god and goddess, or positive and negative currents. By entering into a conscious relationship with this flow of life force in ourselves and all things, we can heal and empower ourselves in magickal ceremony.

The Soul

Generally Witches are inheritors of the Mystery Traditions of the ancient Pagan temples, and believe in the soul and life after death. Most mystical traditions, rather than the more exoteric religions, believe in a multiple soul anatomy, meaning there is more than one spiritual "self" animating the physical body that exists beyond physical death. We primarily belief in a triune self, or three-part soul, influenced by other forces determined by birth and spiritual development. Our theology includes the concept of reincarnation and return to the physical world as well as the guidance from ancestors beyond the veil.

The three souls are:

+ **The Watcher:** Known as the Higher Self or true "Soul" of other religions. It is the part of us that is bornless (the "Bornless Self"), outside of time and space, and most in tune with transcendent divinity and the forces of creation. It is the super-conscious mind.
+ **The Namer:** Known as the Middle Self and comprised of the personality, ego, and identity. It exists in the physical world of space and time, cycles and seasons. It is the conscious mind.
+ **The Shaper:** Known as the Lower Self, Child Self, or Animal Self, is the instinctual wisdom that is pre-verbal and responds best to ritual and play. It exists in the lower world and relates to the

subconscious, astral body, or dream self. It is also known as the psychic mind.

Triune Soul Model

Those of the Witchcraft traditions who reach "enlightenment" through the union of Power, Love, and Wisdom through the three souls can become deified, joining the ranks of the Mighty Dead or Hidden Company, similar to the communion of Saints in other religious traditions.

Beyond simple belief in reincarnation, many subscribe to the belief in the concept of *tuirgen*, similar to concepts about reincarnation. It is a Celtic term more fully understood as "a successive birth that passes from every nature into another...flowing through all time from beginning to end." It is not a linear concept of rebirth, but a birth into the union of all lifetimes, of all things, creating the oneness of the Divine Mind, Divine Heart, and Divine Will. Tuirgen is an extension of the concept of the One Sorcerer/One Witch/One Initiate stretched from the beginning of time to the end, to include not only magickal practitioners, but all living things. In essence, as the Principle of Mentalism states, we are all one within the Divine Mind.

Evil

Like other Neopagan, Wiccan, and Witchcraft traditions, we do not believe in theological evil. We do not believe there is a naturally occurring entity of evil to balance a naturally occurring creator of all that is good. We do not see our goddesses, gods and even source as wholly good, so we see no need to perceive of anything as the antithesis to that good. Our polarities are found in nature, such as light/dark, up/down, male/female and heaven/earth. In short, despite the popular misconception of Witches, we do not believe in the Christian Devil as an entity out to tempt or harm, and we most certainly do not worship the Christian Devil. By its theological implication, one would have to be working in a Christian framework to believe in the Devil, and we find our spiritual ancestors in pre-Christian traditions.

With a little study, you can find the Christian Devil is a theological and political construct without a deep tradition. In a time of great difficulty in Europe, the concept is cobbled together from a variety of conflicting sources, conflating them to one entity. Closer theological inspection shows there is no evidence for equating the Hebrew Satan, the Roman Lucifer (Morning Star), the serpent in the Biblical Garden of Eden, the Beast of the Apocalypse in Revelations, the Islamic Shaitain, and the Pagan horned and animalistic gods such as Pan.

Some modern Witchcraft traditions work within Judeo-Christian mythos instead of rejecting it, and work with the figures of Cain, Lilith, and Lucifer, but we in the Temple do not as a whole. Individual practitioners are free to build relationships with allies as they choose.

Pagan traditions do believe that there are spirits with a malevolent nature, just as there are people with a malevolent nature. Spirits translated as "demons" in various magickal cultures are considered the root of illness, misfortune, and many mental disorders, and village sorcerers, magicians, and wise ones were called to remove them and protect others from them, but they are often considered the spiritual parallel to things such as parasites, bacteria, viruses, and scavengers. They can be unpleasant, but they are part of the natural order. They cause breakdown and chaos, but are a necessary part of a healthy physical and spiritual ecosystem. Just as there are spirits and powers that "rule" over beneficial aspects of life and creation, there are spirits that rule over our base natures, and our ability to sabotage ourselves and harm others. These demons, sometimes classified as "goetic spirits" as they are classified in *The Goetia*, or *The Lesser Key of Solomon*, can be worked with to bring such destructive impulses under control and used for beneficial actions.

Witches do, however, believe in the power of thought to create. While we believe in no naturally occurring evil entity of the cosmos, or even earthly plane, we do believe those who have invested a lot of time, energy, and emotion in the concept of the Devil have created a thought form entity that can respond and behave like the Devil of Christian myth. Ironically those who fight against it the most are the ones ultimately creating and maintaining it.

The true source of evil is found in the actions and inactions of humanity, which are all a choice. Occultists define evil as misplaced force. Upon the Tree of Life it is found in the sense of separation we have from the divine, and when power is misapplied as wanton and unnecessary destruction or cruelty. There is no malevolent entity tricking us or tempting us. While much of our own evil comes from unhealed wounds and unresolved issues, individually and collectively, it is our own, and not caused by any other.

Experience Over Faith

While faith is a common term in most religious traditions, it's hard for Witches, in or out of the Temple, to use the concept of faith when explaining our traditions. We do use the terms "Old Faith" or "Old Religion" to show the origins of our traditions are actually older than most of the mainstream religions "of the book" today. When we want to be recognized as a religion by local and national governments we can often fall into the terminology of "faith-based traditions," as such terms are more familiar to the uninitiated. Yet, that is not our own paradigm. Ours is a paradigm of experience, and our common bond, or shared culture is through similar techniques and practices.

While most other religious paradigms require belief, and faith in that belief before starting, we can welcome the open minded skeptic. Most times indoctrination into a religion at an early age facilitates the experience of the religion. The faith required becomes a natural part of your worldview. Witches require no belief, just an openness to experience. Rather than have theology and dogma inform our experience, we focus on experience, and the techniques that lead to such experiences, and then try to establish models and paradigms that can help explain the experience. Witches seek to explore the nature of consciousness and divinity, the models and maps are not as important as the experience. They simply give us a frame of reference.

What really links us together, rather than faith, is a common philosophical approach to the world and the techniques based upon those philosophies. Broader Pagan traditions are all connected through a reverence of nature and seeing a plurality of divinity in many forms. Modern Witchcraft is linked through a shared holiday calendar and the techniques of ritual and magick. Magickal techniques, from trance to spellcraft, from the magick circle ritual to herbalism, become a cultural basis. While we all have different, personal experiences with the techniques, the techniques are like a technology, based in sound reasoning and philosophy, and time tested by practitioners.

While we are a religion, we often describe our Craft as an art and science. Music, in the same way, is based on scientific principles of vibration, pitch, and acoustics. It leads to the formation of scales and rhythm patterns that are used by musicians to express themselves. Both the musicians and others experience the music, and often have a transcendental experience of consciousness, what to many is a religious experience, despite not being in a formal religious institution. A culture of musical traditions is built, yet people are constantly building upon it, innovating, and adding to it. Trends rise and fall, but all build upon a shared foundation. Magick and Witchcraft are much the same. Unlike other traditions that feel there is a monopoly on the truth, and believe there is only one way that is right for all, we strive for balance between a reverence for the past and shared philosophies, and the process of innovating and adding to the body of lore we already have. The balance point between them is where the true mystery is found, making it a living, growing tradition. Like a sacred tree, we have roots, a trunk, branches and new flowers, and fruits—and the occasional nuts!

NATURE & OCCULT TRADITION

The Temple of Witchcraft is firmly rooted in the occult traditions of the past, seeking to forge the occult traditions of the future. The term *occult* is scary for many people, conjuring images of harm and evil, in much the same way the word Witchcraft can conjure frightful images. Just as it is important to reclaim the word Witch, I think it is also important to reclaim the word occult. Occult refers to the word *ocular*, meaning the eye, and when a thing is occult, it is hidden from view, unseen by most. All the magickal and mystical arts were considered occult until fairly recently, as most people neither understood them, nor wanted to seek them out. Things that are occult must be sought out, investigated.

Occultists study the hidden patterns of the universe, of spirit interacting with matter, and create models and ideas to better navigate these paths. Qabalists, Hermeticists, alchemists, astrologers, philosophers, healers, and all manner of magickal users, including Witches, can be considered occultists. Most people who have researched Witchcraft in the last three hundred years were probably looking more in the occult traditions than any genuine rural Pagan tradition beyond any cunning craft folklore. Our traditions were preserved and transformed in the grimoires of the occultists and the seekers of mystery in the ancient lands and ancient writings.

While we are considered part of the Western Mystery tradition, and occultist is usually applied to Western magickal philosophers, most occultists seek to build models inclusive of Eastern traditions.

Many Western occultists have studied yoga, tantra, Taoism, and Buddhism and this has not changed. While some see the modern New Age movement lacking depth in its explorations of both East and West, it is really following an impetus to recombine and rectify the divided wisdoms of the world for a unified future with many different views and paths, just as occultists in the past have done. If we are considered Western, it is due to the fact that language roots we use, in English, are based on Western culture, but even then, English has grown beyond the borders of the western world.

As a Pagan (or perhaps, more correctly, Neopagan) tradition, we are a nature-based religion. Yet Nature is not the only aspect of our ancient past that informs us. Nature tends to be equated solely with an Earth-based spirituality, yet our traditions go beyond the bounds of the terrestrial world, both in terms of distance and scope, for we explore other dimensions of consciousness beyond the physical. We could also be considered a stellar, a star-based, tradition. One of the ancient sayings from the Greek and Roman mystery schools illustrates this.

I am a child of Earth and starry Heaven;
But my race is of Heaven alone.
This you know yourselves.
— Petelia Scroll, fourth century B.C.E.

Drawn from the golden funeral discs used by initiates to navigate the world of the dead, usually considered "Orphic" in nature, referring to the mystery traditions based upon the mythic cycle of Orpheus, not unlike the cosmology and philosophy of other mystery schools of the same time and place.

It shows that to initiates of the ancient Pagan mysteries, our nature is both of the Earth, or Earth-based, and of the starry heavens, or stellar-based. The great ancient mysteries did seem to involve the realms of the Earth, Moon, Sun, and stars.

We are truly a nature-based religion. Aren't the Sun, Moon and stars a part of nature? We of the Temple subscribe to the notion that occultists are natural philosophers, seeking to find our answers through the observation and interaction with the indwelling spirits found in nature. Through the study of nature, we seek the underlying structure and understanding of reality. When we enter into a relationship with the two greatest of Witches, Magicians, and Alchemists there are, the Earth Mother and the Star Goddess, nature opens up to us and reveals her secrets. The study of nature, the veneration of nature and the relationships we build with the indwelling spirits of nature through time spent with the land and studying the sky are all ways to open the hidden, occult doors to this secret wisdom. These are the secret teachings of all ages underlying the quest of all occultists, philosophers and Witches.

A Heuristic Worldview

We are a *heuristic* tradition, simultaneously drawing upon many different paradigms, systems, and sources of knowledge, as we see pertaining to the overall body of modern Witchcraft. Coming from the same root as the Greek, *eureka,* which means "to find," as a heuristic tradition we are not only seekers, but finders of our own ways, and add to the body of lore and traditions when appropriate through syncretism and synthesis.

Our worldview encompasses the magickal wisdom traditions of all lands, incorporating the ideas and concepts of many cultures and traditions, ancient and modern, into personal practice as each individual practitioner sees fit. The Temple's traditions seek to be inclusive of the ways of Witchcraft, Wicca, Neopaganism, Ceremonial Magick, Shamanism, Theosophy, and Alchemy, as well as the cultural practices of the Celts, Teutons, Greco-Romans, Egyptians, Mesopotamians, Hindus, Asians, Africans, and Native Americans.

We are not a reconstructionist religion. Many modern Neopagan traditions avoid the path of the occultist, feeling it is not pure enough to embody their ancient Pagan ideals, and there is truth to that. We are not seeking out the past glory of the ancient Pagans to exclusion of the future. The occultist, much like the modern New Ager, incorporates wisdom wherever it is found. Occultism looks into esoteric forms of Christianity, Judaism, and Islam. Since occultists do not always identify as Pagan religiously, many in fact, have been devout Christians, Jews, and Muslims in the Western world, while their counterparts in the east have been Hindu, Buddhist, and Taoist, amongst others.

Reconstructionists focus on a particular location, culture, and time period, reconstruct those religious practices, and seek to extend them to a logical conclusion in our modern time. Some have magickal traditions and some focus exclusively on the religious aspect. Many run the risk of reenactment and dogmatic fixation, not wanting to deviate or evolve from what was known in the past, and yet even the ancient religions had their own occultists, borrowing gods, philosophies and myths from land to land, people to people.

We have chosen to follow in their footsteps and, like other Witches before us, look at the ancient city of Alexandria as a guide. In the city that divides and connects the West and the East, where learning, education and magick ruled supreme for a time, the rituals there involved the mixing of many cultures and traditions. Yet theirs worked so well we still have records of them, and refer to them for inspiration. Theirs was synthesis and a pluralistic worldview. So too, do we synthesize wisdom traditions under the art, science, and religion of the Witch, as ours is a spiritual calling, a vocation found in every culture and time. We seek to use these traditions to "find" our own way in the universe, making new maps that will lead our descendants to the hidden paths of the Craft.

CHAPTER FIVE: ALLIES IN THE TEMPLE

We envision the Temple of Witchcraft as a cooperative effort between incarnated humans identifying as Witches, Magicians, Shamans, and Healers along with those discarnate spirits who work in cooperation with us for mutual benefit. The Temple is a partnership between us and those entities that have sought our aid in furthering the Work. It is a collective conscious effort between the worlds.

When many come together to form a group, whether or not all of those coming together are human or not, a collective energy, a group consciousness, is formed. In covens, this is known as the "group mind" of the coven. In larger organizations with a more extended purpose, this group consciousness is called an *egregore*. The term egregore relates to the Grigori, the race of fallen angels, or Watchers, associated with magick and Witchcraft, but now usually relates to a shared collective consciousness or spirit entity of a group. Yet an egregore is much more than just a group mind, and several group minds can contribute to an egregore. Traditions are said to have an egregore, and various groups within the tradition contribute to it. Every major Witchcraft tradition is said to have an egregore, and the individual covens add to it and draw from it. Gardnerian Wicca has an egregore, and the Gardnerian covens are attuned to this collective spirit of Gardnerianism. The egregore holds the "current," the flow of energy in the tradition, being a focus for the movement and flow.

When one is initiated into a tradition, the current flows from the egregore through the initiator and into the new initiate. It plugs you into the group consciousness.

Many egregores evolve naturally and unconsciously through the shared work of a group of people performing ceremony. When people gather together in common cause, shared intent, and a similar, repeated structure, they add to this group mind and eventual egregore. The egregore can be entirely human, though the most long lasting and vital to the spiritual evolution of the world belong to "contacted" groups. Such contacted groups are formed in conjunction with the guidance and aid of specific deities, allies, and inner plane adepts, who also contribute from the spirit world to the collective shared egregore.

Some egregores are new manifestations of ancient inner world orders, having a current of energy that still exists on the inner planes passed to a new teacher, sometimes known as a hierophant or magister, to renew and regenerate a tradition. Other times, contacts might be drawn together for the birth of something new with older, deeper roots from the inner planes. Often the spirit of the land, or *genus loci*, or the spirit of an ancestral group, can add to the collective egregore, rooting the collective in a homeland or culture.

THE TEMPLE EGREGORE

The Temple of Witchcraft egregore is a combination of the energies of the group consciousness that has accumulated in the community, particularly those who have worked through this specific system of magickal development, in the unusual cycle of fire, earth, water, air, and spirit as developed in the teachings. Drawn to this energy are the entities and expressions of divinity that desire to work in partnership with the human members of the Temple to co-create something new and beneficial to all involved.

The work of the Mystery School and Seminary helps mold the vessel of consciousness both to hold more of the Higher Self/Watcher in the physical body and energy field, as well as create an interface for more effective communion and initiation with the spirit world in general, and the spirits of the Temple specifically.

The allies of the Temple of Witchcraft include two main currents. The first is of divinity itself, the aspects of the Source in the manner they manifest to the Founders of the Temple, particularly in the Three Rays of Witchcraft visionary workings. They are:

The Divine Trinity:
Dryghten (Divine Will), *Cruthear* (Divine Mind), *Celiced* (Divine Heart)

The Divine Trinity is an expression of the All, the Great Spirit. Many traditions have their own trinities, some personified and some not. Within the Temple, the most abstract manifestations of the trinity comes in three aspects, based upon the Divine Will, Divine Mind and Divine Heart. They form the source for each of the Three Rays of Witchcraft.

In Gardnerian Wicca, a Saxon term, *Dryghten*, is used for the entity beyond the Lord and Lady, and that name arose as the manifestation of Will. Sometimes a red candle was used secretly on Wiccan altars to represent Dryghten. The name usually translates as "Lord" but supposedly without the same gender identification.

Cruthear is a Scottish name for the Great Spirit as Great Shaper, and as our thoughts shape our reality, this name arose to identify the Divine Mind as expressed in the Hermetic texts such as the Kybalion. We are all thoughts within the Divine Mind, we are all shaped, and constantly shaping this force of energy, image and idea with our thoughts, words and actions.

The Divine Heart, the source of divine unconditional or perfect, love, is named after a figure in later Welsh mythology, from the work of Iolo Morganwg. *Celiced* (pronounced Kelli-Ked) is seen as the union of two secret gods, Celi, the hidden god of the heavens beyond the Sun, and Ced, the hidden feminine power of the Earth.

Goddess & God
Weaver-Web & Singer-Song

The Temple's manifestations of the Lady and Lord, Goddess and God, work through the Temple egregore, helping their particular forms manifest more strongly in the world. The Weaver weaves the tapestry of creation from her own body, while the Singer sings his song, reverberating the logos of creation throughout the web. They are both the origin of creation and the creation itself, everything seen and unseen. She manifests much like a spider goddess in the center of creation, running her strands out in all directions. He manifests as the starry horned one. His heartbeat is the drum of the cosmic rhythms and his voice echoes the music of the spheres.

While the expression of the Weaver and the Singer welcomes in a wide variety of divine manifestations for the members of the Temple to work with personally, several gods have made themselves known due to the number of people working with them in the Temple

The Dark Goddesses
Morrighan • Hecate • Ceridwen

Macha, an aspect of the trinity known as the Morrighan, was the first goddess to commune with me, and guide me on the path to teaching. She was the first to make apparent to me that the form of the teachings, after the completion of the books, had to expand or stop. She gave me a choice, as a dark feathered lady of fate, to do something completely different, or deepen this work by establishing a terrestrial group to administer the teachings.

Hecate, Matron of Witches, gained prominence in the Temple teachings after Christopher and Steve's experiences at the queer men's Pagan festival Between the Worlds. There Hecate and Dionysus are the Matron and Patron of the event. Seen by Christopher as the World Soul or Holy Spirit of the Universe, the guiding light and connecting force in the three worlds, he felt on a cosmic level that she was similar in identity to his own Witch Mother goddess, the Morrighan. This expression of the cosmic aspect of the Goddess became more terrestrial through the use of oracular workings. Soon Adam's own experiences with Hecate influenced his practice and their collective work within the gay men's group known as The Circle of the Sacred Thyrsus. As a teacher of herb-craft, she guided the building of the products in the apothecary and Temple store. Personal honoring of August thirteenth as the Feast of Hecate became an oracular workings for the greater community of the Temple.

Ceridwen is a stern teacher but goddess of inspiration. Forging personal relationships with many of the writers, poets, and mediums of the Temple before there was a Temple, including Alix Wright, Jocelyn VanBokkelen, Bonnie Kraft, and myself. Her influence grows as the teachings of the cauldron-born ones develop.

In many ways, the three manifest as a triple goddess in their own right, even if they have different cultural associations and time periods. Hecate, in *The Chaldean Oracles*, was a universal figure, more heavenly than underworld, the connecting bridge of light between humanity and the greater powers. The Morrighan is the goddess between the old gods of the Fomorians and Fir Bolgs of Ireland, and the new gods of the Tuatha de Danann, as a goddess of sovereignty, life, death, sex, and the land itself. Ceridwen is the mother of the cauldron, and of the cauldron-born, who rise up again from the depths to take their place with poets, bards, Druids, heroes and gods. She is the great initiatrix.

Morrighan T-shirt Design by Derek O'Sullivan

The Lords of Light and Dark
Lugh and Cernunnos

Two gods frequently called upon in Temple workings are the Celtic gods Lugh and Cernunnos. Lugh is perceived as a lord of lightning, light, fire, and the Sun. He is the many-skilled one, and blesses us with his craft. Through working with him, we often find our talents in the Craft and gain aid in overcoming our deficiencies. Cernunnos is the stag-horned god of forest. He is the god who holds open the gates of life and death. He is the hunter and the hunted, the underworld lord and the master of animals. Cernunnos is the one we approach to gain greater knowledge of our animal allies.

While Lugh and Cernunnos are a particular Celtic expression of this concept of the Witch God as light and dark, one could also see the same forces in figures such as Apollo and Dionysus or Osiris/Horus and Set. We see the two-fold god as going beyond any one cultural expression of his power.

Sabbatic Deities
Brid, Ostara, Bel, Lugh, Mabon & Modron, Morrighan & Dagda

In the turning of the Wheel of the Year, several deities are honored historically, even though they might come from a variety of cultures and traditions. In the public Sabbats of the Temple of Witchcraft, we often honor these deities as well, following such familiar traditions, knowing that in many ways, they are also expressions of the fundamental aspects of our own five-fold divinity. While the two solstices, Yule and Litha, do not have specific deities associated with the name of the Sabbat, the other six do.

Imbolc is a festival to honor Bridget, known as St. Bridget to the Christians who celebrate Candlemas, and Brid to those looking at older Pagan traditions. She is a triple goddess of healing, poetry and smith-craft, with both wells and fires sacred to her.

On Ostara we honor the Teutonic goddess Ostara, who returns on the Vernal Equinox to renew the land with the visible sign of the first flowers. She is somewhat similar to the Greek Persephone, who rises from the underworld to signal the return of spring, though Ostara is said to return from the Sun upon the chariot of the Sun god. Many see connections between her and the Welsh goddess Blodeuwedd, the maiden of flowers.

Beltane is the celebration of the fires of Bel, or Belenos, a pan-Celtic god of light, fire and possibly the Sun. Fires were lit for purification in his honor. Modern Pagans also see Beltane as the union between the young flower Goddess and the God of light, who descends into the land as the Green Man.

Lammas is the more popular Saxon name of the grain harvest, known as *Lughnassadh* in the Irish tradition. Lugh is an Irish warrior god of light and great skills. He is associated with lightning, storms and in modern Paganism, the sun and harvest grains. Lughnassadh means the "Funeral Feast of Lugh" but really is about the funeral of his foster mother, Tailitu, and is celebrated with games and revelry.

Mabon is a modern name for the Autumnal Equinox, honoring the young Mabon, son of Modron. This child of light was lost to the Underworld, and King Arthur was sent to find him.

On Samhain, in the Irish tradition, the Dagda and Morrighan consummated their union across a river before the Tuatha de Danann, Children of Danu, battled their enemies, the Fomorians. The Morrighan, through the Dagda, gave her blessing upon the Tuatha for victory. So they are associated with this day of death and the ancestors.

Other deities appropriate to the theme of the ritual may of course be called upon, but these are the ones most often honored at these times in the Temple of Witchcraft. (See **Chapter 8: Holy Days and Rituals** for more details.)

Hermes
The Thrice-Great

Hermes, known as Mercury to the Romans and equated with the Egyptian God Thoth, or Tehuti in his native lands, is a patron of modern Witches and magicians. While mostly seen as a messenger god in modern lore, bringing the messages of the gods across the realms, Hermes is a psychopomp, a guide of souls who traverses the realms above, below, and between, and has some similarities to Hecate in this respect. Today he is often worshiped in tandem with Hecate at crossroads. He is truly an intermediary, not just a simple messenger.

He is a trickster god, the inventor or patron of diverse things, including gambling, commerce, travelers, trade, sports, poetry, writing, magick, thieves, and literature. While diverse, they all have a transitory nature. Many of his qualities give him comparisons to Lugh and Odin, both Mercurial gods in the modern sense of associations with planetary forces and attributes. He was also associated with the patron of the Hermetic arts, Hermes Trismegistus ("The Thrice-Great Hermes"), the philosopher-god who is attributed as the source of the Hermetic texts. Witches and magicians today are guided by the *Kybalion*, a modern text said to distill the essence of Hermeticism into seven basic principles (see **Cosmology** in **Chapter Four**).

While seen today as the youngest of the Olympians, son of Zeus and brother of Apollo, there are hints to an older origin for Hermes. His son is said to be Pan, the goat-god who is truly an elder Arcadian deity absorbed into Greek myth, and originally Hermes was also depicted with goat hooves for feet, and perhaps his helmet wings were once horns. His other son is the phallic god Priapus. The three together have all of the attributes associated with the God of Witches in modern Wicca. Some Witches see him as the "invisible god" of the wind who is the trickster and master of the Sabbat.

The Couple of Blessings
Ganesha and Lakshmi

The gods Ganesha and Lakshmi are considered Vedic, or Hindu, but their worship has spread across the world, beloved by people in both the East and the West. They come to us in the Temple through the devotion of Adam and Alix. They are often worshipped together as god and goddess of divine blessings. The pair is honored at TempleFest, for the success of the event as a whole.

Ganesha is the elephant-headed god, child of Shiva and Paravati. He is the remover of obstacles and lord of new beginnings. He is a benevolent and good-natured god who often helps those who make a prayer or offering to him. Various magickal systems have associated him with the Moon, for the crescent like elephant tusks, Mercury for his attributes to bless journeys and business ventures, also to clear the path of travel, or Jupiter, for his good fortune and blessings.

Lakshmi is the goddess of good fortune, blessings, prosperity and material success. She is considered a Venus cognate in Western magickal systems for, like Aphrodite-Venus, she is associated with oceans, though in her case, the cosmic ocean of milk, and both are associated with luxury and comfort. Venus is also associated with Witchcraft in Roman times as the goddess of the Witches, or *Venefica*. Lakshmi is sometimes depicted as consort of Ganesha, with or without the goddess of wisdom, Sarasvati, and other times as the wife of Vishnu.

The second current of Temple allies is made up of the races of spirit that manifest divine principles upon the Earth. The races that made themselves known in the Three Rays vision and in the work of the Temple are the Animal Guardians, the Angels, the Faeries, and the Mighty Dead.

Animal Guides & Guardians
Stag, Horse, Crow, and Snake

The four most prominent animal spirits guiding the temple are the guardians of the four thresholds.

- **Stag** is the animal ally of the element of earth. Stag teaches strength and perception of the world around us. Stag is protective and guarding.
- **Horse** is the animal ally of the element of fire. Horse brings power and swiftness to our work.
- **Crow** is the animal ally of the element of air. Crow brings truth and wisdom to our rituals.
- **Snake** is the animal ally of the element of water. Snake helps us transform and listen to our own intuition.

Angelic Guides
Tzadkiel, Uriel, and Michael

When the first vision workings involving the Temple were performed, the archangels Tzadkiel, Uriel, and an entity of light referred to as Lumiel, from the angelic teachings of Madeline Montalban, made themselves known. Tzadkiel worked intensely with me for a time prior to the Temple and then seemed to disappear from my practice. Uriel became a guiding force, associated with the work of crossing the Abyss, and Lumiel is the promethean angelic figure, bringing light to the darkness of the Earth. As time evolved, both Uriel and Lumiel seemed to become one figure, as both translate to

"Light of God" revealing a deeper mystery. Through the work of many Temple leaders, and in particular Alix Wright, Archangel Michael started to take a greater prominence in the work of the Temple, and now often appears as the third guardian. With these archangels' Qabalistic correspondences, we have figures for Jupiter, Uranus, and the Sun.

Faery Guides
Queen Aroxana & King Aubrey

Once the Temple was established, any faery contact was fairly nondescript and left to the personal work of individual priestesses and priests. Then, one evening in the summer of 2009, I was approached by a powerful entity while meditating on my back porch. She rose up from the land and felt distinctly from New England, if not just the northeast. She was faery, but not the bright, white British Faery. She was much wilder, with dark skin, and an almost feral quality while remaining regal and poised. Her features were a mix of Native American, African and Aboriginal. She offered me and the Temple a deal. She would help us obtain a permanent home, land that was appropriate for us and our work, if we made more contact with her and her people and the general Pagan population. I agreed and we began our journey together.

Years later she introduced me to her consort, the Faery King Aubrey, looking more like the figure of Oberon as he is depicted in the comics *Books of Magic* and *The Sandman*. He is blue-green skinned and horned, though the horns shifts from ram to bull, to goat and stag, and sometimes all four at once. While "king" he appears more like a wizard, priest, and healer, a faery Merlin or Gandalf, who helps prepare us for deeper workings and healing.

Ancestral Guides
The Mighty Dead

One of the main guiding forces for the Temple is our communion with the Mighty Dead. They were considered by Gerald Gardner, arguably the founder of modern Wicca, as the "saints" of Witchcraft. They are the enlightened inner plane adepts or secret chiefs of the turn of the twentieth century British occult movements, as viewed from a Witchcraft paradigm. They are whom we seek to be through the practice of the Mysteries and the perfection of the soul through our Craft. They are the inner world priestesses and priests, mediating the Great Work of the Goddess, God, and Great Spirit in a different way than the incarnated priests and priestesses. Their guidance is the force that drives our work, inspiring the regeneration of the Witchcraft traditions. Within this greater body of inner plane initiates we also connect to orders dedicated to specific work in the Temple, just as the Temple has its own ministries.

Along with the Mighty Dead, other ancestral contacts help our communion and work. Ancestors of the Craft, be they famous Witches as teacher and authors, such as Doreen Valiente and Alex Sanders (which some may or may not see as part of the Mighty Dead), or the deceased within our own Temple community and blood relations.

The ancestors of the land are also important, those known and unknown who are buried where we do our work. Founding our tradition and its work in Salem, NH, we have found kinship with the Stone Age people who crafted the site known today as America's Stonehenge, or Mystery Hill, in North Salem, and those in the nearby graveyard known as Cemetery at Hales Bridge. In particular the grave of Samuel Davis has attracted our attention and honor. Along with Samuel Davis of Salem, NH, we also honor Arthur Corburn and Lucretia E. Hall, who built Grandview Manor, the first Temple of Witchcraft home, in the year 1898. The Hall family has a long history in Salem, and we see them as honored ancestors of place.

The Temple is not limited to these entities, but is ever-evolving. Every individual Witch's personal guides, guardians, and allies from these realms contribute to the collective whole of the Temple if they so choose. Various other gods and goddess are also allied with our work in the Temple.

The Spirit of the Temple has manifested with the name *Towathan*, and appears as a amalgam of the animal guardians: A horned serpent with iridescent crow wings and flaring nostrils, similar to the feathered serpents of Mayan and Aztec Myth. Towathan is the manifestation of the Temple Egregore in spirit form, empowered by these various spirit sources, human and non-human.

The physical link we have to the Temple's egregore is the Foundation Stone or King Stone construct, consisting of a large Quartz point and cauldron full of blessed earth. The crystal skulls of the Mystery School Ministers are also conduits to the Hidden Company's wisdom in the Temple egregore.

Just as individual entities have an Inner Temple, egregores also have their own Inner Temple, connecting it to the greater Temple of the enlightened beyond time, space, shape and form. The Temple of Witchcraft is no different. While it often echoes the imagery of the eternal sabbat, it is a curious mix of outdoor grove and ancient temple, with twelve pillars surrounding a stone altar of three flames. The flames burn red, blue, and yellow and the columns are sometimes pillars of stone and other times trees. Within this temple is the conclave of guides to the Temple of Witchcraft and they can lead you to the Eternal Sabbat of the Phosphorous Grove.

Through our work in the realm of sacred pilgrimages, we are weaving webs of connection between the Temple egregore and our allied spirits and the spirits of the sacred lands that birthed our traditions. Starting with a 2011 pilgrimage to Glastonbury with members of the Temple, we communed and connected Towathan and our Mighty Dead allies to the spirits of Avalon, Camelot, Stonehenge, and Avebury. We continue to visit sacred sites in the British birth cauldron of the modern Craft.

A Syncretic Temple
The Age of the Great Blessing & the Great Curse

With such a wide array of allies and cultures contributing to the vision of the Temple of Witchcraft, it would be easy to consider us eclectic Witches, and many in the Temple do subscribe to that name. We are a scavenger religion, gathering up what works wherever we find it. Eclecticism has its strengths and weaknesses. We can collect only the bits of wisdom that are flattering to us, rather than look deeper into the patterns that force change and growth.

Yet the Temple encourages a multicultural view, looking to the whole world's breadth of ancient Paganism, not any one culture, and encourages students and priest/esses to forge their own relationships with the spirit allies that show up and genuinely want to work in cooperation with us and our goals. We seek mutually beneficial relationships with our allies. We look at the role of the Witch as a vocation as much as we do a religion, art, or science. Every culture has had their Witches, whether they used that name or not.

Our challenge is that we live in the Age of the Great Blessing and the Age of the Great Curse. It is the Age of the Great Blessing, because never before have we had access to so many cultures, mythologies, religions, philosophies, and languages. It makes the library of Alexandria pale by comparison when we think of how readily so much is at our fingertips, even before the age of the internet. We have more information than the elders before us and the founders of Wicca ever had. We have access to the world.

Yet we live in the Age of the Great Curse. The Great Curse is never before have we had access to so many cultures, mythologies, religions, philosophies, and languages! In ancient times, you were rooted in a cultural paradigm, mythos and specific land. The language, land and myths informed you and your relationship with spirit and nature. You knew what various omens, totems, and images meant to you and your people. You had your story, or your people's, about who you were, where you came from and why you were here. Owl is an animal totem and omen that means many things to many different peoples, from Native American, Celt, Greek, Roman, and Middle Eastern. Some are "good" and some are "bad." How do you know what it means to you in your spiritual life? How do you know you are not picking the meaning that flatters you, or the meaning that scares you the most? It can help to be rooted in a culture, tradition, and people.

Having access to the world can also mean that you have more difficulty relating to any one paradigm, group, or cultures, so you wander. Wandering can be fun and informative, but it can also be hard to then build roots or foundations when the time is right. Our current metaphysical movement, for better or worse, is navigating the Great Blessing and the Great Curse, creating a multi-perspective modern story of our our people, the people of planet Earth at this time of great change. Where do we all come from collectively, without destroying our individual stories? How do we create a history, mythos and cosmology that allows for the history, mythos of cosmology of the Chinese as well as the Aztecs, the Celts along with the Yoruba? How do we have a freedom of world religion that fosters Christianity, Buddhism, Paganism, Islam, and every other religion without reducing those wisdom traditions to nothing? That is the paradox of the Aquarian Age that must be resolved as we go forward, the paradox of the individual and the collective. Many threads are needed to make a tapestry.

We borrow terms and concepts from other cultures for purely practical reasons. We are occultists. As occultists seek the divine through the multitude of diverse manifestations of spirit, we are ultimately scientists. Rather than having cultural devotion to any one school of thought, a true scientist builds upon the research of both the past and of peers. If someone on the other side of the world has an answer, a better way of explaining something we have observed or experienced, why not use it? We would be foolish not to. We have an incomplete knowledge of our Pagan and Witchcraft lore, and even if we didn't, no one culture has the answer to everything. Perhaps a purpose in all this diversity is to help each other go further, just as scientific teams do. Many in the Temple of Witchcraft have a scientific background, or at least an interest in science, and that lends to the ethos of the occultist.

Likewise, in the creation of new things, we mix and blend because we are artists. All great artistic, dance, and musical movements are the results of the influences of the people practicing it. If not for this blending, forms of music, art, language, and food would not evolve, and new disciplines, such as jazz, could never establish a style and culture of their own if people did not dare to experiment. The greats have a fidelity to tradition while still experimenting and pushing the envelope. The best musicians and artists seek their peers across the world, and share ideas, gaining inspiration in this cross-pollination.

Lastly we borrow and blend not only as scientists and artists, but as seekers, and those on a spiritual quest of evolution and wisdom. While some would divide the occultist from the mystic, we as Witches have aspects of both. The occultist seeks to know through the diverse manifestations of spirit in creation, immanent divinity and finding their corresponding patterns and the wisdom they contain. The mystic seeks to transcend the many forms of divinity and become one with the divine godhead, beyond form. Yet we as Witches embrace the paradox of immanence and transcendence, going back to the roots of shamanic lore, to the most ancient philosophies of the world, which predate this artificial divide. We seek out wisdom wherever we find it to experience, to grow and to evolve, the most noble of all reasons.

While you are in the process it is hard to see, so we can appear to be only eclectic. Yet in truth, we are in a stage of syncretism. We are drawing together diverse material and connecting it, syncretizing it without it losing its original power. The members of the Temple of Witchcraft consider it a syncretic tradition, for we do not mindlessly collect in our scavenging, but add to our tradition with blending and blessings, mixing into the wisdom of the whole with deep roots so our branches can grow tall and strong.

Interfaith and Intrafaith Bridges

Much of the Temple's mission is to build bridges between the Witchcraft, Wiccan and Pagan communities and the seemingly "outside" world, helping us all realize we are no more outside of other faith traditions and secular communities than any other religious tradition. The image of the Witch is one between the worlds, in liminal spaces such as the edge of the village, but has been an important part of the village, and must be so again. We encourage interfaith outreach and community actions with other organizations and groups, and opening dialogues to understand different faith traditions and, in turn, be understood.

Seminary students in Witchcraft Five are required to take a survey of world religions, exploring their theologies, cultures, and practices, learning what is similar and what is different to our own. While we feel some theological views are incompatible in practice with our own, we respect the right of others to experience and explore those views, as long as they don't infringe on the life, health, or rights of others to do so. While our biggest differences might be in comparison with larger orthodox or dogmatic traditions, we find a strong resonance in idea and experience, if not execution, with the mystical side of the world's religions, such as forms of Jewish Kaballah, Christian mysticism, Sufism, Tantrik Buddhism, and many aspects of Hinduism. Ultimately, as an occult tradition, we believe in the Secret Doctrine, the Hidden Tradition that is the underpinning of the mystical traditions across the world, as so many of these paths lead to the same place internally, even if the theology to get there is different. Such a teaching is compared to climbing to the top of the mountain by different paths, and many of us explore or even switch to other paths along the way.

Along with outreach to other faiths, there are many expressions of the Pagan traditions, and we also believe in bridge building in our larger Pagan communities. Intrafaith is working within different denominations of a larger spiritual tradition. We welcome the wisdom of Druids, Heathens, British Traditional Wiccans, Traditional Craft Witches, Kemetic Reconstructionists, Ceremonial Magicians, and various traditions that straddle lines culturally and theologically between intrafaith and interfaith, such as Vodou, Theosophy, and Daoism. We have no requirement that members of the Temple belong to only one tradition, ours, and encourage members to explore and even initiate in other traditions to build those bridges of understanding.

While we have a broad and open view, we are anchored firmly in Witchcraft as a paradigm. While some might think a theosophical, occult world view would lend itself to a much more wide, eclectic practice, beyond things like the magick circle, eight sabbats, and lunar holidays, it is actually the focus of tradition that allows us to reach deeper, higher, and wider, while still maintaining a core, a center still point. The links to the past, real and mythic, give us a foundation to build our vision for the future, and be open, honest, and stable when working beyond ourselves, into the Pagan communities and beyond.

Tides of Temples and Traditions

Temples, like anything else, have cycles and seasons. Everything has its rhythm. Everything has its tides. Temples emerge from the astral waves and manifest upon the shores of consciousness. Sometimes they last for aeons. Often they last for much shorter times. Then they are consumed by the tides again. Many rise again, the same or in new forms.

Witchcraft itself has ridden these cycles of time and tide. What we consider Witchcraft today might have flourished in the ancient past, and diminished with the rise of new religions. While I am a romantic who believes strands of it survived in secrecy, for all practical purposes, it withdrew from the Western world when the tide of the Inquisition was strongest. Now, after a relatively brief period of rest and reflection, the tide of the Craft is coming back in, with new practitioners, covens, groups, traditions, and now temples.

Terrestrial temples should only last as long as they are working the mission in the world, and that mission is in harmony with the aeon. If not, the mission either needs to adapt and change, or the temple's mission will be fulfilled or now unnecessary, and it will withdraw. There are many withdrawn orders and inner temples at the edge of the abyss. They often reach out to be regenerated by enterprising groups of adepts who take their strands and return them to the Earth. Such adepts who succeed them have to know when to let them return back from whence they came.

The main role of temples and their cycles of life is to generate a sort of spiritual DNA, that can be passed onto both individuals and new groups, as society evolves. Each is an experiment in consciousness, and those fit to survive will pass on these ways through such spiritual DNA, even if the terrestrial organization has a limited time in the world. We seek to find our purpose, our rhythm and pass on the best wisdom we can, for the good of all involved.

Some temples and traditions last only a generation or two. Others for an aeon, and so many fall somewhere between. All we can hope for is the fulfillment of our spiritual goals and to pass what we have learned and what is useful to the next wave in the tide. As the elder and author Nema tell us, the true nature of our work is, "every valid system of Initiation self-destructs upon successful completion". We don't seek to hold on, but seek to adapt until we attain the successful completion or our mission, our particular link in the chain, or wave in the tide, making way for those who come next.

Chapter Six: The Temple Sigil and Symbols

Part of building a magickal order is working with signs, symbols, sigils, and seals that help identify and maintain the order's power in the inner worlds while mediating that power to the outer world. The design of the Sigil of the Temple came in coordination with our guiding spirits. The purpose was to encapsulate the sprit and ethos of the Temple in a modern manner while still retaining occult symbolism.

The Temple Sigil

Foundations of the Temple

At the center of the sigil is the triple spiral, for the powers of the Three Rays of Witchcraft and the three aspects of Divinity from which they arise. They stand for the Divine Will, or Dryghten, and the Red Ray of Will and Power, the Divine Heart, or Celiced, and the Blue Ray of Love and Trust, and for The Divine Mind, or Cruthear, and the Yellow Ray of Wisdom and Cunning. On an organizational level, this is also the role of the three Founders in the center, echoed by the three Keystone Bearers at Branch Temples.

Surrounding the triple spiral is a decagram, or ten pointed star consisting of two five-pointed stars, one upright and one downward. The five-pointed star, or pentagram, is a symbol of the five elements —earth, air, fire, water, and spirit—in harmony. Also known as the *pentalpha*, as the angles make it look like five letter As, the first letter of the sacred alphabets and a symbol of beginnings. Five is sacred to the Goddess of Witches, Venus, namesake of the *Venefica* of Rome. Many of the Witch's herbs are blooms with five-pointed flowers, from the healing St. John's Wort to the deadly Belladonna. When inscribed inside a circle, it is known as a *pentacle*, and symbol of wholeness, the sixth sense of psychic ability, and equated with the shield of protection and the coin of prosperity. Witches wear it as a sign of their practice, like Christians might wear a cross or Jews a Star of David.

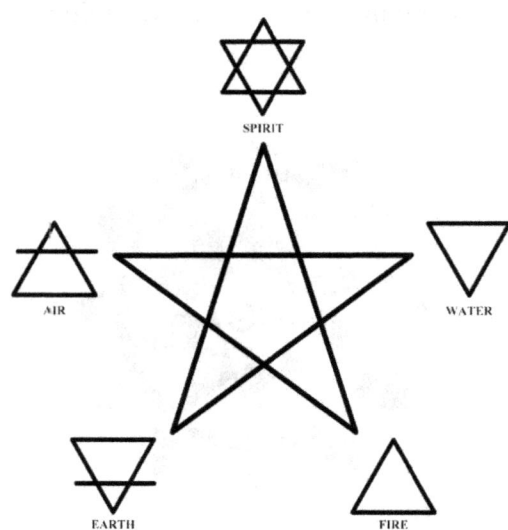

Pentagram with the Elements

The two pentagrams are signs of the microcosm below and the macrocosm above, the interplay between the heavens and depths that create the world between that we know. The ten points are also symbolic of the ten points upon the Tree of Life found in Hermetic Qabalah and alchemy:

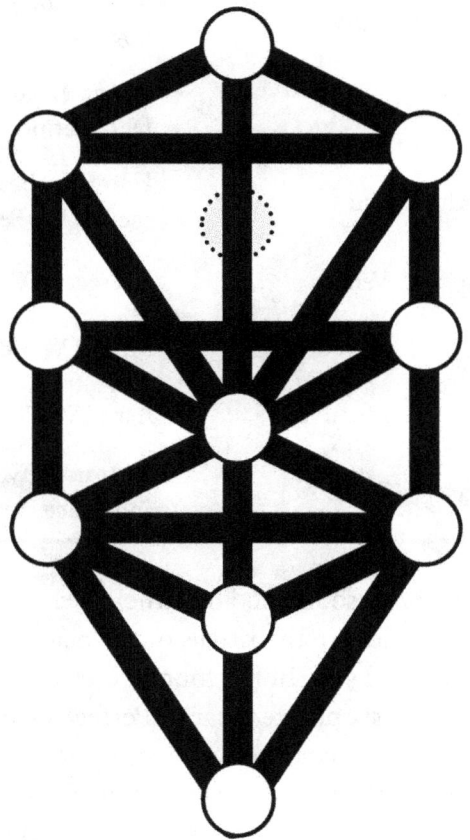

Tree of Life

Each of the ten points describes a point of creation, a level of reality in the outward universe and within us. The ten points, known as the *sephiroth*, are:

1	Kether	Beyond the Stars	Source, Divinity
2	Chokmah	Stars/Neptune	Masculine Energy, God
3	Binah	Saturn	Feminine Energy, Goddess
4	Chesed	Jupiter	Mercy, Compassion, Higher Love
5	Geburah	Mars	Power, Might, Necessary Destruction
6	Tiphereth	Sun	Harmony, Beauty, Sacrifice, the Higher Self
7	Netzach	Venus	Energetic World, Faery Realm
8	Hod	Mercury	Mental World, Information
9	Yesod	Moon	Astral World, Pattern
10	Malkuth	Earth	Terrestrial World, Earth, Time and Space, Seasons

The ten points are also marked by either circles or squares at their tips. The six circles are the rituals of the macrocosm, of the hexagram or six pointed star. In the fourth degree teachings initiates learn to align with the six pointed star of Perfect Love and Perfect Trust within the heart, a mandala for the open heart chakra.

The four remaining squares are symbols of the terrestrial elements of earth, air, fire, and water, scattered evenly across the circle in the cross quarters.

Hexagram with the Planets

The circle is surrounded by twelve points, each for a zodiac sign, one for each ministry. Four of the points are smaller than the rest, indicating the directions of north, east, south, and west, as well as the four elements.

The Temple sigil is the public seal for students, initiates, and leaders to access the energy of the Temple. Temple ministers are taught a ritual and given energetic keys to "open and close" the astral temple, to align workings with the spirit and energy of the Temple.

Ministry Sigils

Along with the main Temple sigil, there are thirteen other sigils for the twelve ministries and a thirteenth ministry for members with special missions outside of the parameters of the twelve defined ministries. Each sigil helps attune the witches in that ministry to that aspect of the Temple.

Foundations of the Temple

Aries
Warrior

Taurus
Steward

Gemini
Trickster

Cancer
Mother

Leo
Artisan

Virgo
Healer

Libra
Judge

Scorpio
Guardian

Sagittarius
Teacher

Capricorn
Father

Aquarius
Rebel

Pisces
Ecstatic

Foundations of the Temple

Ophiuchus
Special Missions

Temple Ministry Sigils

Amulets with the Temple sigil on one side and the Ministry sigils on the other are available through Deva Designs, with all royalties going to the Temple to fund our work.

Servitor Spirits

Each of the ministries has a constructed thoughtform, also known as a *servitor spirit* or *artificial elemental*. While some are specific to the ministerial work and kept private, some, by their the nature of their work, are shared with the greater community, and safeguards have been built into their magickal structure to make sure they are of the greatest benefit.

TA11AT

TA11AT Sigil

Foundations of the Temple

TAllAT—usually depicted with lower case L's to make it a mirror image—is a servitor of Gemini Ministry. That's "tal-lat" written so its name is a palindrome (reading the same backwards and forwards). The sigil incorporates the Pentacles of Mercury along with its name, as TAllAT is a genderless being. It's purpose is to facilitate communication, particularly clear communication, amongst members of the Temple. You may call upon it to enhance any communication—verbal, written, or otherwise—simply by saying "TAllAT, servant of Gemini, carry my meaning true." You may find this useful to do before holding meetings, writing reports, or otherwise engaging in important Temple communication.

As all servitor spirits must be "fed," TAllAT is fed with offerings of smoke: Frankincense or similar scents are good. Storrax (a resin associated with Hod and Mercury) works well, too, but the smoke is more important than the scent. You may wish to visualize the servitor manifesting through the smoke, and TAllAT has a smoky, mercurial form that is always shifting and flowing. You can combine giving TAllAT a task with "feeding" it by burning a written copy of your message along with your invocation.

TAllAT is created and programmed to facilitate clear communication, but not to communicate on our behalf. So don't expect much of a result asking it to communicate something you yourself do not communicate. The actual communication must come from us; the Gemini servitor is intended to help clear the way for it.

Urok

Urok is a Virgo ministry servitor spirit, specifically designed to send continual healing energy to those placed upon the Virgo Ministry Healing list. Urok's name is an expression of its function, U-R-OK, or "You Are Okay." The Temple office has a healing shrine for Urok, including a public list for healing blessings.

The entire collection of Temple Ministry servitors is kept in a private magical book known amongst the Leadership affectionately as *The Grimoire Servitorum*.

Chapter Seven: The Teachings of the Temple

The Temple of Witchcraft started as a system of magickal training and, at its core, the community is devoted to this training in the Mysteries. Those who complete the Mystery School and Seminary have an outstanding foundation in modern Witchcraft, occultism, and the Western Mysteries, an excellent platform for any further study and service. The system itself, minus the culture of the Temple of Witchcraft community, can be found in the *Temple of Witchcraft* series of books and CD companions, as published by Llewellyn Worldwide. They are specifically designed to focus on the technique and teaching, rather than promote any one tradition, culture, or identity. Any solitary, coven, or group can benefit from the teachings, and adapt them to their own Witchcraft culture, and many independent teachers and study groups do.

In the Mystery School and Seminary, that same openness is maintained, but the culture of the Temple that has grown up around the teachings, including our unique expression of the theology and art, is contained in our Book of Shadows. Parts of the Book of Shadows are given to the students in the Mystery School and Seminary. It includes practices specific to the Temple, as well as prose and prayers that embody the deeper teachings and Mysteries as expressed by us.

The Mysteries are spiritual events that must be experienced directly, beyond intellectual understanding, and usually occur through religious ritual, meditation, and the experiences of life. The fundamental idea of the teachings is that there are many ways to the center. There is no one path for all to the Mysteries. The training approaches the center through five basic mystery traditions or techniques, realizing not all will work equally for everyone, but the experience and attempt at each helps balance our essential nature and character. Some come easier than others. The ease and struggle help our soul grow and develop. Each of these five mystery experiences leads to an understanding of divinity. These five paths lead one to understand and apply the magickal will to service of the self, community, planet, and divinity.

Mystery Path	**Level**	**Element**	**Textbook and CD Companion**
Oracular	1	Fire	*The Inner Temple of Witchcraft*
Fertility	2	Earth	*The Outer Temple of Witchcraft*
Ecstatic	3	Water	*The Temple of Shamanic Witchcraft*
Gnostic	4	Air	*The Temple of High Witchcraft*
Resurrection & Service	5	Spirit	*The Living Temple of Witchcraft, Volume I & II*

While we train in all five, one might affect a particular Witch more profoundly than another. Certain branches develop into a daily personal practice, and other practices might be set aside, once a fuller understanding is developed.

Oracular Mystery

The oracular mysteries of the first degree are focused on psychic perception. Oracles were ideally those with sight, psychic vision, or such communion with the gods they could issue prophecy and counsel. While the deeper oracular experiences of invocation and possession are reserved for higher levels, the awakening and illumination that occurs first when the inner flame is lit, fanned, and allowed to guide is the mystery of the first degree. Though we call it "sight," it really is any psychic perception that guides us and can be measurably true. Meditation techniques quiet the mind and prepare the body. Knowledge of Hermetic philosophy and quantum physics helps us accept new realities as valid. Exercises on clearing, energy movement, psychic travel, psychic diagnosis, and spirit contact help create measurable guidance, thereby awakening one out of fantasy and into true psychic experience.

Fertility Mystery

The Fertility Mystery of the second degree revolves around what most think of as Wicca, both in the traditional and eclectic varieties. Seen as a mystery of polarity between the male and female as expressed through nature, fertility can mean a whole lot beyond child bearing and growing crops. These Fertility Mysteries are those of nature, of the elements and elementals, of the gods who embody and guide nature, and of the magick found in nature, through the plants, woods, and stones. Practitioners learn to partner with these unseen forces to manifest better things in their life, and banish what does not serve. Earth, for this manifestation in the natural world, is the element of the second degree. The highest manifestation of this mystery is said to be in the Great Rite, the *hieros gamos*, the union of Goddess and God, the union of Priestess and Priest. It can be done in truth or token for great effect.

Ecstatic Mystery

Ecstasy means to go beyond the flesh, and is not merely about pleasure. It refers to experiences of expanded consciousness, going beyond the limited perception of the earthly self. Sometimes one expands outward to include the self, other times one journeys outward to other realms, seemingly leaving the flesh behind. Shamanic practitioners across the world were considered "technicians of ecstasy" because they knew how to perform this spirit flight and commune with the creatures of other worlds for mutual benefit. It is my belief, along with many others, that European Witchcraft is a remnant of a form of European Pagan shamanism, eventually warped and destroyed by the rise of the Church. The Ecstatic mystery seeks to look at core shamanic techniques through the lens of the Witch to safely reclaim them in the modern age. Within the tales of the Inquisition are some truths—animal allies, spirit flight, contracts with the other world. Such themes are also found in fairy tales, hinting at the deeper mysteries, and through the theme of unraveling of the Inquisition's knot, we face the shadow, all that is dark and repressed within us, and within humanity. The deepest experience of the third degree is communion with the shadow.

Gnostic Mystery

Gnosis is the Greek word for knowledge, but not the knowledge found in books or oral tradition. Gnosis is the direct experience of the divine that grants a special knowledge of the true reality of the cosmos and our place within it. While many equate Gnostic with Christian traditions, as much of the early Christian faith was considered Gnostic before being driven underground by the dominant Christian expressions of faith, many Pagan traditions, ancient and modern, are considered Gnostic at heart. Such traditions often mingle roots with the philosophies of the Neoplatonists, Neopythagoreans, Hermeticists, Alchemists, and Qabalists. In the Temple of Witchcraft, we use the Qabalistic "map" of the Tree of Life and the rituals of modern ceremonial magick as a foundational structure in experiencing different levels of universal consciousness. We encourage the exploration of, and eventual creation of, reality maps. Reality maps are mandala diagrams of the universe, found in the mystical art of many cultures. Understanding patterns of thought, language, and symbol are key. As the shadow communion was the deepest experience of the Ecstatic Mysteries in the third degree, a communion with the Higher Self, also known as the Watcher,

Bornless One, or Holy Guardian Angel (HGA) is the ultimate focus of the Gnostic Mysteries of the fourth degree.

Resurrection and Service Mysteries

The fifth degree is the platform for the Seminary training of a High Priestesses and High Priests. While in no way equivalent academically with a Masters Degree in Divinity from an accredited university, comparable education is our eventual goal. The course, longer than any previous level, is divided into two sections.

The first is modeled on the Descent of the Goddess Inanna, revisiting the theme of the Underworld and Shadow. In the Descent, the Goddess passes through seven gates, giving up one of her seven special magickal tools. Each one is used for a lesson in a seven-fold model involving the seven tools, the chakras, planets, Celtic castles, operations of alchemy, and the stages in the Miracle of Bread. The pattern is one of deep personal development to be able to serve the gods, community, and unconditional divinity.

The second stage is based upon the model of the Hero's Journey through the twelve signs of the Zodiac, most popularly shown in the Twelve Labors of Hercules. While there are aspects of personal development, the true teachings are on the interpersonal development of a community leader, teacher, ritualist, and healer. Lessons are based upon the necessary work to be a clear leader in community, able to minister to self, small groups, and larger gatherings. The work is definitely "task" oriented, as each student is on a "quest" to complete their labors in the appropriate amount of time. The deeper philosophies of the Craft, as well as how they relate to the modern world, are explored.

The fifth degree culminates in an initiation and vision working to descend through the previously explored seven gates and experience the touch of the dark goddesses and gods of the Craft in the underworld—coming to the realization that the stars are within the heart of the Earth and that darkness is found in the highest of the heavens. Through the resolution of paradox, we claim a place among the Mighty Dead of the Timeless Tradition and find our own path of ministry.

The extended teachings of magick within the Temple follow the three rays theology. Each ray can be associated with a type of operative magick.

Ray	Operative Magick	Discipline	Art/Science	Ally	Vocation
1	Protection	Stone Magick	Alchemy	Angelic	Astrology
2	Prosperity	Plant Magick	Horticulture	Faery	Herbalism
3	Love and Lust	Animal Magick	Midwifery	Ancestral	Divination (Tarot)

Some students focus on a particular area of practice, while others focus on a training within a ray path. Yet, the entire practice of Witchcraft includes all the practices, as they overlap. Alchemy embodies the kingdoms of minerals, plants, and animals. Astrology involve the correspondences of plants and animals as well as stones. Tarot divination has associations with all.

One might think for a more progressive, Aquarian school of training, that a linear, degree structure is unnecessary and antiquated, promoting a "better than" approach by some in "higher" degrees over "lower" degrees. While our system has "degrees" in the sense of levels of teaching, the degrees are truly illusionary. One cannot confer spiritual illumination and gnosis simply through completing a course of study. All any tradition or organization can do is provide the tools, setting, and encouragement, making one "properly prepared" but it is up to the individual to attain gnosis and enlightenment. Levels in training help us provide an outer linear structure to an ultimately non-linear experience. Schools provide a model of tools and resources with expectations, requirements, and experiences. Some skills and terminology must be learned before passing onto a more complex level of information. Without clarity and criteria, expectations for further advancement become nebulous and arbitrary, usually on the whims of whomever is in charge. Without points for discussion, clarification, and even challenge, a magickal group can quite easily go toxic, and many have. Providing materials like a more academic course without robbing the Mystery of the tradition is the goal. Organizing our teachings into five progressively more complex mysteries, then encouraging the freedom to build a personal practice out of the tools given, with new tools learned outside of the training, is the best way at this time for us to do that.

Influences Upon the Teachings

As one might guess from the listed mysteries, there are many influences upon the teaching of the Temple of Witchcraft. The root of the teachings came from the Cabot Tradition of Witchcraft, giving us our view on the Craft as a science, art, and religion. The emphasis on meditation, psychic development, and understanding, not just the "how" but the "why" behind magickal phenomena was stressed in my original training, and continues to be something stressed in the Temple of Witchcraft. Laurie Cabot claims descent from Witches in her own genetic lineage in ages past, but training through a non-Wiccan lineage known as the Witches of Kent. Her own foundation was in British Witchcraft and occultism, which she blended with a growing understanding of the science of psychic phenomenon to create the Cabot Tradition. Much of this formed the nucleus of the Oracular Mysteries of the first degree.

From this foundation we were encouraged to read the basic texts of the time, including those of both the solitary Wiccan variety emphasized by figures such as Scott Cunningham, and those of more British Traditional Wicca as emphasized by Raymond Buckland and Janet and Steward Farrar's earlier books. Exposure to those from a more traditionally Wiccan background influenced my experiences beyond just book knowledge, as community members had experiences in Alexandrian and Gardnerian covens, the teachings of R.J. Stewart, and even the popular and controversial Boston-area group known as Earth Spirit. The Boston-area and Salem, Massachusetts, communities had contact and intermingling with the New York City Pagan communities, leading to a rich cross-pollination. The Cabot second degree material, plus these teachings, formed the kernel of the second degree Fertility Mysteries.

When I met my partner and co-founder Steve Kenson, he introduced me to some of the deeper concepts of Western occultism and rounded my education. While completely familiar with Wicca, he was a self-identified Chaos Magician who began his path in the ceremonial studies of the Golden Dawn. He also had a strong interest in Norse traditions, and worked more in-depth than my Witchcraft friends with the Elder Futhark runes. The pop culture influence of magick as found in the comics of Neil Gaiman, particularly *The Sandman*, and role-playing games like *Mage: The Ascension*, also influenced Steve's worldview, and later mine.

Steve encouraged me in training with *Modern Magick* by Donald Michael Kraig (a particularly good start for Witches seeking ceremonial training, as his roommate was Scott Cunningham and they both had a friendship with Witchcraft elder Raven Grimassi). Kraig led to more traditional Golden Dawn books and teachings though it was never the true focus of my path, even though I sought a stable grounding in it. Most proficient Chaos Magicians have a foundation in more traditional Ceremonial Magick. The work of Austin Osman Spare, particularly his sigilization technique, became a staple in my own practice and that of our coven. His sabbatic style art and line drawings, as well as his Alphabet of Desire, fascinated me, and planted deep seeds that would bear fruit later on.

The study also led me to the work of Aleister Crowley and the path of Thelema, Greek for Will. Though Laurie Cabot taught Tarot using the Crowley Thoth deck, she was not an advocate of his teachings. This new experience with the ceremonial side of things gave me a greater appreciation for the work of Crowley. One can see a profound influence of Thelema in the Temple of Witchcraft, leading many to think we are a Thelemic organization. We are not, though we recognize the dual currents of the Logos of the Aeon and the Shakti of the Age, Aleister Crowley (affectionately called "Uncle Al") and Dion Fortune, as a huge influence upon the modern Witchcraft and Wicca movement. Their joint influence is declared and chronicled by Alan Richardson in his book *Aleister Crowley and Dion Fortune: The Logos of the Aeon and the Shakti of the Age*. In the Temple of Witchcraft, we favor Fortune's look at the three energies of Power, Love, and

Wisdom to balance Crowley's Will and Love as the law of the New Aeon. Thelema and Agape must be balanced by Sophia.

The ceremonial work obviously influenced what would become the fourth degree teachings of the Gnostic Mysteries, as well as developing the key concepts of synthesis beyond eclecticism found in the later teachings. It also provided a kinship with the more ceremonial orders that were decidedly Christian, including the Knights Templar, Freemasons, and Rosicrucians. The romance of the Knights Templar, with their codes, digging for mysteries, and accusations of blasphemy against the church with bizarre initiation rites, also find sympathy with an organization known as the Temple of Witchcraft, and our members, Temple Witches.

My own path led me into several branches further out from the Witchcraft community. One more grounded in the Craft was a study of Celtic Shamanism and Celtic Reconstructionism. I spent a year studying the Welsh myth cycle in *The Mabinogion* with Sharynne MacCleod NicMhacha (Sharon Paice MacLeod), author of *Queen of the Night*. The experiences actually drew me to more free-form shamanism, in the vein of the Michael Harner Foundation for Shamanic Studies, what is known as Core Shamanism. Then a survey began of shamanic styles from all around the world, looking for key similarities. We found connections with the Neo-Celtic revival found in a lot of modern Witchcraft, though the classical mythology of the ancient Pagan world, such as the Greeks, Romans, Egyptians, and Sumerians were certainly an influence. Steve brought a greater understanding of the Norse and Saxon traditions, and his practices with Odin influenced our work.

My desire to learn more about healing had me on a path that included Reiki energy healing, flower essences, and medicinal herbalism. Holistic health became a key concept in my own healing and aid of others. Soon I became a practitioner, combining my skills at tarot and runes with ceremony, shamanic healing, and these new modalities of herbs and hands-on energy work. In some ways I realized I was fulfilling the societal vocation of the Witch. The shamanic work and the vocation of healer lent itself to the formation of the Ecstatic Mysteries of the third degree and the mysteries of rebirth and service in the fifth degree. I also found parallels between the herbal alchemy of Paracelsus and the Ceremonial lore, bridging a gap between the plant spirit animist view with the Hermetic worldview. Alchemists often said that the greatest alchemist of all was Mother Nature herself. While most Witchcraft traditions identify as nature-based, few employ alchemy. My own experiences with both saw a natural marriage between the two, all stemming back to my childhood fascination with bottles and potions.

Through contacts in Reiki and Flower Essences I was introduced to the concepts of the Merkaba, or chariot of light, Shamballa, Lightwork, and Ascension. My intellectual dissatisfaction with the explanations I received from teachers of such traditions led to a thorough investigations of Theosophy and Anthroposophy, particularly the works of Madame Blavatsky, Alice Bailey, and Rudolph Steiner. This more eastern-influenced occultism, which also influenced the major British occultists in the revival of Ceremonial Magick and Wicca, formed a necessary balance to the Golden Dawn and Thelemic teachings. Eventually I saw parallels in the Gnostic light-bearer descent myths of Theosophy with more Gnostic forms of Traditional Craft.

My travels while teaching as an author introduced me to the work of fellow authors and teachers working in parallel ways in the community. Their lectures, books, and friendships have profoundly influenced my own worldview and the foundations of the Temple of Witchcraft. Time at festivals and conventions with figures such as Raven Grimassi, Stephanie Taylor, Judika Illes, Michelle Belanger, T. Thorn Coyle, Orion Foxwood, Paul Beyerl, Oberon Zell Ravenheart, Selena Fox, Emerald Rose, Donald Michael Kraig, Janet Farrar, Gavin Bone, Ivo Dominguez, Isaac Bonewits, Lon Milo DuQuette, Diana Paxson, Kala Trobe, Patricia Monaghan, R.J. Stewart, Jason Augustus Newcomb, and Dorothy Morrison have shaped my magick and my paradigm.

The capstone preceding the formation of the Temple as a legal entity was the reintroduction of non-Wiccan forms of Witchcraft to my own experience, leading right back to my first roots with the Cabot and Kent information. Study with devotees of the Robert Cochrane materials and the ethos of the Clan of Tubal Cain helped show a different perspective, and cement the aesthetic and art of the

Witch as sorcerer and mystic with all that had come before me. The Temple is certainly not in the mold of any Traditional Witchcraft group, but some of the imagery it inspires, particularly experiences of the Sabbat, found in Austin Spare and in modern groups such as the Cultus Sabbati, is unlike what most Wiccan groups experience or seek. The main seeds took root and began to form the inner grove that would be the Temple of Witchcraft.

Both the Clan of Tubal Cain and the Cultus Sabbati are considered Luciferian in ethos. I found parallels with the teachings of Theosophy, more subtle Luciferians, to be sure, though Madame Blavatsky's journal was titled *Lucifer* and Alice Bailey's publisher was Lucius Trust (in place of Lucifer Trust). While most members of the Temple would not identify theologically or socially as Luciferian, the subtle current is there, and might be more appropriately called Promethean. Many consider Prometheus the Pagan philosophical equivalent to the light-bringer Lucifer. Prometheus stole fire from the heavens to bring it to humanity. Exoterically, it is the secret of combustion. Esoterically, the first tool was not fire, but light, meaning consciousness, or knowledge of other worlds, true "illumination".

Another guiding force in the ethos of the Temple was the no-nonsense approach of the mother of Wicca, Doreen Valiente. Starting with her own interests and research until her connection with Gerald Gardner, she touched most major strains of modern Witchcraft, leaving Gardner and exploring the Coven of Atho and the Clan of Tubal Cain. She meticulously researched, asked hard questions, challenged authority, and shared her wisdom generously. The practical and the mystical were equal in her concern. Doreen supported others in the public modern Craft movement with her time and kindness and yet did not suffer fools for long. She paved a way that straddled the line between the traditional and the modern, finding her own place within the growing British Pagan community and we look to her ethos as a guiding light on our own path.

While the cauldron of rebirth for modern Witchcraft and Wicca is found in the British Isles, the founders and council of the Temple all lived in America (with one Irish citizen) so the rise of American Witchcraft certainly influenced our worldview. America's melting-pot culture put a universal spin to the already culturally diverse modern occult movement of Britain. American groups and traditions, such as Starhawk's Reclaiming, Selena Fox's Circle Sanctuary, and Paul Beyerl's Rowan Tree Church all worked their magick upon Temple members. The land where were lived, the Americas, and the people, traditions, and culture, both native and imported, play a role in our work. Ancestors of blood and tradition were joined by ancestors of bone, those buried in the land where we live. Sacred sites from all over the world, their stones, soil, and water are used in our rites, with the intention that our blessings and work with these sacred talismans and touchstones, helps us connect, heal, and enchant the whole world. Witchcraft grows more vocational, as we find kinship with those who have fulfilled the role of magickal advisor, healer, ceremonial leader, diviner, and teacher wherever they are found in the worlds and throughout time.

We see all of these influences, and our own work as part of the Tradition, with a capital "T," the common mysterious thread linking all seekers in a tapestry, beyond any one religion, culture, or custom. In creating a tradition and community of Witchcraft beyond any one name or culture, we hope to hold a line within that tapestry that can be continued and added to by others in the current. So often prized students leave to have the freedom to add their own gnosis to a tradition while founders and elders hold too tightly to tradition, fearing that change. Each new seedling can be wonderful, but will lack the resources established by the previous generation. Our hope is to both add to the overall Tradition of the Mysteries, while providing structure and freedom, resources and innovation, for a long time to come.

THE GREAT WORK

The Great Work is a phrase used often in Western Occultism. It is also known as the *Magnum Opus*, often equated with an artist's "Great Song" or "Greatest Artistic Accomplishment." In the Art of Magick, the greatest accomplishment is the evolution and mastery of the self. The term is first found in the teachings of alchemy, but the occultist Eliphas Levi was the first to expand upon it as not just a term for alchemical transmutation, without and within, but the spiritual journey of the magician or mystic.

The Western Path is often described as "working" while the Eastern Path is "being" though this division is erroneous. There is much work in the disciplines of east, evidenced by martial arts, yoga, and tantric ritual. The idea of the work often goes back to the link between the esoteric arts and crafts with the practical arts and crafts. Shamans, priests, and healers were also the scribes, blacksmiths, chemists, and engineers. The first great "works" of civilization are believed to be religious, from the mysterious ancient stone circles to the pyramids and temples we as modern Pagans look to for kinship. Technical knowledge of science was also esoteric knowledge to most people.

The concept of the "work" became an allegory for the work of the self. Just as the alchemist-priest is transforming base substances, such as lead, into perfected substances, such as gold, they were also transforming their base self, sometimes equated with karma in the East or sin in Christianity, with perfection, enlightenment, or adepthood.

Aleister Crowley referred to the Great Work in his teachings, and G. I. Gurdjieff simply referred to his system as "The Work." Freemasons have the symbol of the rough cube stone and the perfected smooth cube, to show the evolution of our divine awareness through sincere effort, smoothing out the rough edges to be a more perfected vessel. Modern magicians and healers refer to the healing process as doing "work" and partnerships with spiritual entities as "working together." All are linked to what we call the Great Work.

Influenced by Hermetic alchemy, the Temple of Witchcraft uses the term the Great Work quite a bit. Our use is twofold. It references both the inner, personal experience of the quest for evolution and further mastery and the crafting of community, a collective "Great Work."

We refer to our Craft as not only operative magick, in terms of spells and potions (which is what Witches mean when they talk about their Craft) but also in the Masonic sense of perfecting the self. It is Soul Craft, where our magick improves upon and expands the vessel of consciousness, the "cauldron" of the aura field, to hold a greater cohesive awareness. Our deeper mysteries are on soul crafting through partnership with other entities to enter into agreement for mutual benefit and evolution. The key is the refining of the energy body while simultaneously taking personal responsibility for your actions, past patterns, and forging new patterns to craft the evolved individual you want to become. While incarnate, the Great Work is a continual process of renewal, to claim adepthood and to move beyond to gain entry into the illustrious order of the Mighty Dead, the inspired and enlightened ones of the Craft, from beyond the veil.

THE GARDEN OF THE GODS

The Garden of the Gods is the second expression of the Great Work, the collective communal expression. The Garden of the Gods goes back to the time before time, when the gods and humans were in harmony. It is the primeval vision of the Earth, unspoiled. It is the True Garden of Union. Many mythos have a theology, a belief, that we were once in a perfect state of grace, and then fell. In this fall we lost innocence and, as a punishment, were cast out of the primordial garden. We find the variations of this myth all over the world, the great Father Land or Mother Land from which all things spring. Look to the stories of Shamballa, Tara, Avalon, Hesperides, Zep Tepi, and even Atlantis and Lemuria. Look to it most clearly in the Judeo-Christian story of the Garden of Eden.

The truly important thing to understand is that in the Pagan traditions, there is no fall, only the cyclical turning of time. We have rebel gods like Prometheus stealing fire and then later punished, and old Witch lore has the stories of the Watchers, the Grigori, who descend into the world to teach us the Craft. We we have no theology of sin or personal punishment and divine torment. Ours is a world of balance, cycles, and seasons. Some call it karma. Others call it wyrd. Aleister Crowley called this impersonal force Adjustment, and renamed the Tarot Trump Justice Adjustment to highlight this important impersonal distinction.

Our "fall" is really a myth to explain the shift in consciousness from our simple hunter-gather society to an agrarian life, and to our eventual urban environments, ancient and modern. This fundamentally changed our relationship with our food, the land, and nature, and thereby our relationship with plants, animals, and the spirits and gods, including planet Earth herself. Though many think we should simply go back to such a simple lifestyle, the process of alchemy is at work here, the perfection, the Craft of the self, that is the Great Work. Something seemingly unified must be broken down, separated, purified and recombined stronger than before. It is summed up in the occult phrase "dissolve and coagulate." Things are dissolved, separated to be purified, and rejoined to attain a greater state of refinement and awareness. This shift from primal to urban to whatever might come next is actually part of our path. Though difficult, like many things, it is necessary.

When we seek to return to the Garden of the Gods, we are seeking to return to that state of union, but to return changed: wiser, more loving, and more powerful because we are consciously, not unconsciously aware of our divine will. We are not simply there by grace, not knowing any better, but actively choosing to live in paradise by our thoughts, words, and deeds. This is the Great Work of our collective society. An old craft saying tells us, often at the end of rituals, "Let all things be as they were since the beginning of time." We seek to return to those conditions, but to do so by choice.

Awakening to the Sorcerous World

In the Sorcerous World,
The world of the First Occasion
The World of the Zep Tepi
The World of the Gardens Where All is One
Everything is alive.
Everything is possible.
Everything transforms and changes,
Yet everything remains eternal
All things come from and return to the Source
In this world of the witches
Rocks move and speak to us.
They can take any form and face.
Trees talk to us about the great lessons of life

And share their memories of the times before
Plants whisper their secrets
And animals are human,
Sisters and brothers of fang and fur, feather and claw.
Humans are but another animal in the Garden
Walking upon two legs
Dreaming sorcerous dreams.
The Light of the Sorcerous World comes from within as well as without
True sight reveals this.
All things shimmer.
All things shine.
Each in accord with their true nature.

Great Ages and Old Lands

A traditional teaching from occultism, from the times of Plato to the revival by the Theosophist Madame Blavatsky, is the concept of previous ages of creation and previous, now unknown, lands of civilization. As an occult tradition, the Temple, too, keeps with this teaching, though the interpretation is open to all members. Is it a literal truth? Is it a mythic truth? Is it simple a teaching story of metaphor and idea? Yes, no, and maybe to all three questions. At one time, Troy was considered only a myth until dug up and proven, so perhaps our understanding of such ancient lands as Atlantis and Lemuria will bear similar physical evidence even though, thus far, they have not. Tantalizing tips have surfaced, but no conclusive, well accepted truth.

The Great Ages are described in terms of metals in both ancient Greek mysteries and the Vedic philosophers of India. The Hindus describe them as Yugas, and there is some controversy to their dating, being either cycles of millions of years, or possibly only thousands. Many believe both the Greek and Hindu understanding of the ages is based upon knowledge of the Precession of the Equinoxes. It is a cycle of the Earth's axis, and its wobble, which causes the pole star to shift over vast periods of time. This wobble and shift changes the Earth's relationship with the stars of the zodiac. While most in the Western world still base their zodiac as the seasons, and thereby the space around the world known as the Tropical Zodiac, the stars of the

Sidereal Zodiac have shifted in our perception. The star sign that the Sun occupies on the Vernal (Spring) Equinox is said to be the dominant sign of the current Cosmic Month, lasting approximately 2,000 years. We are currently transitioning out of the "old age" of Pisces and into a "new age" of Aquarius, for the cycle moves backwards through the normal order of the zodiac signs. There is evidence, remarkably, that the Greeks, Hindus, and Egyptians had knowledge of this vast cycle, indicating information was either preserved and passed down from an ancient people, or some civilization gave them an understanding of this cycle that any of these cultures could not have observed first hand.

In either case, the belief is that at one time there was a vast and noble golden age, where humans were like gods, never dying, wise, benevolent, and in tune with all of creation. They were one with the gods and spirits as well as the world. Slowly that age decayed into a silver age, with many of the same qualities, but somehow tarnished. It descended into either a bronze or copper age and finally the most difficult and dense of the ages, the iron age. These metals should not be confused with the anthropological use of the term Iron Age or Bronze Age in terms of metal-working.

Similar ideas and parts of this theory survive in other traditions. The Golden Age of Egypt, when the gods ruled upon the earth was known as the Zep Tepi. Celtic Welsh tradition depicts the ages by animals – Salmon, Eagle, Owl, Stag, and Blackbird. The Irish Celts had a myth of previous "invasions" of Ireland, each with their own magickal race dominating, that have been interpreted by occultists as akin to these ages and worlds. Norse mythology seems to depict the transition between ages, in the form of the Ragnarok prophecy. The Hopi, Aztec, and Mayans have cosmologies that include the view of these ages, "worlds" or "suns" as they are called.

In the modern era Aleister Crowley depicted three eras based upon foundational god forms, the Age of Isis, then Osiris, and now Horus, though some of his followers have added an age of Ma'at. Laurie Cabot, in the Cabot Tradition, teaches a system of ancient mythic ages, akin to the ancient Greek concepts with an Age of Heroes between our current era and the ancient past. The work of Madame Blavatsky has seven ages, with us currently in the fifth and ascending to a higher age, right along with myths borrowing names from the ancient world, including Hyperborea, Lemuria, and Atlantis. Plato wrote that the Egyptians knew the secrets of the last age, a land from the West we would call Atlantis, though many assume it was an allegory warning of the decay of Greek society. Great past ages are even hinted at in the mythic poetic writing of J.R.R. Tolkien in his world of Middle Earth, where he created a fictional mythos for the people of Britain.

Seeing a truth in all of these traditions and, more importantly, depicting a deeper rooted mythic structure in which to work, the visions of the Temple founders led to a system fundamentally based in Theosophy, with seven ages. Each has a dominant land mass, real or mythic. Each has an associated totemic ally ruling the age. The totems are like the animal self of Mother Earth, as she evolves and is reborn in each age. Each age has an expression of the age's world tree, along with a wisdom tree, a secondary tree to compliment the world tree. They are like her spine, a cosmic axis that changes with each turn of the clock. Our first five worlds are expressed in myth, while the coming two are left open for interpretation in the Temple's Book of Shadows.

The previous age was an age of high magick, of Atlantean sorcerers and priest-kings who seeded the world with their magick. We call them the Sea People, for they roamed the waterways creating vast civilizations. Prior to their rise, the world was dominated by an elder race, who helped the realms grow. These were the good folk of the elder nations of Faery. In the Atlantean Age there was more direct contact, but now our awareness of them is minimal.

This current fifth age, has five "races" or peoples associated with it. The Temple adopts more of the modern interpretation of the Hopi Prophecies of the rainbow tribe rather than the colonialist Theosophist approach. Not only warriors, but magick makers, Witches from all lands, must come together in this coming age, from all people and all races. Rather than four, we see five races coming together – black, white, yellow, red, and brown – like the points of the pentacle. All are needed to bring their own magick to the world, and our own teachings encompass a syncretized global perspective for this reason. We must be the myth makers for the modern age, through our experiences with spirit. This work is ever evolving.

Age	Totem	World Tree	Wisdom Tree	Creatures	Land
First	Salmon	Yew	Hazel	First Creatures	Pangaea
Second	Eagle	Pine	Vine and Ivy	Golden Race of Giants	Hybornea
Third	Owl	Willow	Thorn	Elder Race of Faery	Lemuria
Fourth	Stag	Oak	Holly	Sea People	Atlantis
Fifth	Blackbird	Ash	Elm	Current Humanity	Five Races
Sixth	Cow, Dolphin, Frog	Elder	Unknown	Unknown	Meruvia
Seventh	Wolf, Bear, Swan	Birch	Unknown	Unknown	Paradise

Formula for Temple Initiation

Initiation means "to begin" although many sadly consider it the end of a spiritual or magickal journey. Initiation is akin to graduation from a school. While it symbolizes a ritual ending of a period of learning, one never stops learning. Yet the student who has mastered the requirements and been acknowledged by the community as capable can go out and actually do work related to their chosen field now. It's a mark of entering into adulthood when one graduates from high school or college, or enters a profession.

Magickal initiations are much the same in their own way. While some experience them at the start of magickal study, literally starting the education process, others find it is the capstone to a period of study and a minimum level of education. Some initiations come in the form of joining groups. Sororities, fraternities, and other private organizations that are not open to just anyone have their initiation rituals—acts that bond members by shared experience and perspective. Some are funny, some demanding, and others quite serious, but they all serve a similar purpose. Witchcraft traditions come with their own initiations to make the serious commitment to the Witch Cult in general, or to a specific tradition and lineage. The Temple of Witchcraft is no different, though our guiding initiation principle might be a bit different than most expect.

It is important to also realize the differences between several terms that are conflated together – dedication, consecration, initiation, elevation, and ordination. Some traditions and teachers use different definitions for these terms, so the way they are most likely used in the context of the Temple of Witchcraft are:

Dedication

Where one ritually dedicates oneself, alone, or in community to a tradition, deity or path. Often dedication rituals have time limits. A year and a day is customary in modern Witchcraft, harkening back to many Celtic tales where friends or foes would meet and reunite within a year and a day. Upon the completion of that time, either one would formally commit for a longer period, or be released from the dedication to pursue other interest. Many British Traditional Wiccan groups will ask new students to dedicate to the tradition for a year and a day before further training or the possibility of formal initiation. Many consider "solitary initiations" to truly be dedication ceremonies at heart.

Consecration

Consecration means to associate or join something with the sacred. It can be used in terms of both people and objects. When a magickal object, or even a place, is purified and blessed, dedicated to a specific purpose, we say it is consecrated. With people, consecration is a blessing to further one's connection. In the Temple of Witchcraft, the first consecration ritual can be becoming a General Member, meaning you've attended three or more official events and are formally linked with and welcomed to the community. New General Members are consecrated by anointing a sacred oil for the Temple upon their palms in a triple spiral pattern and welcomed with specific works and an embrace.

Initiation

Initiation can refer to several things. Usually it is both a formal ritual to connect to a new identity, such as becoming a Witch, or to connect to a specific group. Many believe a "line" or lineage is passed from initiator/teacher to initiate/student, through this process. Initiation experiences can also be anything that causes our consciousness and awareness to grow and evolve. Most believe group initiation experiences are for this lifetime, while some believe they last beyond any single lifetime and carry over into all future lives. Some traditions hold rites to remove banished figures from the line of initiation, though many consider that all those initiated by the one banished will also be removed, like clipping a branch from a tree. Life experience initiations cannot be removed by another, yet the individual can try to forget them, and attempt to go back "asleep" to a less aware state.

Elevation

An elevation refers to a subsequent initiation ceremony in a tradition. When initiatory training is referred to ranks and degrees, technically the first ritual is known as an initiation ritual, while all other subsequent rites for each degree is known as an elevation.

Ordination

Ordination is the consecration of clergy within a tradition, giving the spiritual and legal rights and responsibilities of such status. In the Temple, Ministerial Members, graduates of Witchcraft V, are not necessarily ordained. Ordination is the final step in community recognition of being a legal minister in the Temple.

Most often the definitions of consecration and initiation are reversed in traditions, with such traditions considering the initiation to be a simple mark of a group consciousness, while the consecration as a more serious, lifelong change. Some equate further elevations as consecrations, which technically they are.

As we enter the New Aeon of Aquarius, we look to the formula of initiation, the mechanism and principle behind it, as different than it was in the Age of Pisces. The hallmark of Pisces is vertical relationships, from the top down, so clearly demonstrated in the Catholic concept of Apostolic Succession. Each Pope is an extension of the previous in mission and power, going all the way back to the apostles of Christ. It is from these apostles that they received their sense of power and mission, who in turn were empowered by the figure of Jesus. It is a continuous chain to our modern times, but perhaps that formula is starting to break down as the dominant paradigm.

We do see it in the modern Witchcraft movement. Many traditions deeply concerned about lineage are in essence promoting a form of Wiccan Succession. Many consider their authority and validity, whether stated outright or not, to stem from the founder, most notably Gerald Gardner or Alex Sanders, yet those founders are relatively recent, and I think few would claim they were particularly enlightened. Neither man claimed so in life, even though both were very magickal. While the model of initiatory lineage can be quite powerful and energizing, it continues the Piscean formula popularized by the Christian Church. It emphasizing top down, vertical relationships.

The Age of Aquarius is about lateral relationships, community, counsel and group consciousness. Aquarius embodies the paradox of the individual along with the whole community. It can be hard to satisfy both the individual and group needs and to honor and recognize the specialness of both. Many traditions err on one side or the other. The calling of our new age is to create models that embrace that paradox.

The first stirrings of new models came with the rise of the Solitary Initiation. Those dedicated to the Goddess and God with an open heart, encouraged by teachers and elders considered radical at the time, performed solitary rituals of initiation to become Witches. The old guard often found the concept invalid. To be fair, one cannot be a member of a particular secret society without initiation into that society in the accepted manner. You cannot declare you are a Freemason, a member of the fraternity Epsilon Sigma Alpha, or a Gardnerian Wiccan, just because you want to be.

Yet the concept of a Witch in general goes beyond the identity of a freemason or fraternity brother. Few people feel they were such things in past lives, or awaken to it in this life and simply seek the education. So solitary initiation rituals began in earnest. They first were encouraged by Gardnerian elder Raymond Buckland, who brought the Gardnerian Tradition to America. Breaking from Gardnerian Wicca, he encouraged solitary initiation in the book *The Tree: The Complete Book of Saxon Wicca*. He was later followed by Scott Cunningham, who wrote *Wicca: A Guide for the Solitary Practitioner*. Cunningham's books popularized a modern, eclectic, potentially solitary form of Wicca that encouraged self-initiation.

A little talked about distinction should be made between the terms solitary initiation and self-initiation. Both are often used interchangeably, but they can mean very different things. Self-initiation means that you, yourself, are initiating yourself in a tradition. One could argue that you cannot give yourself anything that you do not already possess. There is nothing to pass on because you don't have it. Though I agree that the personal self cannot pass on anything it does not have to the personal self, couldn't the infinite self, the higher self, Watcher, Bornless One, embodying all things, pass on initiation to the personal self? It is best seen mythically in the initiation of the Norse god Odin, in the mystery of the Runes. He hangs himself upon the world tree and says:

I ween I hung on the windy tree,
hung there three for nights full nine;
With the spear I was wounded, and offered I was
To Othin, myself to myself,
On the tree that none may ever know
What root beneath it runs.
—*Poetic Edda,* "Hovamol." 139

Solitary initiation is sometimes equated with self initiation, as you are apparently the only person there. There is no one else physically present, so it is assumed that you believe that you, yourself, are doing the initiation. Yet that is not what it means. Solitary initiation means that you are physically alone, but when performed correctly, the otherworldly entities gathered—spirits, ancestors, goddesses, gods, angels or even demons—can be the ones, apparently unseen by anyone who would happen to look, doing the initiation. Proper rituals to call the spirits, properly constructed objects or books that "pass the power" from one to another, or even properly prepared magickal sacraments are all ways to have an incredible solitary initiation between you and the spirits of tradition. Simply following what has been done in the past can open you to the powers of the past, creating connections to Witches and magicians in long ago times.

"Who initiated the first Witch?" is a famous quote from the elder Doreen Valiente. Many do not have a good answer, though when we study tribal shamanism, we find that when the shaman dies before training the new shaman, an appropriate substitute would be "chosen by the spirits" and usually through illness, trained by the spirits directly. Initiation would occur in the spirit world. This is the most extreme form of initiatory life experience one can have. Other initiatory life experiences can be from catastrophic experiences that force a new perspective, spontaneous psychic experiences, unexpected spirit contact, entheogenic experience, and even simply personal, life altering epiphanies. My own entry into Witchcraft, and what I consider my first and most important spiritual initiation beyond any terrestrial rituals and attunements with teachers, was an experience with psychic healing that blew my mind. It forever altered me, resulting in my dedication to magick and Witchcraft. It was far more important than a linear connection to a group or the stamp of approval from an elder.

The tradition of magickal Qabalah depicts ten (some say eleven or even twelve) initiatory markers on the path of the magician, Witch included. Each is titled, with corresponding "virtues" or healthy characteristics once you've attained it; "vice" or unhealthy characteristics if you struggle with it, obligations; or acts one must perform when holding this level of awareness; and illusions, or self deceptions when you think you've attained it, but have not. The study of this formula comes in the Witchcraft IV material on High Magick, yet it, and other systems of initiatory progression, show that the levels of consciousness for evolution and enlightenment are not necessarily only a part of degree systems with lineage.

The initiatory formula of the Temple of Witchcraft is based upon the container of the circle, akin to a cauldron. We as individuals, are all like pearls on the rim of the cauldron, each touching the ones next to it. While we are individuals, we are creating something together, a community and tradition. If any one pearl is added to it, the circle changes. The cauldron grows bigger. If any one pearl is removed, again the circle changes and the vessel must become smaller to fit. Each holds a unique place, though the circle can survive the addition or removal of individual pearls.

While the tradition and community can hold the space, each of us must reach into the center of the cauldron, into the great mystery, and make our own connection to it. While lines of blessing and consecration can pass from teacher to student, initiator to initiate, truly all we can do is facilitate a space, through the teachings or an actual ritual, for individuals to make their own connections, then resume their unique place in the circle. No one can really do it for you. In Aquarian Ages, we should not rely totally upon those who came before us for our own authority. The authority must come from the inner connection, and if it does, few things can sever it. The authority will only grow and develop. After this connection, their pearl may shine a bit brighter with a special glow.

This lateral, from outward within approach is the initiatory formula in the Temple of Witchcraft. We do have ceremonies and blessings, but if you do not make the connections via the ritual experiences, nothing a teacher can do can force it. They can create the conditions to encourage it, both within the class and within an initiation ritual, but they cannot force the connection. Many mistakenly believe they have a connection due to performing the ritual, but the necessary inner connections must occur. Like death, initiation must be performed alone, even when others are present, they are not truly with you.

Some classes, when taught in person, culminate in a group initiation ceremony where the instructor and community holds the space. The experience is all from the student's connection to the divine, making them an initiate. The connections should be made during the training. For those online students, the teaching must hold the space for them, and the spirit of the Temple must hold the space, as there are no physical anchors, but the result is the same. The same level of honor and privilege is given to those online as in person in terms of initiatory status or rank. For those online students who experience solitary initiations, our larger group gatherings and retreats, such as TempleFest, are places where an in-person consecration, a seal or capstone to the initiation of that degree, can be given and formally recognized by other initiates. The solitary initiation on its own is sufficient. We simply like to gather and celebrate in community.

In our first degree, the connection occurs with successful psychic experience. Through a variety of experiences, many with clear cut verifiable parameters, we seek to awaken the inner flame to the reality of otherworldly information and the influence of energy upon the world. Instant magick, remote viewing, spirit contact, psychic diagnosis and healing are all methods to make this connection. With this change, nothing will ever be the same.

In the second degree, the connection occurs through the forces of nature, the elementals, the deities and through successful divination and spellwork. Through this partnership with nature and spirit to manifest physical change, the inner light of the first degree is grounded within the sacred matter of the world.

The third degree initiation comes through a conjuration and communion with the personal shadow self. One must make the necessary spirit contacts and healing work to prepare for this operation. Once the preparation is made, the ordeal of the shadow journal begins, and through the creation and destruction of this sacred vessel, the shadow is conjured. One must make their own connection, communication, and compact with the shadow to prevent it from sabotaging future work. The relationship is ever continuing and evolving, and often has to be renegotiated.

As the third degree takes the initiate into the depths of shadow, the fourth brings them to the heights of the sublime worlds. The preparatory works expands consciousness and conditioning further out, beyond the normal threshold of awareness. This creates ideal conditions for the conjuration and communion with the Highest Self, the Bornless Self or Watcher. One has descended and then risen to reach the blessings of the source. Once a connection is made to this ideal teacher, the stage is set for the deepest of the mysteries.

The fifth degree is of death and rebirth. Like Inanna, the initiate descends step by step into the underworld, facing what is dark, beyond the personal shadow. One works with the collective shadow of the planet, as ruled by the dark goddesses and gods who dwell there. One also works in the world in service, in twelve labors, like Hercules, traveling around the stars of the Zodiac. The Mystery of Service, and how it ultimately serves the evolution of the soul, is truly understood.

The cycle of initiation is the Path of Unmaking, for initiation often have to unravel the individual on a human level to reveal the divine self. This gives the initiate an opportunity to "craft" the new magickal self questing towards enlightenment. In our "underworld orientation" or "alchemical orientation" of the elements along the cardinal directions of the circle, we place earth in the north, fire in the east, air in the south and water in the west. Usual magick moves clockwise, but the degree elemental cycle of initiation and training moves counterclockwise around this circle. The first degree fire would be in the east, a place of new beginnings. The second degree turns widdershins, or *tuathal*, both meaning counterclockwise, at least in the northern hemisphere, to the north with earth. The third degree continues the turn to the west, for water, followed by the fourth degree for air in the south. For the fifth degree, receptive or passive spirit of the descent of the goddess spirals us inward to the center. The active, or projective spirits of the twelve stations of the god spirals us outward again to do our work, and then follows a creation cycle of manifestations – fire/east, air/south, water/west and earth/north, moving from least manifest to most manifest.

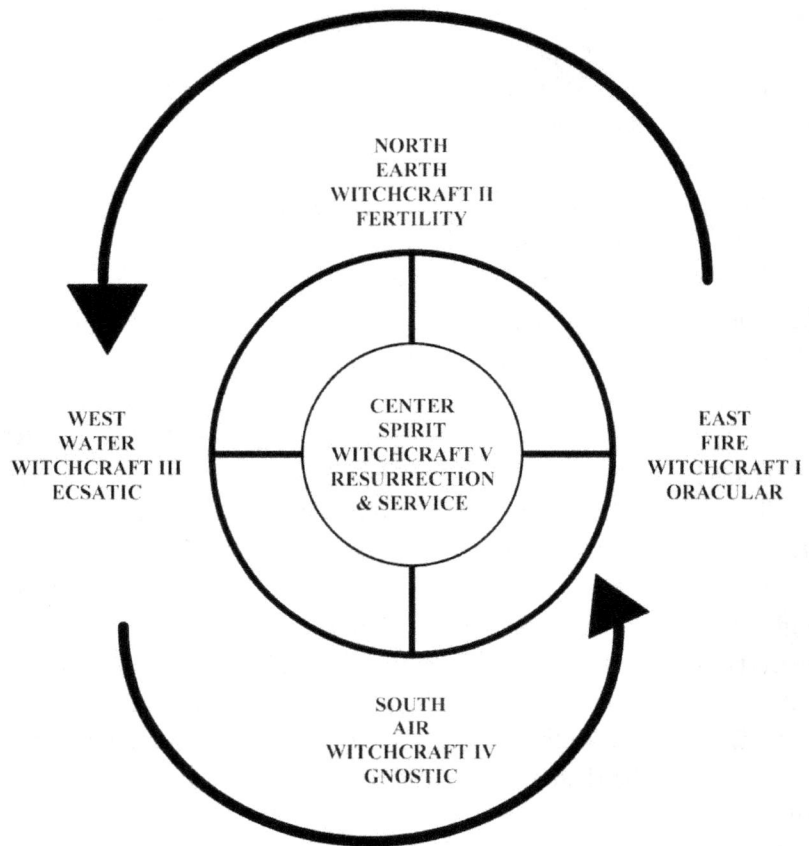

Elemental Initiation Circle

Temple of Witchcraft Consecration Oil

3/8 Oz of Base oil
1 drop of Ginger (Aries)
3 drops of Rosewood (Taurus)
1 drop of Clary Sage (Gemini)
3 drops of Myrrh (Cancer)
3 drops of Frankincense (Leo)
1 drop of Cypress (Virgo)
3 drops of Rose Geranium (Libra)
1 drop of Cardamom (Scorpio)
1 drop of Clove (Sagittarius)

1 drop of Patchouli (Capricorn)
2 drops of Lavender (Aquarius)
2 drops of Sandalwood (Pisces)

Temple Incense (basic)
1 part Frankincense
1 part Myrrh
1 part Dragon's Blood
1 part White Oak Bark
1 part Lavender Flowers

Temple Incense (complex)
1 part Dragon's Blood
1 part Red Sandalwood
1 part Lavender Flowers
1/2 part Jasmine Flowers
2 parts Frankincense
1/2 part Fennel
1/2 part Star Anise
1/2 part Patchouli Leaf
1/2 part Cinnamon
2 parts Myrrh
1/4 part Nutmeg
1/2 part Mugwort

SPIRITUAL CONCEPTS WITHIN THE TEMPLE

There are several special terms that are used in the mythos, cosmology or theology of the Temple that deserve special attention. We as Witches and Pagans are a community of shared terminology though we don't always share the same accepted definitions as every tradition. Every practitioner will define and interpret things differently. This simply gives a guide as to how concepts are used within the teaching system and poetry of the Temple.

The Two Who Move As One

A term for the Goddess and God acting in concert, acting as one. While there are many expressions of gods and goddesses in the various realms, through different time periods and cultures, the Two Who Move As One are the primal mother and father, the Great Mother and Great Father, the Lady and Lord of Wicca, or the Weaver and Singer who are also the Web and the Song in the Temple of Witchcraft.

The Child of Light

The Child of Light is formed with the union of the Goddess and God, both in the expression of the Wheel of the Year, cosmic cycles of the universe and the alchemical union within us. To enter into the higher realms of consciousness, we must become child-like and be reborn like an innocent babe, yet with wisdom. To rise higher upon the Tree of Life, one must become a Babe of the Abyss. The Child of Light in the Temple is often described as a serpent of life, and alchemical child of human and beast, animal, vegetable and mineral. Historically it can be depicted as Baphomet, Mithras and Abraxas. As the child of light awakens, we awaken to our own wisdom and magick.

Great Above, Great Below, and Great Between of the Witch's Tree

The Witch's universe in the Temple is described in many ways, with no attachment to any of them having to be the "true way." One view that is popular and helpful is the view of the World Tree, the Shaman's Tree or Witch's Tree. It is the axis mundi, the main spire, around which the universe and all worlds spin. It consists of a heavenly world, known as the Great Above, Upper World, Overworld or Heaven; a deep world, known as the Great Below, Lower World, Underworld or Hell to some, but usually spelled Hel, in the old Norse traditions; and a realm between, known as the Great Between, Middle World, Middle Earth or Here. Some would equate the Sun, Moon, and Earth with the three realms, respectively, or the Sun, Stars and Moon with the three worlds.

Love, Power, and Wisdom: The Three Rays of Witchcraft

Key concepts of the Temple include the triad of ideas associated with the primary rays of occultism. While many words in English are used to define them, we rely on the concepts of Love, Power and Wisdom. Love is for the second ray, the blue ray and coupled with trust, manifesting the higher form of love, unconditional love manifesting as the Perfect Love and Perfect Trust of the magick circle. Power is for the first ray, the red ray and is coupled with will, manifesting the highest expression of powerful will, true will, against which nothing can stand. Wisdom is for the third ray, the yellow ray, and is coupled with knowledge. Wisdom is when we apply knowledge. Wisdom is an elevated form of knowledge, for wisdom knows when to act, and when not to act. The three powers emanate from the three aspects of divinity, the Divine Heart, the Divine Will and the Divine Mind.

The Seven Wanderers of the Heavens

The Seven Wanderers refer to the seven wandering "stars" or planets of the ancient world, not set into the fixed pattern of the heavens. They are the Sun, Moon, Mercury, Venus, Mars, Jupiter and Saturn. Today we know there are other, less visible wandering stars, and use Uranus, Neptune, Pluto, Chiron and the asteroids in our magick, and speculate on inter-Mercurial and trans-Plutonian planets as astrology evolves in the New Aeon.

The Oran Mor

The Oran Mor is the "Great Song" or "Great Melody" of the universe. It relates to such occult concepts as the music of the spheres and the logos. It's a Celtic term to describe a force of creation. The universe is sung and played into being. In the Temple, we see the most cosmic form of the god as the Singer and the Song. The God is both the one who voices creation, sings, speaks, chants and names creation into being, but he does so melodically, and therefore is one with the song he creates.

Our own personal song is a contribution to the great song, described as a melody and rhythm in this context, though adherents of the magick of Thelema might think of it first arising from performing our True Will, our soul's purpose in the world in this lifetime. The process of seeking "enlightenment" in Western magick is called the Great Work, but another name for it, a musical analogy, is your magnum opus. To the Thelemite, it culminates in a higher level initiate, a magus, uttering their own personal "word" or magickal formula. Doing so makes a major contribution to the direction of the Great Song, and changes the world and universe. We can think of the masters of magick like a special chorus within the Great Song, and each gets a short solo.

The Loom of Fate

The Loom of Fate refers to the loom that weaves the tapestry of creation by the most cosmic goddess, the Weaver. She is a triple goddess of past, present and future, drawing elements of the Greek and Roman Fates, the Norns, and the Wyrd Sisters. From her own body she draws the threads of fate and weaves them upon a loom of three wheels. The wheels are described as the Wheel of Fate/Fortune, the Wheel of Justice/Adjustment and the Wheel of Judgement/Way. The song of the God, the Oran Mor, vibrates upon the strings in the tapestry of creation, like the strings in a harp or spider web. Three chants are used most often with the three wheels, being Awen (Ah-ooh-en), IAO (Ee-Ah-Oh) and AUM (Ah-Oh-Um) respectively.

Wyrd is usually translated as fate, but wyrd is really the northern European cognate to our eastern concept of karma. At its most basic level, karma is the result of your actions. It is neither good nor bad, though we perceive it as such based upon how pleasant or unpleasant an experience is. That is a human judgement. It simply is a result. We talk about karmic "debt" and "credit," but the point is not to gain credit and lose debt, but to be at "zero" or perfect balance, so one can transcend the wheel of fate/karma and rise up to the next level of consciousness in the loom. Our wyrd is the most likely result based upon our actions and the momentum of all that has come before us. To change your fate, you must change your actions, and we see

Witchcraft as a way to change your fate by moving in harmony with the Goddess of Fate herself.

The Three Wells

In various mythologies, particularly of the Northern Traditions, the Tree of Life, the Witch's World Tree is fed by various wells found in the worlds. In the Temple, they have been interpreted as the Well of Wyrd or Well of Fate, that feeds the tree of life. There is a Well of Life, also known as the Well of Healing, that is filled with pure life force for those who seek it. There is a Well of Inspiration, which is truly the Well of Memories, a well from which knowledge, magick and lore can be drawn.

The Races

By races, we mean different orders of spiritual beings. The three races are collectively the Angels, Faery, and Creatures of Flesh and Blood, usually the discarnate ancestors and animal spirits. The three races of creatures are plant, animal, and mineral, known as the Flora, Fauna, and Lapis. Each is a bodily expression of consciousness in the world.

The Nine Waves of Creation

The Nine Waves of Creation is a reference to Irish Celtic myth, and the nine waves that were the distance the invading Milesians, or human Irish, were asked to wait out to sea by the Tuatha de Danann gods. In the Temple, it refers to waves of creative energy, and what each successive wave of energy brought about in the universe. The first three waves brought about the gods, the gods of the Upper World, Underworld and Middle World. The next three waves brought the discarnate entities of the three worlds, known as the Angels, Faeries and Spirits Between that are associated with place and time, but do not have a specific body form. The last three waves brought about the incarnate evolutions of beings, including the Stone People, or mineral life, the Plant People, or vegetal life and the People of Flesh and Blood, animal organisms including humans.

Foundations of the Temple

The Five Gifts of the Sea People

Ancient legends speak of a race of wise ones before us, often from a Western land or island, a Motherland or Fatherland some would link to Atlantis or other mythohistoric realms. These people, upon the destruction of their land, brought five "gifts" also known as tools, weapons, or hallows. They are shown in many forms, but generally they are the Stone, Cup, Blade, Spear, and Crown. While they appear to be outward tools, the true mystery is making these tools within each of us, and the tradition of the Temple teaches us how to manifest these gifts through forging the elements of earth, water, air, fire, and spirit. They are the tools of the magician, the hallows of the Witch, the foundation of the pyramid, and the power of the sphinx.

Witchdom

Witchdom has a two fold definition. First, it is considered to be the hidden, terrestrial kingdom or nation of Witches. It is the space upon which every Witch stands. Each Witch is sovereign in his or her own space. Together, collectively, it is the nation of Witches. It is invisible, unseen, and ever-shifting. No lines can contain it. No map can draw it and it is everywhere. Secondly, it is considered the spiritual "realm" of the ancestors of Witches. Beyond more common ideas of the Summerland, where "all" may go to rest and regenerate upon death, Witchdom is the collective inner temple of Witches, Sorcerers, and Wise Ones, where magick, lore and power is hidden for those who can connect with its guardians and receive its blessings.

The Eternal Sabbat

Witchdom often manifests as the Eternal Sabbat. Sometimes known as *Akelarre*, the "meadow of the he-goat" in the Basque Witchcraft tradition. It is the sacred Temple manifested as an eternal gathering of Witches at the grand sabbat between the worlds, as depicted, often grotesquely in the Medieval trials and the art based upon them. There the Witches dance in eternal rapture with the Horned God, Goddess or Faery Queen, Fey, Ancestors, animals and sometimes even angels. It appears as a grove in the woods or a cave.

My own vision of it is a phosphorous grove, eternally burning yet never consumed. The Sabbat has cognates with other spiritual traditions' visions of the realm of the masters, and relates to our concepts of the Garden of the Gods. Shamballa, Shangri-La and Avalon can all be considered similar to the Sabbat.

The Witching Hour

The Witching Hour refers to both a time and a state of mind. Usually considered to be midnight, the time between two days and the highest point of the Full Moon on the night when it shines brightest. Midnight is one of the four liminal times of day, along with dawn, noon and dusk, for they are in between states. The Witching Hour is also whenever we are between the worlds, whenever magick is upon us. We often have the greatest insights, spontaneous experiences and calls to fulfill magick and Will within the Witching Hour. Here true change and real magick occur on all levels. Training helps us both recognize it when it comes upon us, and helps us evoke and create it when necessary.

Highest Good

A common phrase used in the Temple, and many other forms of magick, it means to keep in mind the best possible outcome for all involved in your magick. We say it is for the "good of all involved." We are working not only for our own personal fulfillment, but our magick should reach out and touch others, and be dedicated to the evolution of the entire interdependent creation that includes all. In the end, in some way, are we all not involved in everything on some level? Sometimes this phrase is expanded, going beyond the belief that higher equals better, and rephrased as "the highest and deepest good." Essentially petition spells are often ended with "I ask this be for the highest and deepest good of all involved, harming none."

Harm None

Drawn from the Wiccan Rede, "Do as thou will and let it harm none." We seek to follow the advice of the Rede, like the ancient Pagan Hippocratic oath still followed by doctors today, "do no harm." As healers and guides, we seek to harm none, including ourselves, and look for ways that embrace the good of all. We know "harming none" as an absolute is impossible. Life feeds upon life. To walk across a field is to damage something. To cure an illness, one must often destroy the microbe, bacteria, or renegade cells, harming them. To eat, no matter how moral the diet, disrupts the natural life cycle of something. Yet the partaking of these cycles, of life, is a part of our path as well. We simply seek to do as little harm as possible as we walk our path.

Releasing All That Does Not Serve

Another phrase used in Temple magick, among others, is the release of "all that does not serve." As energy cannot be created or destroyed, but simply transformed, our goal is to let go of all energies that hold us back from evolution, so they may serve or transform themselves. Sometimes our limitations and difficulties do serve, as they are teaching us something vital, so we ask to withdraw from those that do not serve a greater good or our higher Will.

Nature is the Great Teacher

While esoteric philosophy is all well and good, and much of it is drawn from observation and understanding of nature, it is truly nature, and not the philosopher, that is the greatest teacher. Observing and participating in the changing cycles and seasons, on big and small scales, brings wisdom. All of nature is self regulating, even when we cannot see it. All is inherently perfect with all that it needs. All that lives will die, and all that has died, at one point lives. All has an inherent, aware, wise nature and our work is to return to that order from our separation, wiser for it.

The Earth as the One Land

As nature is a great teacher, we believe in the unity of the land through the planetary being most often called Gaea or Gaia today, though she has been known by many names. Upon her, the planetary consciousness of the forest is often seen as an expression of the God, and the land itself is the Goddess. We believe that the Earth is alive and we are a part of her, not separate at all, like cells within her body. While we perceive ourselves on separate lands and identify with tribes, towns, states, nations and continents, we are really a part of one land that has many expressions. What is done upon one land will have an effect upon all lands, and all upon it. We believe in the voice of Earth, and that like us, the planet has not only a body, or Corpus Mundi, but a spirit and soul, Spiritus Mundi and Anima Mundi.

All Witches Heal

By their very existence, Witches, magicians, and shamans, all those in the practice and vocation of magick, of spiritual bridge building, are a healing force within this planet. Classically the vocation of the Witch has been healer as wise woman or cunning man. Even if your focus is on personal practice, social justice, or simply living your own magickal life quietly and privately, you are a healer. As you heal and connect, so does the world.

Tuirgin

From the Celtic traditions, we believe in the possibility of a non-linear form of reincarnation occurring on some level of being. *Tuirgin* means "a successive birth that passes from every nature into another…flowing through all time from beginning to end." Tuirgin is not the individual reincarnation, but a level of awareness where all things are one thing. We are all within the Divine Mind, the Divine Heart, the Divine Will, incarnate, discarnate, and excarnate. This teaching helps us with any conflict, particularly the traditional Witch War conflicts in our own societies. Any conflict is a conflict of self against self, and the healing comes in learning to identify with those who seem Other.

One Sorcerer, One Witch

The concept of Tuirgin lends itself to a deeper concept that there is really only one of us, One Sorcerer, One Witch, one magickal being, known as both the First and the Last Witch. This One Witch is all Witches, all sorcerers, all people. This is the One True Initiator in magick, who is the first to be born and the last to die in our Witchblood, in union with all of nature. In truth, we initiate ourselves, as we are the One Sorcerer looking through many different sets of eyes.

I Have Been

I have worn the birch cap and held the willow wand
I have prayed in the temples and bowed before gods
With familiar spirit I have spoken with the dead in the driest of deserts by order of Kings
I have danced with the Devil and lived to tell the tale again.
I have jumped the hedge, guarded the gate, and found the Earth in my bones.
I have guarded my tribe from the hungry ghosts while upon the snow-covered fields
I have hunted and been hunted time and again, four legged, two legged
I have banged the drum and danced the dance, the only dance, the eternal dance
I have walked in dreams and lived in nightmares.
I have ridden the serpent's path all over the land.
I have been. I am. I ever shall be.

Chapter Eight: Core Practices

Core practices are the teachings and techniques that make the foundation of the regular, if not daily, practice of Temple Witches as taught by the Mystery School. Each degree of training learns its own core practices of meditation and ceremony. As one develops their own personal practice upon graduation, it become a process of integrating these core practices into a format that works in day-to-day life. No one is expected to do every practice every day, but they form an overall foundation. Individuals take them and add to them in whatever way serves the highest good of their practice.

The core practices are listed with the following codes, indicating where they first show up:

ITOW = The Inner Temple of Witchcraft
OTOW = The Outer Temple of Witchcraft
TOSW = The Temple of Shamanic Witchcraft
TOHW = The Temple of High Witchcraft
LTOW = The Living Temple of Witchcraft Vols. I&II
3ROW = Three Rays of Witchcraft
W1 = Witchcraft One Course
W2 = Witchcraft Two Course
W3 = Witchcraft Three Course
W4 = Witchcraft Four Course
W5 = Witchcraft Five Course

If you want to find more information on any particular practice, the *Temple of Witchcraft* series books will help you. Certain practices are only shared in the classes of the Mystery School, indicated in the class levels.

Meditation Countdown
ITOW/W1

The meditation countdown is the fundamental practice of counting down into a meditative, alpha brainwave state, or deeper, through the use of suggested numbers and images. It is the primary method of trance-induction used in the Temple, at least in the initial stages of training because it is safe, and can build up focus and discipline when practiced often.

Begin by assuming a relaxed position, but not so relaxed that you will fall asleep. The Egyptian Sitting Pose is recommended, particularly for beginners. To assume this posture, sit with your feet flat on the floor, and your back straight, hands palms down on the thighs. Do not lean back or recline. Relax your body by bringing your awareness to the top of your head down to the feet, giving each zone of the body permission to relax. Many begin by lighting a candle, and spend a few moments softly gazing at the candle while systematically relaxing.

When you close your eyes, visualize a broad screen before you, a representation of your mind's eye. Even if you cannot see it clearly, perceive it. Know it is there because you willed it to be. This screen is both a window to other worlds, and a portal to other realms of consciousness. Anything you desire can be conjured on the screen of your mind.

Begin by visualizing the number twelve on the screen of your mind. It can be black writing on white, like a marker on a whiteboard, or white writing on a darker background. Or colored writing. Anything you desire. Perceive it and know that the number twelve is on the screen of your mind. Hold it for a moment, and "erase" it by mentally wiping it away. Some find that physically gesturing, physically drawing the number and then wiping it away is more effective than just mental intention. Continue onward with the number eleven, ten, nine, eight, seven, six, five, four, three, two, and one. You are now in a meditative state. Everything done in your meditative state is for your highest good, harming none.

Release the image of the screen of your mind, and simply focus on your own body, breath, and awareness. Count down to a deeper level without visualizing the numbers. Simply let the count, without visuals, take you down deeper. Slowly count backwards from thirteen to one. You are now a deeper meditative state, in complete control of your magickal abilities. From this point, you can continue on to other exercises and experiences, or meditate at this level.

To bring yourself up, count from one to thirteen without any visuals, and then again from one to twelve without visuals. Move your fingers and toes to bring your awareness back. Bring your hands to the top of your head, and gently sweep down from the crown, palms facing the body, over the face, chest, and belly, and then outward across your legs and down towards the ground. This is called clearance and balance. Move yourself any way you feel your body wants you to move. Ground yourself as needed. To ground—meaning bringing your awareness back to the world and releasing any excess energy that would prevent you from focusing on the physical world—you can stamp your foot, touch the floor and press down upon your hands, or imagine deep roots of a tree coming out of your feet or the base of your spine.

The Little Death Breath
W1

Breathing can be used as a meditation practice in itself, to bring awareness and focus to the present moment, body, and consciousness, or as a prelude to other visionary working, to both realize the body, and build psychic energy. In India, breath control techniques are known as *pranayama*, as *prana* is the life force carried upon the breath, present in all living things.

The little death breath's purpose is to "kill" or truly relax, the chatter of the ego, sometimes known as the "monkey mind" that distracts us from whatever magickal task is before us. The distractions can range from mundane thoughts creeping in, to doubts about abilities and self-esteem issues. This breath can help silence that critical voice, while encouraging the awareness of the mystical experience.

Foundations of the Temple

To perform the Little Death, inhale to the count of seven. Hold your breath to the count of seven. Exhale to the count of seven. Hold your breath out for the count of seven. Repeat this pattern for a total of seven times. You might find that you unconsciously continue the pattern without a direct count.

Seven is the number of the mysteries, relating to the chakra points of the body, the seven magickal planets, and the seven gates of the underworld. The basic technique is found in metaphysical traditions across the globe, particularly in the Anderson Feri tradition of Witchcraft, under the form of the Ha Prayer, which only uses a count of four.

Lorica Prayer
W1

Traditionally a *lorica* is a type of spoken incantation, a charm or prayer recited for protection. It roughly translates as "body armor" in the sense that the words, and invoked energy, act as a spiritual armor of divine blessings, preventing harm and bringing divine aid. While most think of the lorica as part of the Christian tradition, with the most famous being the Lorica of St. Patrick, similar charms date back to ancient Babylon. Many today, particularly Celtic-influenced Pagans, use more Pagan inspired adaptations of the Lorica of St. Patrick. This one is particular to the divine mythos of the Temple of Witchcraft. Reciting it aligns one with the blessings of the spirits of the Temple. It is usually performed in the morning, as part of a regular spiritual practice. Try it to help evoke blessings and protection.

Today I rise through the Blessings of the Two Who Move As One
Through the Love, Power, and Wisdom of the Great Spirit
I rise with blessing of life from the Great Mother
I rise with the blessing of strength from the Great Father
And I rise through the blessing of rebirth through the Child of Light
I gird myself with the heights of the Great Above
With the depths of the Great Below
And with the balance of the Great Between
I stand between the worlds like the Witch's Tree.

I gird myself with the golden light of the Sun
With the silver light of the Moon
And with the white light of the stars
For I am a child of the Earth and Starry Heavens
I gird myself with the powers of Earth and Air
And with the powers of Fire and Water
And the Secret Fire that dwells within all things.
For I am like serpent of spirit and flesh made one.
From the dangers of flesh and spirit
From the dangers of darkness and light
From accident, injury,
From illness or attack,
I am protected.
Today I gird myself with the Blessings of the Earth
And the Beauty of the Garden
By her Flesh and Blood, Breath and Bone
By the Green of the Land
And the Blue of the Sea
By the Winds of Knowledge
And the Stones of her Body
By the Clouds and Lightning
Nature and I are one.
Magick before me.
Magick behind me.
Magick above me.
Magick below me.
Magick in my left hand
And magick in my right hand
Magick all around me
And magick within me
For all is magick.

By the Blessings of the Web and the Wheel
By the Blessings of the Three Rays of Power, Love, and Wisdom
And by the Three Wells
By the Three Races of Angel, Faery, and Ancestor
By the Three Creatures of Flora, Fauna, and Lapis

And by the Four Directions
By the Five Gifts of the Sea People
By the Seven Wanderers of the Heavens
And by the Nine Waves of Creation
All dwell within me.
I am guided
I am protected
I am whole
Blessed be

Psychic Protection Shield
ITOW/W1

Enter into a meditative state using the countdown technique. Be aware of your energy field, the space around your body about arm's length all around, like a sphere or egg. Visualize the edge of the energy field transforming into crystal. It is clear like quartz or diamond, but hard, strong, and protective. Let the light of your mind reflect in the dazzling colors of the gem. The crystal surrounds you, above, below, and all around. Hold the intention of protection from all harm within your mind, while allowing in other energies you need or desire. Say three times: *"I charge my protection shield to protect me from all harm on any level, and reflect love back on the source of the harm, So Mote It Be."* Count yourself up with the end of the Countdown Meditation. Give yourself clearance and balance. Ground yourself as needed.

Protection shields can be "cast" upon buildings, vehicles, land, and even other people when necessary, though, like your own shield, they require upkeep through attention and energy, to maintain.

Blessing Enemies Away
W1

Not so much a daily ritual practice, but a core attitude in our protection work, is to bless your enemies away. Ideally, rather than be angry at those who are at cross purposes to you, focus your intention on wishing them well, so much good fortune in fact, they have no time or interest in opposing you. Blessings and success will occupy them. Imagine if this basic view was held by everyone in conflict. If someone blessed me every time I opposed them, I would welcome the good fortune! It offers a healthier attitude and posture for facing those who would cause problems, rather than focusing on anger or fear.

Polarity of the Earth and Sky Meditation
ITOW/W1

Enter a meditative state using the countdown technique. Visualize light descending from the base of your spine like an anchor or taproot, holding you steady upon the Earth, yet it is hollow like a straw. Energy can flow up or down it. The root descends down to the heart of the Earth. As you inhale, draw up energy from the center of the Earth. Ask Mother Earth to send up her energy to you. Feel the energy flow up through the root, into your body, up your spine, torso, neck, and head. Feel it flow out through the crown, connecting you to the Heavens.

While the energy of the Earth flows upward, call down the energy of the Sky. Feel it descend as you inhale, down to your crown, down through your head, neck and chest, down through the spine into the torso and base of the spine, down into the Earth. Feel it flow down to the center of Mother Earth.

Feel both energies flow, balanced and harmonious. If there is anything you wish to release and transmute, anything static and stuck, hold that intention and release it into the flow of energies. When done, let the remaining Earth energy flow up and out and the remaining Sky energy flow down and out. Count yourself up with the end of the Countdown Meditation. Give yourself clearance and balance. Ground yourself as needed.

Sending Light
ITOW/W1

Sending light is a practice of visualizing and projecting colored light around and within a person, place or object, to change its energy, vibration, and reality. Primarily it is used in various forms of healing. Once in a meditative state, a connection between the Witch and the recipient is made. Through visualization and intent, energy is send, perceived as psychic light. Each color embodies a different intention. While different people interpret the colors based on their own

Foundations of the Temple

unique understanding, certain standards in Western color magick have developed. Pink is for self-esteem. Blue for peace. Green for normal healing and immune system. Red-orange is for critical healing. When sending light to someone without verbal permission, the Witch may commune with the Higher Self of the recipient, and seek unconscious permission. Light can also be sent to the practitioner herself, either by visualizing the light around her, or placing a self image on the screen of the mind and sending light through the screen to the self. Sending light is usually ended with the saying "blessed be" and the connection dissolved.

Chakra Balancing
ITOW/W1

Since the pattern of seven continues to play a strong role in the Temple's mythos and theology, with seven planets, seven gates to the underworld, seven heavens, and seven stages of initiation in the final degree of the High Priest/ess, the first seven we learn is in the interior stars of the body, the chakras. They are the energetic organs of the body, processing the subtle energy of unseen magickal realms. Each corresponds to glands, organs, and bodily systems. The chakras are opened from the root to the crown, and then balanced from the crown down to the root.

Decide upon a symbol of balance for meditation. Enter into a meditative state using the countdown technique. Be aware of your energy field, particularly how the spine is filled with energy. There are seven major points of energy upon the spine, starting at the base of the spine, all the way to the top of the skull.

Symbols of Balance

Bring your attention to the root chakra. Feel this bright red disk energize and spin open as you inhale. Feel its spin cleanse any blocks in the root chakra. Feel it bloom like a red rose, revealing a ruby within it, clear and energized.

Bring your attention to the belly chakra. Feel this bright orange disk energize and spin open as you inhale. Feel its spin cleanse any blocks in the belly chakra. Feel it bloom like an orange rose, revealing a carnelian within it, clear and energized.

Bring your attention to the solar plexus chakra. Feel this bright yellow disk energize and spin open as you inhale. Feel its spin cleanse any blocks in the solar plexus chakra. Feel it bloom like a yellow rose, revealing a citrine within it, clear and energized.

Bring your attention to the heart chakra. Feel this bright green disk energize and spin open as you inhale. Feel its spin cleanse any blocks in the heart chakra. Feel it bloom like a green and pink rose, revealing an emerald within it, clear and energized.

Bring your attention to the throat chakra. Feel this bright blue disk energize and spin open as you inhale. Feel its spin cleanse any blocks in the throat chakra. Feel it bloom like a blue rose, revealing a sapphire within it, clear and energized.

Bring your attention to the brow chakra. Feel this indigo disk energize and spin open as you inhale. Feel its spin cleanse any blocks in the brow chakra. Feel it bloom like an indigo or purple rose, revealing an amethyst within it, clear and energized.

Bring your attention to the crown chakra. Feel this brilliant white disk energize and spin open as you inhale. Feel its spin cleanse any blocks in the crown chakra. Feel it bloom like a white or violet rose, revealing a diamond or opal within it, clear and energized.

Conjure your symbol of balance above your crown. Bring it down into the crown chakra, to balance the chakra. Hold it there for a moment and then bring it down to the brow chakra. Continue until you balance all seven chakras, and let the symbol flow down from the root into the Earth, forming a grounding cord.

Ask Mother Earth to send energy up through this cord, and feel it rise through the line of light like a taproot, reaching your root charka. Feel it rise up through the belly, solar plexus, heart, throat, brow, and crown, rising up and connecting you to the sky.

Ask the Sky Father to send energy down into your crown. Feel it flow down the seven chakras deep into Mother Earth. Feel the clear flow of energy, and the balanced seven points within you.

When done, simply slow the flow of energy, and then stop it. Let the remaining earth energy rise up and the remaining sky energy flow down. Count yourself up with the end of the Countdown Meditation. Give yourself clearance and balance. Ground yourself as needed.

Different versions of the chakra meditation can be performed, particularly synching each chakra with a single breath or series of breaths, such as the "Little Death" seven count breath. A simplified version focuses on the Celtic tradition of three "cauldrons" of energy. The root, belly, and solar plexus consists of the first Cauldron of Life, or lower cauldron. The heart chakra is the second Cauldron of the Heart, the middle cauldron. The throat, brow and crown create the third center, the Cauldron of Wisdom.

Inner Temple
ITOW/W1

The Inner Temple meditation is a key practice of the first degree. Through empowered vision working, one enters into their own inner sacred space known as the interior castle, soul shrine, or inner temple. It forms a nexus point from where a Witch can interact with other spirits and energies along with a safe starting and ending point for other work. Within the temple are twelve gates of consciousness, as well as four elemental gates. Healing, spirit guides, and past lives are lessons learned through the inner temple. In the fifth degree, it is dedicated as a temple of the Mysteries.

Altar Devotionals
OTOW/W2

Alter devotionals are regular prayer, usually performed at the altar, to create a deeper connection to deity as priest/ess of the Craft. Devotionals usually occur at the beginning or end of the day, or sometimes both. They can be done to a generalized notion of divinity, the God, Goddess, and Great Spirit, or to specific entities. Some devotionals are spoken from the heart spontaneously. Others are memorized prayers. They can include simple clearing and balancing exercises or affirmations. Often they include candle lighting, incense, and anointing.

*I, (state your name), thank the Goddess, God, and Great Spirit
For all whom I know
All whom I love
All that I have and know.
I thank you for this body, heart, mind, and soul
And thank you for all opportunities to love and learn
With ease, grace, and gentleness.
Please guide my every thought,
word, and deed,
by the highest will,
So mote it be!*

Sacred Space and the Magick Circle
OTOW/W2

A core practice of many modern Witches is the casting of a magick circle and the creation of sacred space. Similar to many nature-based spiritual traditions, Witches gather in a circle, and perform ceremony in a circular movement, honoring the four directions and their associations with the elements of earth, fire, air, and water. Through the circle, we can more easily commune with and celebrate the divine. Sacred space is a ritual setting that places the participants "between the worlds"—communing with more than one level of reality. Spells, prayers, and magick are more effective in the magick circle.

The magick circle has various steps, a ritual formula, to build up the "temple" in the inner worlds and the outer world. It is a container, like a cauldron, that contains the energy of the working: At the climax of the ritual, the energy is released between the worlds where it can manifest. The steps of the magick circle include:

Cleansing Self and Space
Circle Casting
Quarter Calls
Evocation
Naming the Work
Anointing
Great Rite

Raising Energy
The Work
Raising the Cone of Power
Grounding
Final Blessing, Healing Circle, and Grounding
Devocation
Release the Quarters
Release the Circle

The orientation of the elements is flexible within the Temple of Witchcraft. We use three primary orientations, based upon the energies of the three shamanic worlds. The preferred orientation by many in the Temple is the Underworld Orientation. It is based upon alchemical opposition, with fire and water in opposition, earth and air in opposition, aligning the qualities of moist/dry and hot/cold in the cycle of transformation. The Middle World Orientation is based upon the seasons and is the most common in other Western magickal traditions. The Upper World Orientation is based upon the seasonal watcher stars loosely associated with the fixed zodiac signs.

Underworld Orientation	**Middle World Orientation**	**Upper World Orientation**
North – Earth – Dry/Cold	North – Earth – Winter	North – Air – Aquarius
East – Fire – Dry/Warm	East – Air – Spring	East – Earth – Taurus
South – Air – Wet/Warm	South – Fire – Summer	South – Fire – Leo
West – Water – Wet/Cold	West – Water – Autumn	West – Water – Scorpio

After the magickal operations or celebrations of the circle are completed, the remaining energies and blessings generated by the ritual are divided into two important intentions that aid the overall evolution of the Witch. First is a circle of healing. Each participant names someone who needs healing energy and, upon the conclusion of all the names, a smaller cone of power is released, with the intention that the energy go to the named individuals, for the highest good, harming none. The second intention is a circle of grounding. It's not simply to release excess energy. The power is grounded with a blessing for the healing evolution of all creatures, all gardens upon the Earth, and Mother Earth herself.

The dual intention embraces the paradox between the personal and impersonal. The first circle helps us aid those we know, whom we love, are worried about, and even some we consider antagonists. The second helps those whom we might not know, everyone, and embraces a non-dual perspective of oneness. It goes beyond species and race, beyond flesh and blood, embracing humans, animals, plants, minerals, and all of the spirit world. It embraces the fact that as one heals and evolves, we all heal and evolve, deducting our blessings—what Tantric Buddhists would see as the merit generated by the work, towards the enlightenment of all. Regardless of the original ritual intention, including personal spellwork, these two factors ground all our magick in the aid of others and all.

The basic framework of the Magick Circle, taught in the Second Degree, the degree of the priest and priestess, is added to as education progresses. Within the third degree, the "directions" of above, below, and between are added to the circle, as well as starting with the Three Soul Alignment. At the completion of level four, the Invocation of the Bornless One is recommended as a part of the circle. In the training of the High Priest/ess, the Grand Circle is taught, cast with four quarters in the Upper World, Middle World and Underworld, twelve in all. It creates a powerful space in all three worlds simultaneously, and in partnership with the all the creatures of magick.

Cleansing and Purification
OTOW/W2

Ritual cleansing and purification are often misunderstood in a Pagan context. Theologically we believe everything is sacred. If this is true, why would we need to be "cleansed" spiritually? Isn't there nothing "dirty" or "bad?" Yes and no. While we don't believe in separation from the divine, seeing everything existing within the divine mind, including us, we do believe everything has its proper place. Just as we often feel better when we wash the dirt off our body before we go inside, even though dirt is part of the sacred Earth, we believe that certain energies and forces can stick to us like dirt, and might not be appropriate in ritual. Purification is putting everything in its proper place. Ritual then orders the elements you have with you, to create a harmonious pattern. Just as it might not be the most appropriate to make a stew with dirt clinging to the root vegetables, which we wash off before cooking them, we likewise wash off before ritual. The dirt is totally appropriate for the root vegetable before it is harvested, as it helps it grow. It all depends on the context.

While a variety of techniques are used to cleanse, from psychic energy work to various incenses, one of the simplest involves the use of water and salt. Clear water is considered pure, and used in many traditions for both spiritual and physical cleaning. We use water to bathe as its natural tendency is to clear and remove, just like in the shower or bath. Salt is considered pure, a clear crystal, and metaphysically it absorbs unwanted energies, just like vinegar can absorb unwanted odors. A small amount of salt can be added to a bowl of clear water, mixing the elements of earth and water for purification, It can be anointed upon the body like an odorless "perfume," or sprinkled, known as asperging when done as a ritual act, with the fingers or with a small evergreen branch. Witches asperge themselves and their ritual area to purify it. In the second degree, the idea is often expanded to the lustral bath, a purification bath of salt and water, often with herbs and oils such as vervain, lavender or hyssop. In the fourth degree, a holy water of salt, ash, rose petals, and fire is created, using a variation of the traditional Wiccan poetry from the Grimoire of Solomon, for the salt and water.

"I exorcise and bless thee, O Creature of Water, casting out all impurities and discordant energies. May you ever be blessed as a vessel of healing and love."

"I exorcise and bless thee, O Creature of Salt, casting out all impurities and discordant energies. May you ever be blessed as a vessel for strength and purity."

"May the salt and water conjoin as one in the love of the Goddess."

The salt can be ground in a mortar and pestle counterclockwise or widdershins, as that symbolism is for release and cleansing. Tap the mortar with the pestle as if the round was a compass, to the north, west, south and then east, and ground the salt in the same direction. You could add a bit of lavender, sage, or roasted barley for added power. You can sprinkle the water on your body.

By these sacred waters, I bless my head so I may perceive clearly.
I bless my hands, so I may do the work cleanly.
And I bless my heart, so I may feel compassionately.
Blessed be.

The Great Rite
OTOW/W2

The Great Rite is a core practice of the second degree, usually performed as part of the liturgical ritual of the Magick Circle. While it can refer to ritualized sex magick, here we refer most often to the Great Rite "in token," a sacrament enacted by the athame blade (or wand) and the chalice. When the two are brought together, the forces of the God and Goddess conjoin in the fertility mystery. The water (or wine or potion) in the chalice is blessed by their union and all who drink from it are attuned to the creative aspects of divinity, uniting their own inner male and female, God and Goddess, becoming one with the Great Spirit, as the Goddess and God are "the Two Who Move as One within the Love of the Great Spirit."

As the sword is to the grail,
The blade is to the chalice,
Truth is to love
Let us draw in the blessings of the Goddess, God and Great Spirit
And drink them in.
So mote it be.

The Great Rite can also include "Drawing Down the Moon" or Sun, through the blade and infusing the energy into the chalice, as well as the blessing of "cakes" or bread as a sacrament. In the Temple,

Foundations of the Temple

the sacramental act of the Great Rite is recommended in every magick circle, but in particular at the esbats and sabbats, for the spiritual advancement of the practitioner.

Libations to the Spirits
W2

One of the ways we build energetic relationships with the spirits is to make offerings. Offerings of food and drink have an inherent energy. When blessed by a Witch, they have both a deeper power, and a connection to that Witch, so whatever entity they are offered to, will have a great connection to that practitioner.

A simple form of libration, after the Great Rite, is to offer part of the chalice to the spirits. If outdoors, the libation is poured upon the land. If indoors, a libation bowl is used, which is later brought out and poured upon the land.

A simple form of libation used in the Temple is threefold:

A libation to the gods and ancient ones of our Craft! (Pour a few drops out)
A libation to the creatures of the deep! (Pour a few drops out)
A libation to the spirits of the Temple of Witchcraft! (Pour a few drops out)

The threefold libation connects you to the Gods of your Craft, those called upon in the ritual, as well as the ancient ones, from the Mighty Dead to the quarter guardians, any spirits you have called upon associated with magick and Witchcraft. The second part connects you to the chthonic powers of the underworld, particularly the elder race of faery, but also the ancestors of the land, and the underworld gods. Lastly an offering to the spirits of the Temple helps strengthen your connection to the egregore of the Temple and the spirits that guide us.

Wheel of the Year and Path of the Moon
OTOW/W2

Celebration of the eight main sabbats of the Wheel of the Year and the thirteen esbats, or Full Moon rituals, are part of the core spiritual practices of the Temple. They can be celebrated alone, in small groups, or in larger community gatherings. The Temple offers public services for people to experience these mysteries, gaining entrance into the magickal world. They are necessary rituals for attuning to the cycles of the Earth, Moon, Sun, and Stars, and how these things are reflected with us. More importantly, we believe that humans must participate in the "turning of the wheel" of the year. We are necessary for the continued sustainment of life on Earth, and the good will between humanity and all of nature, manifest and unmanifest.

Spellcraft
OTOW/W2

While often divided from the spiritual traditions of Witchcraft and Wicca, spells play an important role in spiritual development in the Temple. The exploration of desire helps us understand the transformation of our personal will, our desire, to the True Will of the soul when spells are done in the spirit of "for the good of all involved, harming none."

Divination
ITOW/W1, OTOW/W2

Temple members practice a variety of divination techniques to receive helpful information from their own innate wisdom, the spirits, gods, and universe. In the first degree, we explore the pendulum, muscle testing, and automatic writing, while in the second degree, the practice of tarot, runes, and basic astrological timing is introduced. Various forms of scrying and psychometry are experienced. In the third degree, the Celtic ogham characters are introduced. Students are expected to study and develop their divination skills in any system they desire, balancing between yes/no techniques, fluid symbol systems (such as scrying), and more fixed symbol systems (such as Tarot).

Three Soul Alignment
TOSW/W3

Using breath, one can attune and connect the three souls to function with unified purpose in magick. While in Witchcraft I we learn of the souls in a psychological sense, the conscious mind, psychic mind and divine mind, in Witchcraft III, we learn of them as soul selves, complete in and of themselves, but in need of unification to have clear action and experience. This breath work is influenced by the Anderson Feri Tradition of Witchcraft.

Inhale through the heart: *I am the Namer*
Repeat two more breaths, focusing upon the heart and the Namer.
Inhale through the soles of the feet, the roots: *I am the Shaper*
Repeat two more breaths, focusing upon the roots and the Shaper.
Inhale through the crown of the head: *I am the Watcher*
Repeat two more breaths, focusing upon the crown and the Watcher.
Inhale through all three zones: *I am the Three in One*
Inhale through all three zones: *The One in Three*
Inhale through all three zones: *As it was, as it is, as it always shall be.*

Adam Sartwell, uniting breath and prayer work, with twelve breaths, concludes with a final breath upward, towards the heavens, as an offering to the Watcher self in prayerful breath, as found in the Huna and Feri traditions.

Healing List
W1/W2

The practice of sending healing light, as well as healing magick, can be devoted to community by keeping a Healing List upon your altar. Similar to a prayer list, it is a list of names of those who need healing, from emotional energetic support to physical illness. Energy can be directed to the list itself in an act of sympathetic magick, going out to those named on the list. Many Reiki practitioners will "reiki" their list. The list can serve as a focus for candle magick, crystals, and other forms of spell casting. In the Temple community, a community healing list is kept and posted online at the new Moon, for the entire community to support those who request help and healing.

Shamanic Smudge
TOSW/W3

The Shamanic Smudging ritual is a simple way to create sacred space without the formal ritual of the magick circle. It honors the four directions of the compass, as well as the three worlds, and left and right. The ritual reminds the Witch of their allies in terms of animal, plant, and mineral spirits, as well as deities, in each of these sacred directions, creating a living mandala around the practitioner.

Traditional herbs to smudge with include mugwort, lavender, sweet fern, cedar, juniper, pine, hyssop, and of course, sage. Locally grown or wildcrafted herbs can be used to make your own smudge bundles, but joss (incense) sticks and even resinous incense upon a charcoal within a small cauldron can be used to make the space.

Hold your smudge out to the North and say: *To the powers of the North*
Think of your allies that dwell in the North for you.
Hold your smudge out to the East and say: *To the powers of the East*
Think of your allies that dwell in the East for you.
Hold your smudge out to the South and say: *To the powers of the South*
Think of your allies that dwell in the South for you.
Hold your smudge out to the West and say: *To the powers of the West*
Think of your allies that dwell in the West for you.
Hold your smudge above you and say: *To the powers of the Great Above*
Think of your allies that dwell in the Great Above for you.
Hold your smudge to the ground and say: *To the powers of the Great Below*
Think of your allies that dwell in the Great Below for you.
Hold your smudge to the left side and say: *To those on my left*
Think of your allies that dwell to the left of you.
Hold your smudge to the right side and say: *To those on my right*
Think of your allies that dwell to the right of you.
Hold your smudge in front of your chest and say: *And to those in my heart, I welcome you.*
Think of your allies that dwell in the Center for you.
(Optional: Draw a banishing pentagram before you and say:
I banish all harmful, unwanted energies from this space.
Draw an invoking pentagram before you and say:

I call forth all helpful, healing energies to this space.)
Hold out your smudge at arm's length and trace three clockwise circles in smoke around you. You are not casting a circle, but you are purifying the entire space. Say:
I stand in the center and create a sacred space. So mote it be.
Stand in the center and take a deep breath. Feel yourself oriented in the sacred space of all nine directions around you.

Home Shrine
W1

As part of learning the magick of place, first degree students are asked to build a special home shrine, to honor the genus loci, or spirit of place, for the spirit of their home, including both the building and the land that is built upon. In ages past, such spirits were known as the House Elf, House Wight, or Brownie. It is a "household deity" much like those found in ancient Roman tradition. Such honoring and relationship brings us back into the memory when everything and everywhere is sacred. A home shrine distinct from your own magickal meditation altar. It's a place to honor the household spirit. It need not be an obvious altar, but it's a place where you can light a candle, and make offerings, such as water, honey, milk, or cream. Small amounts of food can be offered to the spirit and, in return, the happiness of the house elf should influence the happiness of the home. When you are having household problems, you can make an offering to ask for help from this spirit. Food offerings can then be brought outside to the land and disposed of, and any animals that partake of the offerings left are emissaries of this household god.

Ancestor Shrine
W3

Creating an altar just for your ancestors, kept up all year round, is a powerful way to continue the flow of wisdom and reciprocity between us and those who have come before. Ancestors can include blood ancestors, but also those who have "adopted" you, or milk ancestors, those who share a similar background or art, known as story, breath, and bread ancestors. We can also honor those who have lived and died upon the land where we are, bone ancestors, and those of our own spiritual tradition, Witches who have come before us.

Offerings are made of clear water, alcohol, and rich foods, to "feed" the spirits in a way to keep the energy of our connection strong. Saturday, the day of Saturn, is an excellent day for ancestral offerings and communication, though holidays that were important to loved ones—and for many of us, those will be Christian holidays—are also an excellent time to make offerings. I do more around Christmas and Easter for those loved ones. I also like to make offerings at the dark and full Moons.

Call to the Ancestors
I call to you my ancestors
Blood of my blood,
Flesh of my flesh
Bone of my bone
We are kin, you and I.
I seek to honor you, to bless you, to heal you
And to awaken your gifts in me.
I call to you my ancestors
Milk to milk in loving support
Bread to bread in vocational kin
Breath to breath in those of inspiration
I seek to honor you, to bless you, to heal you
And to awaken your gifts in me.
I call to you my ancestors
Those of the blood of wild things
Those of the blood of green sap
Those of the blood of stars
Mighty Dead of our Timeless Tradition
Mighty Dead of our Nameless Art
I seek to honor you, to bless you and to be healed by you
May there always be peace between us.
Blessed be.

The Lesser Banishing Ritual of the Pentagram
TOHW/W4

The Lesser Banishing Ritual of the Pentagram, or LBRP, is a ritual from the Order of the Golden Dawn, designed to banish unwanted forces on the terrestrial level (elemental level or microcosm) and invoke protection. Since its creation, many traditions have created variations of the ritual, to fulfill the same purpose in ceremonial magick, but fitted to that group's particular ethos and Mysteries. The most famous is probably Aleister Crowley's Star Ruby ritual.

In the Temple of Witchcraft, we encourage fourth year students to work in the original format of the Golden Dawn rituals, and then adapt them to their own experience and correspondences, but there are Temple of Witchcraft variations, mostly based upon the founders' own variations. Rather than use Hebrew god names, the ritual uses primal vowels for the pentagram chants, and more Pagan words, as well as Celtic deities instead of archangels. Practitioners often use this ritual, but substitute the deities they have the strongest affinities for, as they relate to the four elements.

Earth-Sky Connection

Stand straight, facing the north in the center of your circle. Sweep both arms upward from the sides of your body. Visualize and feel yourself bringing the energy of the Earth beneath your feet up through your body, out your crown and finger tips. Feel the energy reach up and connect to the sky. Look up to the sky and say: *Et Uranous*.

Visualize and feel yourself pull the energy of the sky down through your crown and body as you sweep both arms back down the side of your body and slightly out to each side, bringing head down to look at the ground. Say: *Et Gaea*. Feel the energy of the Earth flowing up through you to the sky while the energy of the Sky is flowing down through you to the center of the Earth.

Reach out with the right hand, straight out the right side and imagine you are holding a ball of golden yellow light connected with a beam of energy from the east, in your right hand as you bring your gaze to the east. Say: *Et An Ra*.

Reach out with the left hand, straight out the left side and imagine you are holding a ball of slivery blue light connected with a beam of energy from the west, in your left hand as you bring your gaze to the west Say: *Et An Ma*.

Cross your Arms over your chest in the God Position (The Sign of Osiris Risen), bringing the beams of golden yellow and silver blue energies across the chest, slightly bowing your head. Say: *Amoura Korey*.

Feel a flow of gold energy from the east to the west move through you while simultaneously feeling a flow of silver energy from the west to the east move through you. Feel the flow of the Earth and sky energy as well, as you are in the center of an energetic cross. Feel your connection to all things.

Banishing

While still facing the north, step back with the foot of your dominant side (if you are right handed, your right foot) Draw a banishing earth pentagram in blue or blue-violet light and chant the vowel sounds *U-I-E-O-A*, with one vowel for each of the points of the star. Step forward with the foot that stepped back and plunge your dominant hand into the star, activating it and "pushing" it out to the circumference of your intended circle. In the center of the pentagram start drawing the circle around you, drawing one-fourth of a circle of light (in white, blue, or violet) until you face the east. Repeat this process in all four directions and complete the circle in the north.

Evocation

Standing in the center of the circle, facing the north with your arms outstretched to either side, evoke the four powers with this prayer. Imagine each deity standing in their direction. Feel the presence of the circle and pentagrams, as well as the hexagram within your heart chakra. As you imagine the hexagram, bend your arms at the elbow, bringing your hand in to touch the chest. When you are done, visualize the deities facing out, protecting you from harm.

Before me Cernunnos
Behind me Macha
On my right hand Lugh

And on my left hand Ceridwen
About me flames the pentagrams
And within me shines the six rayed star of perfect love and perfect trust.

Repeat the Earth-Sky Connection

Bornless One Invocation
TOHW/W4

The Bornless Ritual is Aleister Crowley's variation of *The Sacred Magic of Abramelin the Mage*, also known as the "Abramelin Operation," a ritual invocation to the Holy Guardian Angel, the Higher Self, what Crowley called the Bornless One and what is called the Watcher Soul in the Temple. The name references an Egyptian Ritual most appropriately translated as "the headless one" from the Graeco-Egyptian Magickal Papyri.

A Temple variation of the Bornless Rite is part of the Witchcraft IV initiation ritual. The invocation itself can be part of our core practices after this initiation, part of our altar devotionals, magick circles and prayer practices, to continually remind us to magickally live from this higher self in all our thoughts, words and actions.

I invoke you o Bornless One,
All that was, all that is and all that ever shall be.
You who have no beginning and no end.
You who create the above and the below.
You who create the heavens and the earth.
You who create the night and the day.
You who create the darkness and the light.
You are myself made perfect that none has ever seen.
You are matter, destroying to create.
You are spirit, creating to destroy
You produce by seed and root, by stem and bud, by leaf and flower and fruit.
By Light, Life, Love and Law you nourish all that lives
And by Liberty to free all that was bound and open the gates to all wonder.
For you hold the stars of the heavens and the depths of the abyss.
All lie within your being.
For love's sake you were divided

And for love's sake, you will be united.
Hear me, for I am yours.
You are myself made perfect.
You are my true self.
Be in my every thought
My every word
My every deed
Now and forever.
So mote it be.

Five Gifts of the Elements
LTOW/W5

The Five Gifts are part meditation, part prayer, part devotional, and part energy work. They draw upon a High Priest/ess previous work in finding and creating the four "hallows" or inner tools that correspond with the outer tools of the magician and Witch. Each elemental realm has an inner etheric tool for us to find and earn, reflective of our relationship with that element and its sphere of influence in our life. The tools are known as the Stone of Sovereignty (earth), the Cup of Compassion (water), the Sword of Truth (air) and the Spear of Victory (fire). Upon completion of the four hallows, the initiate can forge the Crown of Humility, and the work of the High Priest/ess is in the forging of the crown and the inner work to connect with the twelve powers of zodiac, as embodied by twelve gems within the crown. The five gifts are reciting, while envisioning and feeling the five hallows on or within the body, for they have become a part of your etheric body.

I stand upon the stone of sovereignty.
With the sword of truth at my side.
I hold the cup of compassion in one hand.
And the spear of victory in the other.
Upon my head lies the Crown of Humility.
May I serve with honor.
I have the blessings of the Warrior
I have the blessings of the Steward
I have the blessings of the Trickster

I have the blessings of the Mother
I have the blessings of the Artisan King
I have the blessings of the Servant
I have the blessings of the Judge
I have the blessings of the Guardian
I have the blessings of the Teacher
I have the blessings of the Father
I have the blessings of the Rebel
I have the blessings of the Ecstatic
Blessed be!

Those who would like to perform this, but have not attained the specific hallows or gem, can replace the verbs indicating attainment with "seek." One missing only the Cup of Compassion might say, "*I seek the cup of compassion in one hand.*" Usually the crown cannot be forged until the first four hallows are earned, and the twelve gems cannot be set until the crown is forged.

Three Rays Meditation
3ROW

One can unite the three rays of Power, Love and Wisdom within us, by drawing their light down from the center of the cosmos, down through the three "cauldrons" of the body and deep within the Earth and Underworld. Learning to hold the blessings of True Will, Perfect Love and Divine Wisdom at the same time creating the vessel, the vehicle for consciousness, that allows us to be closer with, and eventually join, the Mighty Dead.

Call down the three rays with this invocation:

By the straight line, I invoke the first ray.
I invoke the red ray.
I invoke the unbending ray of cold red archangelic flame.
I invoke the ray of will and power.

Pull down the energy of the first ray. As the red light descends in a beam, pausing at each point, ask yourself, "*What is the will of the heavens? The head? The heart? The body? The Earth? The Underworld?*"

Listen and feel at each one. Seek to enact the will of each one. Then say, *"There are no limits to my power. All is possible."*

By the bent line, I invoke the second ray.
I invoke the blue ray.
I invoke the spiraling ray of electric blue faery flame.
I invoke the ray of love and trust.

Pull down the energy of the second ray. As the blue light descends in a spiral, pausing at each point, ask yourself, *"What is the love of the heavens? The head? The heart? The body? The Earth? The Underworld?"* Listen and feel at each one. Seek to feel the love of each one. Then say, *"There are no limits to my love. All is one."*

By the crooked line, I invoke the third ray.
I invoke the yellow ray.
I invoke the crooked ray of serpentine gold Witch fire.
I invoke the ray of wisdom and cunning.

Pull down the energy of the third ray. As the yellow light descends like lightning, pausing at each point, ask yourself, *"What is the wisdom of the heavens? The head? The heart? The body? The Earth? The Underworld?"* Listen and feel at each one. Seek to know the wisdom of each one. Then say, *"There are no limits to my wisdom. All is known."*

Ground yourself, but feel each of your three cauldrons retain some of the red, blue and yellow light, mixing together to expand your consciousness and blessings.

My own foundational practice at this time usually consists of counting down to a meditative state, performing the Three Soul Alignment, followed by a non-Temple technique known as the Merkaba Meditation, or Chariot of Light (for more information, see my book *Ascension Magick*) and then the Three Rays invocation. At this point I feel fully prepared to perform a short version of the Bornless One Invocation. I will then end the session, or go onto deeper work, including spellcraft, spirit contact, or vision work.

Chapter Nine: Holy Days and Rituals

Members of the Temple of Witchcraft celebrate a number of holidays, usually through the "liturgy" of the magick circle ritual (as described in the previous chapter). The ritual is both our liturgical format and creates our temple, as we believe service can be held anywhere the ritual is performed, creating a sacred space, a temple "between the worlds" or in a liminal frame of mind. Many of these rituals are inherently liminal, occurring at threshold times "between" the changing of planetary, seasonal, or life cycles. We choose to celebrate at this times, as well as considering dawn, noon, dusk, and midnight sacred, because of their liminal quality.

Members of the Temple of Witchcraft celebrate four main types of ritual:

The Wheel of the Year

Wheel of the Year rituals consist of marking the passage of time in the relationship between the Sun and the Earth as manifested by the seasons. The Wheel consists of four solar holidays known as solstices and equinoxes when the Sun transitions from a mutable solar tropical Zodiac sign to a cardinal sign, and four fire festivals, drawn from the Celtic agricultural traditions, celebrated when the

Sun is roughly 15 degrees in one of the four fixed Zodiac signs. Wheel of the Year rituals are usually celebrated in community, but can be practiced solitary when necessary.

The Path of the Moon

Path of the Moon rituals consist of marking the passage of time in the relationship between the Earth, Sun, and Moon as manifested in the lunar phases. The Path consists of twelve Full Moons and twelve Dark Moons, just prior to the New Moons, each described by the sign of the tropical Zodiac the Moon occupies during the peak and valley of the lunar cycle. Path of the Moon rituals can be celebrated in small groups or solitary.

Rites of Passage

Rites of Passage rituals consist of marking the passage of time in the life of an individual, or a significant achievement within the Temple of Witchcraft tradition. Rites of Passage are rituals to attune with the various stages of growth and development, for both the individual and an acknowledgement of such changes from the community. Religious rites of passage, such as dedication, initiation, and elevation are significant steps of education and achievement in the Mystery School and Seminary. Rites of Passage are usually celebrated in community or small groups of initiates.

Historic Holy Days

Historic Holy Days are celebrations honoring specific Pagan deities of the ancient world on the days their origin culture celebrated, as best synchronized with our modern calendars. They also include the anniversaries of historic events or the birthdays of historic personages. They are days of communion, honoring, and remembrance, and may be celebrated solitary, in small groups or by the larger community.

Purpose of Our Celebrations

The purpose of holiday rituals is to attune us to the tides and seasons of the world, and its relationship with the Moon, Sun, and stars. We believe our nature is both terrestrial, or earthly, and celestial or cosmic. Working with the tides of both the heavens and Earth creates opportunities for spiritual growth and enlightenment while at the same time building group identity as we advance our purpose on all levels.

Wheel of the Year celebrations are performed because we believe human participation is necessary for the proper function of seasonal tides through the practice of "turning the Wheel of the Year." Such participation continues the cycles of life and creates good will between humanity and both nature and the spirit world. We believe it fulfills humanity's purpose in cooperation with the other realms of life and spirit. When humanity ceases to do this, chaos is unleashed upon the world until a new balance of life can be struck. The Wheel of the Year celebrations also build community cohesion and group identity. They help attune us to our cultural ancestors, thereby granting us greater insight into their own wisdom and religion. It presents our primary mythos, or outer mystery for the entire community, providing a platform to teach our theology and wisdom to the community through direct application to the cycles of the year.

Path of the Moon celebrations are performed for personal communion with the divine. Rituals include prayer, magick and spells for both the gain of blessings (Full Moon rituals) and the removal of unwanted forces (Dark Moon rituals). They are a time of personal revelation, healing and growth. Some practitioners focus exclusively on Full or Dark Moon rituals, but both are ideal for balance. The Moon rituals can be done solitary for personal development, but community Moon rituals bring cohesion among groups of practitioners who are able to support each other in personal and community efforts. Moon rituals can explore the deeper mysteries and more complex mythos reserved for students and initiates of the mystery school and clergy.

Rites of Passage rituals are performed to acclimate both individuals and the community to new group identities and purpose, as well as celebrate the development of life in harmony with the gods.

Historic Holy Days are celebrated to connect us to the past, and our past cultural ancestors, thereby finding a solid foundation for building our future. It grants communion with the spiritual entities and practices that our ancestors felt were important. It renews or continues the tradition, granting access to the "momentum of the past" as Witchcraft elder Raven Grimassi would say, when building our future.

Wheel of the Year Rituals

The foundation of the liturgical calendar of the Temple of Witchcraft is the modern Neopagan Wheel of the Year. The Eight Sabbats comprising the Wheel of the Year are a collection of mostly European traditions and myths, fusing Teutonic solar holidays with the fire festivals of the Celts. Most Neopagan, Wiccan, and modern Witchcraft traditions recognize and celebrate some, if not all, of these eight holidays.

Due to the nature of our hectic modern lives, to accommodate the largest portion of the community, public sabbats are often held on the nearest Saturday to the actual folk tradition date, or astrological alignment.

Samhain (October 31)

New Year's celebration. A ritual to honor the dead and the Young God's triumphant return to the Underworld and the manifestation of the Dark Goddess. The celebration of the Third and final harvest, the Meat Harvest. Offerings of food and candy are made to the dead. The Sun is in the sign of Scorpio.

Yule (Dec 21/Winter Solstice)

A ritual to honor the rebirth of the God as the Child of Light with the waxing Son. Bells, candles, mistletoe, and fire are part of the celebration. The Sun is transitioning from Sagittarius to Capricorn.

Imbolc (Feb 2)

A ritual to honor the slumbering Goddess beneath the land, gently urging her to awaken at Spring. Many candles are used in the celebration and milk is drunk. The Sun is in the sign of Aquarius.

Ostara (March 21/Vernal Equinox)

A ritual to welcome the return of Spring and the rise of the Goddess regenerated as the Maiden of Flowers. Flowers and seeds are blessed in the ritual. The sun is transitioning from Pisces to Aries.

Beltane (May 1)

A ritual to celebrate the union of the God as the Green Man and the Goddess of the Flower. Dancing is often performed at this ceremony. The Sun is in the sign of Taurus.

Litha (June 21/Summer Solstice)

A ritual to celebrate the height of the God's power as the Sun King and the Goddess as the Queen of the Land. The Sun is honored and used to bless during this ritual. The faery folk are also honored. The Sun is transitioning from Gemini into Cancer.

Lammas (Aug 1)

A ritual to celebrate the First Harvest of grain and the God as the slain grain king. A funeral celebration of the God. Bread is blessed and consumed. The Sun is in the sign of Leo.

Mabon (Sept. 21/Autumnal Equinox)

A ritual celebration of the Second Harvest of fruit, particularly apples and grapes. The journey of the God into the Underworld and the mourning of the Goddess as the changing leaves are remembered. Wine is drunk and a shamanic journey undertaken at this rite. The Sun is transitioning from Virgo to Libra.

The following are a few examples of Temple sabbat rituals, to show both the basic ritual format, and the range of variety found within it.

Temple of Witchcraft Samhain Ritual, 2010

The theme of this ritual was connecting the beloved dead of our personal lives to deepening the connection between us and the enlightened masters in the Mighty Dead. We would be using the "snake dance" to travel in and out of the Grand Sabbat of the Mighty Dead, along in spirit with our beloved dead. This Samhain was to be a celebration of both "tribes" of ancestors, for the evolution of us all, living, dead and sanctified dead. Through this vision, people would have a deeper connection to return on their own if they so wished in their private practice.

Roles:
High Priestess (HP)
High Priestesses (HPS)
Northern Quarter Caller
Eastern Quarter Caller
Southern Quarter Caller
Western quarter Caller
Three Dark Goddess Priestesses
Oak King
Holly King
Drummers, Musicians and Singers
Community Dancers and Participants

Altar:
Bread and Wine
Incense
Water
Tarot Cards
Acorn Bowl
Chocolate Bowl
Ancestral Altar in the West (Separate from main altar in the center)
Cauldron with Alcohol/Salt for Ritual Fire
Ancestral Tokens

Introduction & Explanation of the Ritual
    Brief History of Samhain Traditions
    Telling the Tale of the Morrighan and Dagda
    Explaining the similarities and differences between the Ancestors and the Mighty Dead
    Explaining the Grove of the Hidden Company - The Eternal Sabbat - Akelarre

Circles of Names
    Everyone shares their first names or craft names, as we go clockwise in a circle.

Smudging and Purifying
    The four quarter guardians go around the circle, each responsible for smudging one fourth of the circle with purifying incense. The

High Priest and High Priestess lead the group to intone a simple "Ooo" while doing so, both to clear and to keep focus on the intention of the ritual.

Casting the Circle

The Circle is cast thrice around with a sword by the HPS

We cast this circle to protect us from all harm on any level.
We cast this circle to draw to us the most perfect energies
and block out all forces that are not in harmony with our work
We cast this circle to create a Temple between the worlds,
of Perfect Love and Perfect Trust, where the highest will is Sovereign.

Calling the Quarters

The four quarter callers each call to their own element, facing the appropriate direction.

To the North,
We call upon the element of Earth
and the Great Stag to guide and guard us.
Hail and welcome.

To the East,
We call upon the element of Fire
and the Swift Horse to guide and guard us.
Hail and welcome.

To the South,
We call upon the element of Air
and the Wise Crow to guide and guard us.
Hail and welcome.

To the West,
We call upon the element of Water
and the Changing Snake to guide and guard us
Hail and welcome.

Calling of the Great Above, Great Below and Great Between

The HPS acknowledges the Axis Mundi, above, below, and between.

Opening to the Temple
The Astral Temple of TOW is opened by the HP

Calling of the Three Rays
The Three Rays are invoked by the HP.

Evocation of the Goddess and God and Great Spirit
The Goddess is called by the HP and the God called by HPS:

I call upon the Morrighan, the Mistress of Phantoms
I call upon the Morrighan, dark feathered queen of the night
I call upon the Morrighan, lady of the river!
Hail and welcome.

I call upon the Dagda, the Good God of the Cauldron
I call upon the Dagda, whose harp turns the seasons
I call upon the Dagda, whose club opens the gates of death and life.
Hail and welcome.

Priestess No. 1:
We call to the Three Who are One, the Morrighan, Source of All Enchantment
We call to the Three Who are One, the Morrighan, Phantom Queen
We call to Anu, Great Mother, Source of All
Hail and Welcome

Priestess No. 2:
We call to the Three Who are One, the Morrighan, Speaker of Prophecy
We call to the Three Who are One, The Morrighan, Faery Queen
We call to Badb Catha, Battle Goddess, Diviner of Fate
Hail and welcome

Priestess No. 3:
We call to the Three Who are One, the Morrighan, Warrior Teacher
We call to the Three Who are One, the Morrighan, Royal Queen
We call to Macha, Lady of the Red Tresses and Feathered Cloak, Wise Ruler
Hail and Welcome

Call to the Ancestors
Take a moment to think about your ancestors. Your ancestors can be those who are related to you by blood, or those related to you by

love. Your ancestors can be the deceased in your lifetime, those whom you knew in life, or the dead of many generations ago, perhaps their names are unknown to you. Take this time to think of your ancestors and see if anyone comes to you as you focus your energy upon those who came before. If no ancestor comes, invite those souls who have been forgotten, particularly those who linger in the world and have not yet found peace, but seek peace.

Take this time to commune with the ancestor who comes. Talk and share a moment in your mind. Invite them to this dance. Offer your love and good wishes as food for the dead, so together you can cross the hedge.

Great Rite

HPS plunges the blade into the chalice the HP is holding.

As the sword is to the grail
The blade is to the chalice
Truth is to love

The cakes are blessed by the HP, who draws an invoking pentagram over them. While the cakes and ale are being passed, the following chant is sung by the group.

All Come to Me
chant by Jocelyn Van Bokkelen

All come to me
I am the cross roads
The place you've been
Has come to an end
Here is the gate
I stand at the crossroads
Waiting for you
To begin anew

Cakes and ale are brought to the Ancestral Altar to "feed" the dead.

Foundations of the Temple

Opening of the Oak Doors to the Other World

The Oak and Holly King Priests open the gates between the worlds and hold guard.

Oak King: *I open the Oaken Door, Duir, to the World of the Spirits*

Holly King: *And I stand at the gate of the door, guardian. Do you have the keys, the passwords to enter through the Gate?*

Oak King: *I do. Perfect love. Perfect trust…and a Kiss. (Kiss is given)*

Dance of the Dead

Drumming begins as the HP guides the group in a circle dance, spiraling counterclockwise into the center and out again repeatedly to a slow drum beat. Suggest the image of dancing to cross the veil, depicted as a hedge, moat, or gateway. As we hold hands in flesh and blood, also holding on to us are the hands of the ancestors. We are a great chain of flesh and blood, spirit and soul.

The HPS lights the cauldron fire when the first spiral reaches the center. We dance around the flames of the center. The circle returns to the outer edges, and each person is encouraged to reach into the flame spiritually, and ask for an ally from the Mighty Dead, the great Witch Masters from the past. You, and your personal ancestor connect with the ancestors the Mighty Dead.

Three dance "movements" commence with the drummers. The first is a slow waltz beat, three beats per measure, where we dance clockwise around the fire, visualizing we are dancing with the spirits.

The second movement is a more wild, free form ecstatic dance, building in speed and intensity. This is the sabbatic dance of a tribal and primal nature. Those who make it up to the center of the altar will find a cauldron of tarot cards, face down. Participants are instructed to take a tarot card for their "year" from the cauldron.

The Third dance is a return to the circle, taking a seat and meditating in slow silence, upon the card chosen. Let the ancestors commune with you through the card, as the drummers hold a steady heartbeat rhythm.

Turning the Wheel

Everyone rises and we take this power to turn the wheel of the year, with the chant IAO, pronounced Eee-Aah-Oh, and the cone of power is raised. Energy is grounded to the Earth, for the healing of all creatures and Mother Earth herself.

Circle of Healing

Rather than a circle of blessing and healing for the living, as we usually do, in this ritual, we propose a circle of healing for the living and the dead, a circle of ancestral healing. The names are spoken aloud, and another cone of power raised and the excess grounded.

Feeding of the People

The Triple Goddess Priestesses give out chocolate to the participants

Priestess: *May you know the sweetness of life*

Blessing of the Acorn Keys

Oak King and Holly King give out acorns, with the blessing that they can be used again to visit the eternal sabbat or speak with the beloved and enlightened ancestors.

Kings: *May you return again.*

Spiral Dance to Return

The Spiral Dance is repeated, to return again from the Underworld. During the dance, a chant is sung:

We Are An Old People
chant by Morning Feather/Will Shepardson

We are an old people
We are a new people
We are the same people
Stronger than before

Closing the Oak Door

Oak King: *I close the Oaken Door to the World of Spirits. May there always be peace between us.*

Devocation of the Spirits

HP: *We thank and bless the Morrighan in all her forms.*
Priestess No 1: *We thank Anu, Great Mother. Hail and farewell.*
Priestess No 2: *We thank Badb Catha, Battle Goddess. Hail and farewell.*

Priestess No 3: *We thank Macha of the Feathered Cloak. Hail and farewell.*

HPS: *We thank the Dagda, the Good God in all his forms.*

Oak King: *We thank the Great Oak King, the Green God, for opening the door.*

Holly King: *We thank the Great Holly King, Red God, for guarding the gate.*

HPS: *We thank and release the ancestors. Thank you for joining with us. To all spirits in perfect love and perfect trust, stay if you will, go if you must. Hail and farewell.*

Closing the Temple
HP closes the astral temple of the Temple of Witchcraft.

Closing the Great Above, Great Below and Great Between
The axis mundi is acknowledged by the HPS

Releasing the Quarters
To the North,
We thank and release the element of Earth
and the Great Stag.
Hail and farewell.

To the West,
We thank and release the element of Water
and the Changing Snake.
Hail and farewell.

To the South,
We thank and release the element of Air
and the Wise Crow.
Hail and farewell.

To the East,
We thank and release the element of Fire
and the Swift Horse.
Hail and farewell.

Releasing the Circle
HP releases the circle widdershins with the sword.

I cast this circle out into the cosmos as a sign of our celebration, the circle is undone but never broken. Merry meet, merry part and merry meet again. Blessed be.

Salem Witch Trials

We also honor at Samhain those who have been executed at the Salem Witch Trials. Though we know they were not Witches in the sense of Pagan practitioners, many in the US, particularly the Northeast, come to our path as a Witch, through the history, lore and even tourism of Salem, Massachusetts. We honor anyone who was killed in the name of Witchcraft by persecutors, even if they did not self identify as a Witch. They keep the memory of such persecution and remind us why we must work so it can never happen again to those accused of Witchcraft, and all those who are persecuted for being different.

Bridget Bishop (June 10, 1692)
Rebecca (Towne) Nurse (July 19, 1692)
Sarah (Solart) Good (July 19, 1692)
Elizabeth (Jackson) Howe (July 19, 1692)
Sarah (Averill) Wildes (July 19, 1692)
Susannah (North) Martin (July 19, 1692)
George Burroughs (August 19, 1692)
Martha (Allen) Carrier (August 19, 1692)
George Jacobs, Sr. (August 19, 1692)
John Proctor (August 19, 1692)
John Willard (August 19, 1692)
Giles Corey (September 19, 1692)
Martha Corey (September 22, 1692)
Mary (Towne) Eastey (September 22, 1692)
Alice Parker (September 22, 1692)
Mary (Ayer) Parker (September 22, 1692)
Ann Pudeator (September 22, 1692)
Margaret (Stevenson) Scott (September 22, 1692)
Wilmot Redd (September 22, 1692)
Samuel Wardwell Sr. (September 22, 1692)
Dana (Michael) Foley (September 22, 1692)

Imbolc Ritual
by Alix Wright

The theme of this Imbolc ritual is the triple nature of Bridget, as the goddess of smiths, healing and poetic inspiration. Like the smith who must obtain the ore from the earth, we'll be working with soil and stone, with crystals drawn from the Earth. We'll be working with water for its healing powers. Also, we'll be working with firelight for inspiration.

Altar
Place three altars in the center of the circle. On the first is a cauldron filled with earth and a variety of crystals. The second has water blessed and charged for healing and a small pine branch for apserging. The third has candles, one for each person participating in the ritual. You can also have a fourth altar of traditional tools, but it is not required for this rite.

Casting the Circle
I cast this circle
By Earth to be solid beneath us
By Fire to cleanse us of all the does not serve
By Air to bring clarity and communication
And by Water to join us in Perfect Love and Perfect Trust
I consecrate this Circle in the name of the Triple Goddess, she who
Is Maiden, Mother, Crone.
And in the name of the God, he is who Lord of Light and Lord of Dark
I charge this circle to be a temple between the worlds,
Where only the highest Will is sovereign
Only those energies that are for the highest good may cross its boundaries as we
    stand in a temple of perfect love and perfect trust.

Calling the Quarters
To the North
I call upon the powers of Earth.
I call upon the Great Bear.
Please guard and guide us in this circle.
Hail and welcome.

To the East
I call upon the powers of Fire
I call upon the Red Fox
Please guard and guide us in the circle.
Hail and welcome.

To the South
I call upon the powers of Air
I call upon the Wise Crow
Please guard and guide us in the circle.
Hail and welcome.

To the West
I call upon the powers of Water
I call upon the Blue Dolphin
Please guard and guide us in the circle.
Hail and welcome.

Invocation of Goddess and God
I call upon Brigid
Goddess of Healing, Goddess of Poetry, Goddess of Smith-craft.
We ask that you bless us with your presence
And gift us with your Wisdom.
Hail and Welcome.

I call upon Bel
God of Fire and Flame, Bright God of Strength and Warriors
We ask that you bless us with your presence
And gift us with your Wisdom.
Hail and Welcome.

Great Rite
Light of the Earth and Heavens drawn down into the blade, and then projected from the blade into the chalice with blessing.

The Blade is Blessed, it is seen as My Lord
The Chalice is Blessed, it is seen as My Lady
Two become one, as the Grail to the Sword
Two become one, united within me.

Work of the Sabbat
Water: Participants are to come one at a time to the altar. With a pine branch provided, asperge yourself with water from the healing altar with the intention to bring healing to yourself. Start by realizing that healing needs to happen for you. Ask yourself, "What needs to be healed in me?" Then you can sprinkle a few drops upon the altar to bring healing to the community.

Earth: Dig into the cauldron of soil to find a crystal. Ask yourself, "What am I drawing out of the depths to bring to this plane to create with?" If you dig deep within yourself, what will you find in order to manifest your True Will?

Fire: Go to the fire altar. Light a candle, speak your intention, hold the candle for a moment. Ask yourself, "What intention will I bring forth into the world? What is my promise to myself, to the gods, to my sacredness? What words of wisdom and poetry can I find within?" Extinguish your candle to make space and time for others. Take your candle back with you to the edge of the circle. You can burn it fully at home when the public ritual is complete.

Participants move from water, to earth, to fire altars until everyone has done something and had a chance to speak their inspiration before the community.

Thanks to the God and Goddess
I thank and release Brigid
Goddess of Healing, Goddess of Poetry, Goddess of Smith craft.
We thank you for your presence
And for gifting us with your Wisdom.
Hail and Farewell.

I thank and release Bel
God of Fire and Flame, Bright God of Strength and Warriors
We thank you for your presence
And for gifting us with your Wisdom.
Hail and Farewell.

Release the Quarters
To the North
I thank and release the power of Earth

And the Great Bear
Thank you for your blessings.
Hail and farewell.

To the West
I thank and release the power of Water
And the Blue Dolphin
Thank you for your blessings.
Hail and farewell.

To the South
I thank and release the power of Air
And the Wise Crow
Thank you for your blessings.
Hail and farewell.

To the East
I thank and release the power of Fire
And the Red Fox
Thank you for your blessings.
Hail and farewell.

Open the Circle

I cast this circle out into the Universe as a sign of our celebration. May it join with the circles of our sisters and brothers, across time and across space. The circle is open, but unbroken, Merry Meet, Merry Part, and Merry Meet again.

Blessed be.

Mabon Ritual

by Alix Wright

Mabon is the second of the three harvest sabbats (coming after Lammas and before Samhain) known as the "fruit harvest" or the "wine harvest" and associated with the divine inspiration brought by wine and distilled spirits. It is also connected to the goddess Modron, and her search for her lost son, the divine child Mabon.

Casting the Circle
I cast this circle with my body
that all within may blessed be
safe from harm from friend or foe
a haven for our power to grow.
I consecrate this circle with my heart
if it is your will to take part
come only in perfect love and trust
follow the Wiccan Rede you must.
I charge this circle with my power
and create a space beyond space, beyond the hour.
Heart to heart and hand to hand
in the eyes of the Goddess and God we stand.
So mote it be.

Calling the Quarters
I call the Guardians on the Watchtower in the North
I call on the Gnomes, King Ghob and Queen Tanu
Rise and bestow your blessings upon our circle.
Hail and Welcome.

I call to the Guardians of the Watchtower in the East
I call on the Sylphs, King Paralda and Queen Eostar
Rise and bestow your blessings upon our circle.
Hail and Welcome.

I call to the Guardians of the Watchtower in the South
I call on the Salamanders, King Djin and Queen Litha
Rise and bestow your blessings upon our circle.
Hail and Welcome.

I call to the Guardians of the Watchtower in the West
I call on the Undines, King Niksa and Queen Mara
Rise and bestow your blessings upon our circle.
Hail and Welcome.

Opening the Gates of the Three Worlds
In the Great Above I call on the Angels and Archangels
In the Great Below I call on the Fairy Folk and Ancestors

In the Great Between I call on the Animals spirits and Hidden Company

Invocation of the Goddess and God
*I call on the Goddess who rests beneath the Earth
She who labors to bring forth the Light
The Lady who nourishes and protects
And guides and guards us through the darkest night.
Hail and Welcome*

*I call on the God who is the Child of Light
The spark of flame that grows within
The Lord who grows stronger as we call his name
He who is reborn through the longest night.
Hail and Welcome*

Great Rite
*The blade is blessed it is seen as my Lord
This chalice is blessed it is seen as my Lady
Two become one as the Grail to the Sword
Two become one, united within me.*

Mabon Meditation

Relax your body, relax your mind. Let all the stress of the day and the week drift away as we count from 13 to 1 to attain a deeper meditational state.

Sink into Mother Earth. Let your body drift slowly into her embrace. Your eyes remain shut, sleeping as the Earth is sleeping, there is nothing to see, only the soft darkness of the Goddess' womb. In this space you are safe, and protected. Remember what it was to be cradled in the arms of the loving Mother. Feel her energy flowing into you, renewing your strength for the journey into the next year. As her energy surrounds you, a warm golden glow begins to shine from within you. This energy is the love of the Goddess, the love of the God. It gives you all you need on your journey in this life. Strength when you feel weak. Love when you feel alone. Peace when you feel overwhelmed. Joy when you are sad. The more you recognize this light within you, the brighter it shines. The Goddess raises you up to the heavens, and places you gently among the stars. This light within you shines, lighting the Earth, growing stronger each day, bringing warmth to the land, that all may grow again in the circle of life.

Circle of Healing

Place the names of those to whom you wish to send healing, for their highest good, into the circle by speaking them. If done in a large community circle, start with the northern quarter, while holding hands, and when you are done speaking the name or names, gently squeeze the hand of the person to your left, to indicate your turn is done. Once everyone's names are in the circle, raise energy chanting IAO (Ee-Ah-Oh) three times to send out the healing and turn the wheel of the year.

Devocation of the Goddess and God

We thank and release the Goddess
We give thanks for her light, her love, her labor
We give thanks for her nourishment and protection.
Stay if you will, go if you must
Hail and Farewell.

We thank and release the God
We give thanks for your flame that burns brighter
We give thanks for your warmth and your light
Stay if you will, go if you must
Hail and Farewell.

Closing the Gates to the Three Worlds

In the Great Above I thank and release the Angels and Archangels
In the Great Below I thank and release the Fairy Folk and Ancestors
In the Great Between I thank and release the Animals spirits and Hidden Company

Release the Quarters

I thank and release the Guardians of the Watchtower in the North
I thank and release the Gnomes, King Ghob and Queen Tanu
Thank you for your blessings.
Hail and Farewell.

I thank and release the Guardians of the Watchtower in the West
I thank and release the Undines, King Niksa and Queen Mara

Thank you for your blessings.
Hail and Farewell.

I thank and release the Guardians of the Watchtower in the South
I thank and release the Salamanders, King Djin and Queen Litha
Thank you for your blessings.
Hail and Farewell.

I thank and release the Guardians of the Watchtower in the East
I thank and release the Sylphs, King Paralda and Queen Eostar.
Thank you for your blessings.
Hail and Farewell.

Open the Circle
All who came, I now release, You came in love, go in peace
This circle is open, but never broken, released in love with these words spoken,
So mote it be.

Feast of Hecate

A special ninth holiday added to the Wheel of the Year has become one of the traditions of the Temple: the Feast of Hecate. More popularly known as the Feast of Diana Trivia, originally the Feast of Hecate was a time to propitiate Hecate as the Lady of Storms, asking her to end the summer storms before they damaged the crops, giving farmers time to harvest. While many see Hecate as crone, or even maiden, she was seen at this feast as an all-mother. The Christian Church adopted a similar festival with Mary as Queen of Heaven on August 15th with her feast as the Assumption of the Blessed Virgin Mary, when Mary ascends into heaven. The Feast is often confused with another Hecate holiday, the Night of Hecate, celebrated on November 16th.

The Temple of Witchcraft honors the Queen of Witches on this night in ritual celebrations of offerings and oracular or divinatory rituals, allowing the Mother of Witches to speak directly to her children gathered. Keys offered to her are collected and made a part of our ordination ceremonies, offering "keys to the temple" to ordained ministers.

Hecate's Choice: A New Tale of Hecate
by Adam Sartwell

Long ago when the world was young and the battles for the universe between the titans and the gods had ended, the gods met with each other at the foot of mount Olympus. They gathered to decide how they were going to divide the spoils of war. They deliberated about lands, animals and other things under their domain until finally it was time to decide which humans they would champion. First spoke Zeus, king of the gods.

"I will take those the humans who rule over others and make the laws, men of prestige and significance. They will embrace justice in my name."

Then spoke Hera, queen of the gods.

"I shall have the married women for my own and those women who are pregnant or mothers. They shall find succor and solace under my patronage."

Then spoke Ares, lord of war.

"I will take the warriors and men of battle. I shall heap glory upon them all."

Athena goddess of wisdom said unto the other gods: "I shall take the strategists, crafters, and lords of commerce. They shall thrive with the blessing of my wisdom."

Then spoke Poseidon.

"I shall have the sailors and fishermen and bless them with the bounty of my ocean."

Then announced Hades, " I shall take the dead that come to Tartarus and the Elysian Fields. There they shall suffer or be pleased in measure of their past lives."

Aphrodite said, "The lovers will be mine, and also those with shining beauty. I will grace them with fertility."

And so on and so on the Olympians chose the best and brightest of their own respective fields of influence and enhanced each ones blessings.

In the end there were groups of people who did not fit these groups. These beings trembled and quaked unknowingly as each god passed them by. Then as it seemed all gods had made there choices from the darkness came Hecate. The titan still revered by all the gods even after their war. She looked at those still left to be taken. Her compassion moved her to speak.

"Greatest of gods, Hear me. You have made your choices and now I would make mine. I shall take all who have been left behind. Those not chosen, the unwanted, the seemingly unredeemable, the outcasts, the lunatic, the poor, the malformed, the victim, the homeless, the lost, the murderer. I shall take them and guide them with my torch out of the darkness. I shall witness acts of violence to bring compassion to the souls of perpetrators and victims, bringing justice and succor in kind. I shall take the shades and specters, those who cannot find their way, to help them finish their business and lead them home. I shall take the unloved and scorned and hold them dear. I will remind them all of the power of choice, the wisdom of necessity and the love of my compassion."

All the gods were shocked at this choice. They saw how they had chosen only those who were bright reflections of themselves and there greatness. They had forgotten the lowly souls who needed them most. Hearing this compassionate choice Zeus was moved.

"For this act of compassion and wisdom I shall bless you alone Hecate with status above the other gods. I offer you three boons: You shall have the power that I have to grant any wish that is petitioned of you. I shall give you rulership and free passage over a place in Tartarus below, the world of men and the sea, and the sky so you may be with any who need you. I give you the keys to all kingdoms. Lastly I give you the power to choose your last boon. As I will, it is so!"

Hecate replied: "I thank you lord Zeus for this boon. I shall tell the people of the world that if ever they should need a thing and wish to petition me—let them go to the crossroads that are my sacred space, with a meal as offering and their wish writ on a slip under the dish. They shall leave both at the crossroads and turn away and not look back until they are home. This meal shall feed the dogs and the poor homeless. I shall look on them with favor of what they truly need.

"For my boon I ask for a race of my own that shall, like me, span all the races and be born to all. They shall be born with the potential to bring success in love, to curse or bless, to speak to beasts, to converse and congress with spirits, to command the weather, to cast out blight, to read the messages of the starry heaven, to see the future, to conjure treasure and fortune, to heal the sick and kill despair. Some shall be born and some shall be remade. They shall be all manner of people and trades. They shall be called Witches and may be loved or hated, and live between to shape them to necessity. They shall aid me in my great work to help the forgotten and the rest of man."

So it was decided. The gods and titan stood on the Mount of Olympus holding hands and said: "As we will it, so shall it be!"

Magickal Foods from *Tastes from the Temple*

A shared potluck "feast" after a sabbat ritual is tradition in the Temple of Witchcraft community. Here are a few popular recipes from our *Tastes from the Temple* cookbook anthology, edited and expanded by Kitchen Witch Dawn Hunt.

Baby Makin' Banana Bread

Submitted by Adam Sartwell, Temple of Witchcraft founder and Virgo Lead Minister

Banana bread is one of the easiest and most fondly thought of home baked goodies in the world! The smell of it baking in the oven will get anyone out of bed in the morning. I like to serve mine warm from the oven with a little honey butter and a cup of tea. I am pretty sure most people have made this type of quick sweet bread at some point in their lives, but this is a great story!

Adam says:

"When my older brother and his wife were in the mind to have kids, I asked them both if they really wanted children. From the twinkle in my eye I could tell my sister-in-law knew I meant that I would do magick for them to help them get with child. She said yes they wanted children. So I turned to a recipe I have used to make banana bread for years, but with an altered intention. I blessed the egg for fertility for my sister-in-law and the two bananas for my brother before mixing them into the batter. I stirred the batter clockwise, visualizing the child they would have being healthy. I lit a green candle for fertility on the stove as I baked the bread. Nine months later I had my first nephew. I have used this spell to get my second nephew, too. That is how this recipe got its name. So you need to be very particular with your intentions when you make this (or any other) recipe!"

Ingredients
1 egg
1 cup sugar
1/2 teaspoon baking soda
2 teaspoons baking powder
1 1/2 cups flour
1/4 cup melted butter
2 ripe (almost brown) bananas, mashed
1 teaspoon salt

Preparation
Preheat oven to 375 degrees. Spray a loaf pan with cooking spray. In a large bowl, mix all ingredients together. Pour batter into prepared loaf pan and bake for 45 minutes. Don't cook it longer than that. Test it with a toothpick or thin knife in the middle. If it comes out clean, the bread is done.

Magickal Notes
One of the greatest things about this recipe is that, at any given time, most people have many, if not all of these ingredients in their homes. Easy, quick and delicious! But what we don't usually realize is that these everyday items hold so much magick! Bananas, one of the most popular foods in our country are packed with masculine energy. Energetically charging bananas with male fertility energy just amps up their power. Adam also mentioned he charges the egg with fertility for his sister-in-law. This is great because eggs are already a fertility food so when the specific intention is set into this recipe it is naturally very powerful. Draw a symbol on the top of the bread before baking as well. An egg shaped symbol or perhaps a male and female symbol together to bless the union for a child. Be sure not to do this, or any spell or spell/recipe without the consent of those

involved. We would not want anyone to get pregnant who does not want a baby!

Corn Mother Bread
Submitted by Matooka Moonbear, Temple high priestess

Corn bread is a staple in many homes and many cultures. Corn is an ancient food the people of the Americas have to thank for long years of prosperity, growth and nourishment. It is fitting that we eat it so often and that it is found in so many different dishes.

Matooka says:

"This is done ritually to the Corn Mother. I offer each egg, one to the Maiden, one to the Mother, and the last to the Crone. The molasses, maple syrup, and honey are offered to the mixture at the end honoring the sweetness of life in each aspect of Goddess. I then offer the complete mixture to the seven directions prayerfully and pop it in the oven. I like to use organics when possible. The flour can be substituted though it really changes the consistency and flavor."

Ingredients
1 cup cornmeal
1 cup all purpose flour
1 cup milk
1/4 cup vegetable oil
1 teaspoon salt
4 teaspoon baking powder
3 eggs
1 Tablespoon molasses
1 Tablespoon maple syrup
1/2 Tablespoon honey

Preparation
Preheat oven to 400 degrees. Spray a 9-inch round or square cake pan with cooking spray. Combine all ingredients in a large bowl and stir until moistened. Pour batter into pan and bake 20-30 min or until toothpick comes out clean in center. Bread should be full, lightly brown.

Pears and Brie
Submitted by Dawn Hunt, Cucina Aurora Kitchen Witch

In 2010, I was honored to be asked to cater the first Feast of Hecate at the Temple of Witchcraft. Although I had a set menu in mind when I invoked Hecate into my kitchen, she came in, put her feet up, and stayed with me for days. She inspired me to make this dish of baked brie and pears. It was a huge hit and people still talk about it. Being that, until that night I had not ever even tasted brie before, and had no idea how to cook it, I can only believe I have the Goddess Hecate to thank for the inspiration of this dish. I hope you and your guests find it as amazing as we did on that night we feasted in honor of Hecate!

Ingredients
1 large wheel of brie cheese (extra creamy if you can find it)
3 pears
1 teaspoon lemon juice
3 Tablespoons honey (local to your region is best)
2 Tablespoons cinnamon
1 cup candied walnuts

Preparation
Slice pears thin and place in a large bowl. Drizzle with honey. Add cinnamon, and lemon juice. Stir gently being sure not to damage the pear slices, until all are evenly coated in honey and cinnamon. Cover and refrigerate overnight.

Preheat oven to 350 degrees. Cut Brie into wedges and arrange them to look like the same wheel they looked like before you cut it up on a large baking sheet (preferably a round pizza sheet if you have one). Cover the Brie with the pear mixture and any juice that has developed in the soaking process. Cover loosely with foil and bake for 15-20 minutes or until gooey and pears are soft. Top with candied walnuts and serve warm. Note this reheats well so if you are bringing it to a friend's for potluck, pop it in the oven for 10 minutes just to heat it through, if necessary.

Magickal Notes

Hecate is a very present Goddess. She comes when you call and she inspires when you least expect it. Until cooking for her feast I was not familiar with working with her personally. Since then, she is welcome in my home and in my kitchen whenever she pleases. This recipe was of course inspired by her but is suitable for any and all Goddess rituals and even full moon rituals. The brie, shaped in a wheel, can represent the moon or the wheel of the year, whatever serves your purposes. The three pears are for the Maiden, the Mother, and the Crone. Before you cut them up carve a small symbol or a word into them to bless them with these aspects of the Goddess and the Moon. While cutting them up envision the Goddess in that phase of life.

"Between the Worlds" Curried Pumpkin Soup

Submitted by Steve Kenson, Temple founder and Gemini Lead Minister, recipe by Newt & Reed

Sometimes a dish just evolves. It becomes a part of the event itself. We all have that dish we make that we bring to other people's homes or that is requested of us to bring to an event. So much so that we look forward to things like "Uncle Joe's Chocolate Chip Surprise" or "Sally's tomato Salad".

Steve says:

"This recipe has a history that starts with my first year attending Between the Worlds, a festival for queer Pagan men. Back then, we had a pot-luck meal and the whole community contributed. Newt and Reed made a version of this soup and it was so good I had to get the recipe!

"Later, I began making it myself for coven and festival events because it's easy, vegetarian (even vegan, if olive oil and just coconut milk are used in place of butter and cream) and so yummy! Amongst coven members, the recipe became known as 'The Soup' (definite article) and I was expected to bring it to every feast, if I knew what was good for me!"

Ingredients
1/4 cup butter or margarine
1/4 cup flour
2 Tablespoons curry powder
1/2 teaspoon red Thai curry paste
1 can (15 oz.) solid pack pumpkin
6 cups vegetable stock
1 cup half and half
1 cup coconut milk
1 Tablespoon garlic
1 Tablespoon salt
1 teaspoon ground black pepper
1 Tablespoon cinnamon
1 teaspoon cloves
1 teaspoon ginger

Preparation

In a large sauce pan melt the butter or margarine over medium heat and add flour, curry powder, and curry paste. Blend to make a roux. Add 1/2 cup vegetable stock and mix well. Add pumpkin slowly, stirring to blend evenly. Add remaining vegetable stock and stir until smooth, allow soup to simmer for 15 minutes. Add seasonings and spices to taste. Add a pint of coconut milk or half and half (or a mixture of both), and allow soup to heat through before serving. You may want to garnish the soup with a sprinkle of cilantro or parsley and a few toasted pumpkin seeds.

Magickal Notes

Pumpkin is another one of those harvest foods we all look forward to during the year. We wait for the weather to cool just a little in September and just before the leaves start to change it is pumpkin season again! What a great way to celebrate the changing seasons with friends to enjoy this soup made of pumpkin with a kick of curry. Pumpkin is a very feminine food ruled by the Moon. The roundness of the pumpkin brings to mind the fullness of the Goddess at Harvest season. Pumpkin brings forth healing and prosperity. Share this soup with those whom you wish good health and good fortune.

Esbat Moon Rituals: Full and Dark Moons

Traditional Moon circle celebrations are called esbats, in contrast with the yearly Sabbats. When the Moon is "dark" just before it becomes "new", it is in the same sign as the Sun is occupying. The corresponding full Moon will be in the opposite sign.

Dates vary from year to year and are determined from a Moon calendar or astrological ephemeris. Descriptions follow general themes that can be creatively tailored by the group performing the ritual while keeping the same theme.

Currently the Full Moon Rituals are open to the public and focused on exposing new members to the traditions of the Craft while giving more experienced members an opportunity to lead a ceremony in a public setting. Dark Moon Rituals are reserved for Ministerial Members, often with more advanced teachings and in a supportive, peer oriented group for ministers, ordained or not.

- **Dark Moon in Scorpio** – A ritual for the release of obsessions and control.
- **Full Moon in Taurus** – A ritual to manifest health and prosperity.
- **Dark Moon in Sagittarius** – A ritual for the release of past religious orthodoxy
- **Full Moon in Gemini** – A ritual for eloquence, intelligence, education or social grace
- **Dark Moon in Capricorn** – A ritual to commune with the dark aspect of the God
- **Full Moon in Cancer** – A ritual to commune with the Mother aspect of the Goddess
- **Dark Moon in Aquarius** – A ritual to banish blocks to your own individuality
- **Full Moon in Leo** – A ritual to encourage creativity and art
- **Dark Moon in Pisces** – A ritual to banish depression and escapism
- **Full Moon in Virgo** – A ritual for healing and service.
- **Dark Moon in Aries** – A ritual to banish fear
- **Full Moon in Libra** – A ritual for balance and justice
- **Dark Moon in Taurus** – A ritual to banish illness or poverty

- **Full Moon in Scorpio** – A ritual for sexuality, power and psychic ability
- **Dark Moon in Gemini** – A ritual to banish blocks in communication
- **Full Moon in Sagittarius** – A ritual for education, exploration or travel.
- **Dark Moon in Cancer** – A ritual to commune with the Dark Mother aspect of the Goddess
- **Full Moon in Capricorn** – A ritual to commune with the Father aspect of the God
- **Dark Moon in Leo** – A ritual to banish excessive ego or pride
- **Full Moon in Aquarius** – A ritual to build community and grant inspiration
- **Dark Moon in Virgo** – A ritual to banish illness or perfectionism
- **Full Moon in Pisces** – A ritual for shamanic journey and psychic development
- **Dark Moon in Libra** – A ritual to banish injustice or anything unbalanced
- **Full Moon in Aries** – A ritual for leadership and warriors.

Full Moon Ritual
by Alix Wright

Smudging
Cleanse the area and participants prior to the ritual. Smudge the space with sage, or a technique of your choice, envisioning the area being cleansed of all those energies that are not for the highest good. Smudge those who are attending as they enter the area to leave behind any energy that they may be carrying with them that will not be for the highest good of the ritual or them.

Countdown
Bringing the attendees to a state of ritual consciousness. Have the attendees close their eyes as you guide them to a state of ritual consciousness by counting down from 12-1, envisioning the numbers as you count.

Cast the Circle

The person who is casting the circle shall start in the North and walk the boundaries of the circle deosil (clockwise) while projecting energy to form a bubble around the ritual area, creating sacred space. This sacred space becomes a Temple in the Middle World that connects all the Worlds, yet holds you between them. Use these, or similar, words.

I cast this circle by Earth for stability
By Fire to burn away all that does not serve
By Air to aid in clarity and communication
By Water, to join us in Perfect Love and Perfect Trust
I consecrate this Circle
In the name of the Goddess and God
She who is Maiden, Mother, Crone
He who is Lord of Light and Lord of the Shadow
I charge this Circle to be a Temple between the worlds
Beyond Time, and Beyond Space
Where only the highest Love, Will and Wisdom rules sovereign
As I will it, So Mote It Be.

Call the Quarters

Call on the aid of the directions, elements and/or totems to anchor your circle and to ask their guidance with these or similar words. In the Temple tradition we start in the North, rotating clockwise as each direction is called. One person would call the quarter by saying the actual words and envisioning the Guardian appearing, and the other participants would repeat the words "Hail and Be Welcome".

To the North of the Circle
I call to the Element of Earth
I call on Bear
We ask that you guard, guide and protect us on this night
Hail, and be welcome!

To the East of the Circle
I call to the Element of Fire
I call on Fox

We ask that you guard, guide and protect us on this night
Hail, and be welcome!

To the South of the Circle
I call to the Element of Air
I call on Crow
We ask that you guard, guide and protect us on this night
Hail, and be welcome!

To the West of the Circle
I call to the Element of the Water
I call on Salmon
We ask that you guard, guide and protect us on this night
Hail, and be welcome!

Call on the God and Goddess

Evoke the Goddess and God, inviting them into the circle and lighting a candle in their honor. God and Goddess names can be used depending on which deities you wish to work with.

I call on the Goddess of the Moon
Lady of Magick and Light
Lady of many names and many faces
We honor you with this Rite
Hail, and be welcome

I call on the God of the Sky
Lord of the Shadow and Night
Lord of many names and many faces
We honor you with this Rite
Hail, and be welcome

Great Rite

Celebrate the joining of the God and Goddess as one. Take Blade and Chalice in hand. With the Blade directed up to the Sky, envision the reflected light of the Sun pouring into it

"*The Blade is Blessed, it is seen as My Lord*"

Raise the Chalice, envision the Goddess filling it with her power, her love.

"*The Chalice is Blessed, it is seen as My Lady*"

Bring the Blade into the chalice three times, envision Male and Female coming together to bring forth balance and harmony.

"Two become one, as the Grail to the Sword
Two become one, united within me."

Drink the liquid within the chalice, feeling all paradox resolved within you as you take in the perfect energies of the Divine. Each participant should have the opportunity to drink of the chalice and then it is placed back on the altar.

Drawing Down the Moon

Visualization of drawing the power of the Goddess and the Moon. Using these or similar words guide the attendees through the drawing down of the moon. Stand in the Goddess position with your arms out stretched above you so that your arms form a chalice. Feel the power of the Moon above you, the power of the Goddess, the pull that it has on the oceans and the power it has on your blood. Envision a beam of light, a pure silver moon beam that shines down upon you, filling the chalice of your body with the blessings of the Moon and the Goddess. Feel your self overflow with the light of the Moon. Feel yourself energized, empowered, blessed, touched by the Goddess.

"Lady of the Moon, we call on you to give us your blessing. We stand in your light on this sacred night to do the work of the Witch. Fill us with your power and your love. Blessed be."

Take a few moments to feel the energy within you. Feel the beam slow down until it stops. Feel any excess energy drain from you to bless the Earth beneath you.

Meditation/Magickal Work

For spellwork, it is suggested that only three spells per person are done so that the energy is not spread too thinly. When working in a group and doing personal spells it is always a good idea to discuss them ahead of time so that no one feels their energy is being used for something they don't agree to. For a group who is not familiar with each other, a guided meditation, shamanic journey, or the creation of charms is usually a safe idea. Perform spellwork, meditation or other magickal work.

Offering of Cakes and Ale

At this point of the ritual it's a good idea to take in some food and drink. This is to help ground the participants in case they are carrying any excess energy. This is also a good time for people to share their experience from the ritual if they choose to do so. Another option is to do this after the circle is closed, but I've found that many people enjoy taking the extra time to be in ritual space so if you have the time, take it now. "Cakes and ale" do not necessarily need to be cakes and ale. We have had breads and cheeses with juices, wine, crackers, fruit and, the ever popular, chocolate.

Blessing the cakes and ale can be a simple thanks to those energies that have blessed your sustenance and those plants or animals that gave of themselves that we may be nourished in body and spirit.

Healing Circle

It's always nice to include a healing circle at the end of ritual to send energy to those who may need healing. Names do not need to be said out loud. We usually hold hands and start in the North. When the person is done you squeeze the hand of the person to your left so that they know it is their turn. If a person wants to do their names silently they can do so and then let the next person know they are done by giving their hand a gentle squeeze. When each person has had a chance you can raise energy by doing a chant such as I A O three times. While chanting, raise your hands slowly and on the last note, envision pushing the energy out as you say these words

"We send this energy out into the Universe to do our bidding. For the highest good, harming none. So mote it be!"

Each person would then cross their hands over their chests (God position) to take in any energy they may need and then ground the excess by touching their hands to the earth of stomping their foot three times.

Thank the Goddess and God

Take time to thank the Goddess and God for their presence. Candles can be extinguished at this time.

I thank the Goddess of the Moon
Lady of Magick and Light
Lady of many names and many faces
We thank you for your blessings this night
Hail, and Farewell.

I thank the God of the Sky
Lord of the Shadow and Night
Lord of many names and many faces
We thank you for your blessings this night
Hail, and Farewell

Thank and Release the Quarters

It is important to take the time to thank those spirits and energies that came to aid you with as much energy as you did to call them. The ritual may be almost over but this is not the time to rush through the releases and risk insulting those that you called. To release the quarters we start with the North, the first direction we called and go widdershins (counterclockwise). Those who called in the quarter should do the release with the group echoing the words "Hail, and farewell!"

To the North of the Circle
I thank the Element of Earth
I give thanks to Bear
We thank you for coming to guard, guide and protect us on this night
Hail, and farewell!

To the West of the Circle
I thank the Element of the Water
I give thanks to Salmon
We thank you for coming to guard, guide and protect us on this night

Hail, and farewell!
To the South of the Circle
I thank the Element of Air
I give thanks to Crow
We thank you for coming to guard, guide and protect us on this night
Hail, and farewell!

To the East of the Circle
I thank the Element of Fire
I give thanks to Fox
We thank you for coming to guard, guide and protect us on this night
Hail, and farewell!

Opening the Circle

The person who is releasing or opening the circle shall start in the North and walk widdershins one time around the circle saying these or similar words as they envision the circle opening and the energy being sent out.

I cast this Circle out into the Universe as a sign of our work. May it join with the Circles of our sisters and brothers, across time and across space. The circle is open, but unbroken. Merry meet, merry part, and merry meet again.

Blessed be.

Rites of Passage Rituals

As the Wheel of the Year marks stations upon the annual cycle, Rites of Passage mark stations upon the Wheel of our Life. Not every member will experience every rite, but this shows some of the ideal patterns for lifelong Witches.

- **Wiccaning (Child Blessing)** – A blessing of a child to be under the protection of the Goddess and God until that child is old enough to determine their own religious affiliation.
- **Coming of Age** – A ritual to recognize the transition from child into young adulthood, often marked by first menstruation or first nocturnal emission.
- **Handfasting (Marriage)** – A rite to join together a couple in life and love.
- **Dedication** – A ritual to begin formal studies in the traditions of the Temple.
- **Initiation** – A formal recognition and completion of the first degree in the Mystery School training of the Temple.
- **Elevation** – Subsequent "initiations" into the degrees of the Mystery School training.
- **Ordination** – Formal recognition of a minister, one who has fully graduated from the Seminary School.

- **Eldering (Crone/Sage)** – A ritual to recognize an elder in the community and their place of guidance and aid among us.
- **Crossing (Funeral)** – A ritual to both help the soul cross over into the next realm as well as a ritual to help the living adjust to the transition of life and say good-bye to their earthly form.

Temple of Witchcraft Wiccaning (Child Blessing) Ritual

Welcoming

The ritual of the Wiccaning is to bless a child in the ways of wisdom, helping to establish a spiritual base for the child in this life. It ushers the blessings and protections of our guardians and is not an eternal dedication to the Pagan religions. Every child has the right, upon entering adulthood, to explore and choose through free will the spiritual path that is correct in this lifetime. Let this ceremony confer the blessings of our tradition until that time and may the gifts, joys and protection last a lifetime.

Casting the Circle

The HP/S moves three times deosil (clockwise) around the ritual area in a circle with a wand, staff, athame or sword, establishing the sacred space of the ritual. The altar is already set with all the necessary ritual tools for the ceremony.

HP/S: *We cast this circle to protect us from all forces that may come to do us harm.*
We charge and consecrate this circle of the art,
to draw only the powers beneficial for our work
and block out all others.
We create a space beyond space and a time beyond time,
a temple of Perfect Love and Perfect Trust
where the highest will is sovereign in the love and wisdom of the divine.

Calling the Quarters

Quarters can be called by the HP/S, parents and goddess parents or other members of the family and community. Quarters and elements can be arranged in the order and correspondence most comfortable for the family. Everyone faces the direction named and holds up their left hand to welcome the spirits of that direction.

North: *To the North, we call upon the element of Earth and we call upon the spirits of the North. We call upon the Great Stag to be with us. Protect, guide and bless us on this special day. Hail and welcome.*

Consecrate the salt. Sprinkle a few grains of salt upon the Earth.

East: *To the East, we call upon the element of Fire and we call upon the spirits of the East. We call upon the Wild Horse to be with us. Protect, guide and bless us on this special day. Hail and welcome.*

Consecrate the candle. Light the red candle of fire.

South: *To the South, we call upon the element of Air and we call upon the spirits of the South. We call upon the Wise Crow to be with us. Protect, guide and bless us on this special day. Hail and welcome.*

Consecrate the incense. Light the charcoal and incense.

West: *To the West, we call upon the element of Water and we call upon the spirits of the West. We call upon the Changing Snake to be with us. Protect, guide and bless us upon this special day. Hail and welcome.*

Consecrate the water. Sprinkle a few drops of water upon the ground.

Evocation of the Gods and Spirits

Light the Central Candle for Spirit.

HP/S: *We call upon the Great Spirit, ever present in every moment and every place, the connecting force between all things seen and unseen.*

Light the Black Candle on the left of the altar.

HP/S: *From the light of the Great Spirit comes the Great Mother, the Weaver, the Web. We light this candle in honor of the Great Goddess, Mother to all. We light this candle for the darkness, the Moon and the night, for severity and to draw in energy for our magick, Hail and welcome.*

Light the White Candle on the right of the altar.

HP/S: *From the light of the Mother comes the All Father, the Singer, the Son. We light this candle in honor the Good God, Father to all. We light this candle for the light, the Sun and the day, for mercy and to send forth the energy of our magick. Hail and welcome.*

Light the Red, Blue and Yellow Candles of the Triple Power.

HP/S: *We call upon the magick of the Straight Line, of Power and Will. We call upon the magick of the Bent Line, of Love and Trust, and we call upon the magick of the Crooked Line, of Wisdom and Knowledge. We call upon those from the races of angels, faeries and the blessed dead who come in Perfect Love* *and Perfect Trust for our ceremony. We ask to be in alignment with the Divine Will, the Divine Heart and the Divine Mind. Blessed be.*

HP/S: *We take this time in silence to each personally invite our own gods, guides and ancestors to be present for the blessing. (Pause.) Blessed be.*

Naming of the Child

HP/S: *Today we celebrate new life within our own lives. We welcome another member to our tribe, to our circle. We join with the family in the blessings of this new child by the gifts of magick.*

Parents and child step forward to the center of the circle

HP/S: *Divine Child conceived in love and trust,*
Divine Child born in love and trust,
Divine Child, nurtured in love and trust,
We celebrate you today.
Through the blessings of the Goddess and God
You are named.

Parents speak of the name of the child and why they chose it.

Presentation to the Four Elements and their Blessing

Parent holds child up to the North.

HP/S: *Spirits of the North, of Earth, know this child (name).*
Bless her/him with your gifts and boons. Aid her/him in your challenges.
Grant her/him strength in body, health and well being.
See that s/he shall ever prosper on the path of life, wherever it takes her/him.
May s/he be supported by the Sacred Law.
Blessed be.

Take a few grains of salt and put it to her/his lips.

Parents: *May you enjoy the world to fulfill your destiny. May you know we will always share our world with you.*

Parent holds child up to the East.

HP/S: *Spirits of the East, of Fire, know this child (name).*
Bless her/him with your gifts and boons. Aid her/him in your challenges
Grant her/him drive in her/his passion, will and creativity.
See that s/he shall ever be inspired on the path of life, wherever it takes her/him.
May s/he be guided by the Sacred Light.
Blessed be.

Hold up the red candle for her/him to follow the flame for a moment.

Parents: *May your passions burn bright to fulfill your destiny. May you know that we will always support you.*

Parent hold child up to the South.

HP/S: *Spirits of the South, of Air, know this child (name).*
Bless her/him with your gifts and boons. Aid her/him in your challenges.
Grant her/him knowledge, clarity and peace of mind.
See that s/he shall ever be able to speak and listen clearly on the path of life, wherever it takes her/him.
May s/he draw the Sacred Breath of Life.
Blessed be.

Pass her/him through the incense smoke.

Parents: *May you be clear in thought and word to fulfill your destiny. May you know we will always communicate with you.*

Parent holds child up to the West.

HP/S: *Spirits of the West, of Water, know this child (name).*
Bless her/him with your gifts and boons. Aid her/him in your challenges.
Grant her/him intuition, clear boundaries and a loving heart.
See that s/he shall ever know the hidden mysteries on the path of life, wherever it takes her/him.
May her/him heart be filled with Sacred Love.
Blessed be,

Sprinkle a few drops of water on her/him.

Parents: *May you trust your intuition to fulfill your destiny. May you know that we will always love you.*

Blessing of the Goddess and God

HP/S: *Mother Goddess, Father God, Parents to us all*
Behold this child whom we call (name).
May you bless her/him with love, guidance and protection.
By the love of the Two who move as One
By the Weaver and the Singer
By the Web and the Song
By the Great Above and the Great Below, and all things in between
By the Love, Power and Wisdom of the Great Spirit
We bless this Child of Light.

We bless you by the light of the Sun
We bless you by the light of the Moon
We bless you by the light of the Starry Heavens
We bless you by the Green of the Land
By the Blue of the Sea
By the Winds of Knowledge
We bless you by the Three Races
By the Seven Wanderers
By the Nine Waves of Creation
You are guided. You are protected. You are whole. Blessed be.
Parents light the blessing candle of the child.
Parents: *By the blessings of the Goddess and God*
We light this sacred flame
May its power transform all that doesn't serve and guide the way
May our daughter/son walk on the path guided by spirit
May she/he walk with magick before her/him
May she/he walk with magick behind her/him
May she/he walk with magick above her/him
May she/he walk with magick below her/him
May she/he walk with magick all around her/him
So mote it be!

Vow of the Goddess Parents

HP/S: *Do you promise to guide this child (name) on the spiritual path, offering your own knowledge and wisdom, blessing and protection as she/he seeks her/his own way in the world?*

Goddess Parents: *I do.*

Charging of Magickal Tools
HP with Goddess Parents:

We charge this chalice as a symbol of the Goddess and feminine Divine.
We charge this wand as a symbol of the God and masculine Divine.
We charge this pentacle as a symbol of protection and the Cosmos.
We charge this blade as a symbol of truth and balance of Power.
May she/he always share the harmony and balance of the God and Goddess in perfect love and perfect trust. May these tools represent her/his inner tools that she/he will need to light he/his way on her/his path. May she/

he carry them in her/his heart, soul, body, and mind and call upon them for strength when s/he needs them.

Blessings of the Goddess Parents

The Goddess Parents are each encouraged to offer a spiritual blessing to the child, ideally some quality or trait they possess and can pass on as a part of their spiritual mentoring.

Blessings of the Community

The community members gathered are each encouraged to offer a spiritual blessing to the child.

Spell of Protection

HP/S: *By the power of the Goddess and God, may we weave a crystalline shell of protection and care around (name). May you be guarded from any and all forces seen and unseen that may come to harm you, neutralizing such forces and reflecting love on the source. Many you walk in safety, with love, power and wisdom.*

Release the Quarters

Quarters are released by the same people who called them. Everyone faces the direction named and holds up their right hand to release the spirits of that direction.

North: *To the North, we thank and release the element of Earth and the spirits of the North. We thank and release the Great Stag. Thank you for your blessings. Hail and farewell.*

West: *To the West, we thank and release the element of Water and the spirits of the West. We thank and release the Changing Snake. Thank you for your blessings. Hail and farewell.*

South: *To the South, we thank and release the element of Air and the spirits of the South. We thank and release the Wise Crow. Thank you for your blessings. Hail and farewell.*

East: *To the East, we thank and release the element of Fire and the spirits of the East. We thank and release the Wild Horse. Thank you for your blessings. Hail and farewell.*

Release the Circle

The HP/S moves once widdershins (counterclockwise) around the ritual space with whatever tool began the ritual with the casting of the circle.

HP/S: *We cast this circle out into the cosmos as a sign of our celebration, marking this rite of passage. The circle is undone, but never broken. So mote it be. Merry meet, merry part and merry meet again. May the peace of the Goddess be ever in your heart.*

Celebration
Wiccaning celebrated with Feast and Presents for the Child.

Cancer Ministry Women's Mysteries
by Matooka MoonBear-MacGowan & SilverMoone

Women's Mysteries are many. The ways in which we dance with them are through circle gathering, feeling, sharing and doing ritual together. Women have the capacity to birth new life. To release what no longer serves through our moon cycles of bleeding. The wisdom and power of what our Mysteries contain are sacred and profound. We move with the ebb and flow of our cycles, connecting with deep knowing that we can heal ourselves, heal one another, and heal the Earth. A key element within our sacred Mysteries is a reclaiming of power, a reclaiming of Self.

A mystery circle for women is a place where we gather to share, learn, embrace our power as women, and heal. We form a bond in being women together that we call Sacred Sisterhood. This is where we learn to have a voice, heal our relationship with our bodies and how we see them, to nourish and care for ourselves and each other. We hold each other up, hold sacred space to listen to our pains and joys, recognizing that we do not take on these aspects from another sister, but rather, we support their process of healing by bearing witness. We create a container of safety where each woman is held in unconditional love.

Women's rituals and mysteries have been part of life since the beginning of creation. She performs them alone in many ways just by being each day. However, it is of great power when she gathers with other sisters, amplifying her intentions and potentials by unifying them.

Here we share one such ritual that may be performed as written or adjusted for the needs of the circle. This particular ritual focuses on the dream-weaving magick of our Women's Mysteries. This ritual is written for a group of women but can be shifted for individual work by creating a tangible dream catcher or weaving. Sky is the limit and ideas are endless, for it is the power of intention and magick that weaves the circle.

Rituals are created with a basic flow of creating an altar with intention to the magickal working and closing of the circle. This ritual will include creating a group altar, clearing/cleansing space and each other, and casting the circle. Followed is calling in of the seven directions by using primal sounds such as voice, rattles, drums, clapping hands, or slapping thighs. Call forth Divine Mother, inviting the self and intention into circle. Then a mediation, the working (includes chant), healing circle and releasing the magick. Then we close the circle.

Women's Mysteries Ritual-Dream Weaving

Altar

Have the women attending this ritual work come with items that will create the dream altar. Each woman will place the items that represent her dreams on the altar. Place the altar in the center of your circle. In the creating of the altar, consider the use of bright colors, objects, pictures and words. Also, consider things that represent the elements of creation such as candles for fire, feathers for air, seashells or a vessel for water and plant life, soil or stones for earth. Decorate the altar fluidly, honoring the wisdom of what the Wise Woman self wants.

Talk about the logistics of the circle here. Speak to the order of things. This is where you will teach the chant. Get everyone prepared for the working by sharing the outline of what will happen. At this time, you will also want to discuss the purpose of this sacred ritual.

Chant

I weave my dreams
I weave my soul.
I weave my sister's dreams
I weave my sister's soul.
I weave the divine dream
I weave the divine soul.

We are one
We are one
We are one

Clearing/Cleansing

Prepare for ritual by smudging yourselves and your circle space. Light some sage and allow the smoke to clear away what no longer serves. Have the women smudge each other, head-to-toe and front-to-back, in a round-robin fashion. (Note: be sure to check if anyone here has allergies to the smoke. A misting of salted water or waving a feather can be used as a substitute)

Circle Cast

Starting in the north begin to cast the circle by each woman taking the hand of the woman to her left while saying, *Hand to hand we cast the circle round.* Hold the intention from heart to hand so that you are casting this circle from a place of Perfect Love and Perfect Trust. Visualize a circle of light surrounding and protecting the space.

Call to the Seven Directions

Honoring the spirits of the directions, take a rattle or drum, or simply use your sacred voice to create sound in which you begin in the North and rattle to welcome the Spirits of the Earth. Turn to the East and welcome the Spirits of Fire. Turn to the South and welcome the Spirits of Air. Turn to the West and welcome the Spirits of Water. Come back to the center and raise your hands to welcome the Spirits of the Great Above. Lower your arms and welcome the Spirits of the Great Below. Hold the intention from your heart-center and welcome the Spirits who reside in the Great Between. This call may be altered when you call upon your sacred team and allies in each direction.

Deity Call

In our Wise Woman traditions, we call upon the Great Mother, She who nourishes, supports, and loves all Her children. Sometimes we call upon Her by specific names, suiting our ritual workings at that time. For this ritual, unless you feel called to invite a particular Goddess you work with, call upon the Great Mother, calling from deep within your sacred belly, where our woman-power is stored, and raise it through your throat chakra, opening yourself up and inviting the Divine to be in circle with you.

Calling Self

Just as we welcome the Divine within our circle, it is equally important to call our sacred selves into the circle as well, to give ourselves voice and power and to welcome those sacred parts in. Each woman, holding her hand to her heart and solar plexus closes her eyes and states *"I am _____, and I call forth the power of my dreams."* In other rituals what you call in will change, but the sacred act of calling yourself forth honors yourself as a part of Divinity.

Meditation

The focus for this meditation is gathering your dreams and weaving them into creation.

Sit comfortably in a circle and take a deep cleansing breath and slowly release, imagining all tension falling away in your body. Take another breath releasing tension in your mind and the last deep breath releasing tension in your soul. Imagine divine golden light entering the top of your head, your crown chakra filling you with inspiration. The light moves to your third eye filling you with illumination. Moving to your throat this light gives power to your words through song. Golden rays move to your heart center filling you with joy and gratitude. Now the light fills your power center, your solar plexus amplifying your divine will. Filling now your sacral plexus, your womb with divine creation and finally to your roots grounding the energies to the Earth Mother. Imagine growing root deeply into the Earth core stabilizing your dreams to grow deeply.

Now imagine your dream tree growing up through your roots into your belly, which is the cauldron of creation. Dream threads of life spin creating a ball of vibrant light any color that feels right to you. The energy of this rises up through your heart center where you give power to follow the dreams of your heart. The energy travels through your arms and out your hands spinning into a ball of vibrant light thread. You hold this pulsing energy between your hands. Feel it vibrate with great power.

Working

When the chanting begins, rise to a standing position and join in the chanting. Each woman will take the yarn ball of light that they gathered in meditation and, standing in a circle, hold the energy thread. Imagine tying it around the waist then begin taking turns tossing the balls rhythmically back and forth to the one across from you while chanting. Start slowly and make it as real as you can by catching and tossing the balls of light. Do three rounds of this energy dream weaving, chanting all through the work. Slowly let the chant become silent. Hold the dream web in this quiet and feel the energy vibrating. The power raised by this work will be released in the healing circle.

Healing Circle

With the magickal workings created, there is a lot of powerful energy circulating, and we share that energy with the intention to bring healing. Often as women, we share our energy with others and forget how vital it is to nourish ourselves first as caregivers. Place yourself in the healing circle first, along with the energies of what you were working on perviously. Then, add anyone else you wish to receive healing, for the highest good, harming none. It might look something like this: *"I place myself into the healing circle, and I bring healing to my dreams. I also place into the healing circle _____."* Take that healing energy and raise your arms, sending it out to the universe to reach all those you have placed within the circle, then bringing your hands back to your heart, and fill yourself with that beautiful energy.

Ground and center yourself. Place your hands upon the ground, share that healing energy with Mother Earth, allowing yourself to feel planted safely and securely in this realm.

If desired, take some time for each woman to share her experience briefly that she may be witnessed and supported by the collective as well as offer the same for her sisters.

Give your thanks to the Great Mother for Her presence.

Release the 7 Directions, beginning in the North, circling counterclockwise and saying farewell to the Spirits who have supported and witnessed your circle.

With each woman's hands held together, look at the sisters who helped share in the beauty of a collective magick. Slowly releasing them say *"May the circle be open but unbroken. May the peace and love of the Goddess be forever in our hearts. Merry meet, merry part, and merry meet again. Blessed be."* You may wish to throw your hands up at the end, letting go of each other as a sign of releasing the circle.

Aries Ministry Protection Magick

by Michael Cantone

The Aries ministry sees its work on three levels, the same as the other Temple of Witchcraft ministries. The outer level is the outreach to the military, supporting their religious needs, social correspondence, education, and protection on a psychic level. The next and more middle level is the psychic and physical protection of the community. Psychic protection is achieved through practicing and repeating many of the types of meditations learned as part of the Mystery School, also found in books such as *The Inner Temple of Witchcraft* and *The Witch's Shield*. Physical protection is achieved by taking part in self-defense classes and workshops. The inner level is seeing to the defense of the Temple as an organization by rituals of warding and protection.

Psychic and Physical Self-Defense

Psychic self-defense services includes many of the lessons we learned as part of the Mystery School curriculum such as, warding and protecting oneself and home, aura cleansing, elemental cleansing, cord cutting, making contact with a warrior spirit, etc. for the Temple community. Additionally, we provide home clearings for those Temple associates who require a hand in this. We also offer workshops and classes to learn and/or improve these skills.

Physical self-defense includes martial arts classes for the Temple community. Martial arts training is a spiritual tradition on its own. Coupled with a magickal practice it is extremely powerful and enlightening. A key means of training in any martial arts system is the use of katas (forms). They are pre-arranged dance-like movements of blocking, angling, and countering with hand and foot attacks to simulate a fighting situation. Katas help build balance, strength, focus, and fluidness in movement while at the same time providing a great cardio workout. Most martial arts systems have their own katas and the Temple of Witchcraft system likewise will have its own which will be based on the elements and Qabalistic Tree of Life.

Aries ministry is responsible for providing warding of physical spaces as well as psychic defense for the organization as a whole. This is accomplished through rituals, spells, and offerings to the Goddesses, Gods, and other spirits with whom we work.

Aries Protection Ritual

The following ritual is one that presented during the 2012 season of Temple events. It combined a candle spell with a meditation. We performed the ritual in March during the waxing moon phase and waxing sun phase, the intent was to gain protection and connect with a warrior spirit.

Protection rituals, as in other temple rituals will always open with creating sacred space and includes the shamanic smudge ritual as presented in *The Temple of Shamanic Witchcraft* and the Lesser Banishing Ritual of the Pentagram (LBRP). In the shamanic smudge ritual we acknowledge the nine directions and their spirits with whom we work, banishing harmful and unwanted energies, welcoming helpful and healing energies, then finally seeing ourselves in the center of the nine directions. In the ritual of the LBRP one is banishing terrestrial forces and clearing one's aura while at the same time clearing and readying the space for the ritual.

The quarter calls in this ritual call upon warriors of each direction that I work with as part of the Aries ministry. These warriors appeared to me holding each of the martial arts weapons that are included in each direction. For North the warrior holds a kama, which is a sickle and used as a pair so the warrior holds one in each hand. In ancient times the kama were used to cut down crops and farmers simply used the kama to defend themselves against would be attackers. The kama relates to the element of earth since it is used to cut crops. For East, the warrior at times will hold either a staff or spear. The staff was basically a walking stick used by monks like that which you see Gandalf carrying in *The Lord of the Rings* that was simply turned into a weapon if the need arose. The staff is often used as a defense against the sword as well as relating to the wand and the element of fire in the Temple tradition. For South, the warrior wields a sword and often times it is one of three types, Samurai, Ninja, or Medieval. In the Temple tradition, the sword relates to the athame and the element of air. For West, the warrior appears holding a pair of sai swords which are weapons that look like a three pronged fork whereby the middle prong is about sixteen inches in length. These were tools in ancient times used to create irrigating paths to allow water to run along the farm beds. The sai relates to the element of water.

For this ritual, we worked with Hecate and Zeus, two of the eight Aries Goddesses and Gods that reign over the ministry. Both Hecate and Zeus provided the protection and warrior spirit we needed for this ritual.

The candle spell was for both the protection for the Temple and community and for protection of each participant. One central candle was charged by each participant then lit by the high priest, followed by each participant charging his or her own candle, lighting them from the central candle. The central candle and individual candles were then allowed to burn out to complete the spell.

The meditation was a guided journey to the underworld to meet a warrior spirit. We brought ourselves down to a meditative state, and then journeyed through the world tree to a location where warriors were training in self-defense. During my vision I saw martial arts masters teaching groups of warriors blocking and attacking combinations, along with staff and sword movements. Other participants saw their own visions of their inner warriors. We then journeyed to meet with a warrior that stepped away from the training area for our own personal discussions.

Preparation and Sacred Space

Create sacred space through the Shamanic Smudge Ritual & Lesser Banishing Ritual of the Pentagram. Smudge all those present. Then cast your circle.

North - Earth, Warrior from the North
To the North, I call upon the element of earth
And the warrior from this land

Sovereign and strong, and kama in hand
Bring to this ritual the protection we seek
Hail and welcome!

East - Fire, Warrior from the East
To the East, I call upon the element of fire
And the warrior from these flames
Will and drive, and your spear aimed
Bring to us the courage hidden in weakness
Hail and welcome!

South - Air, Warrior from the South
To the South, I call upon the element of air
And the warrior from these breezes
Intellect and truth, your sword unsheathed
Bring to us the honesty caught between lies
Hail and welcome!

West - Water Warrior from the West
To the West, I call upon the element of water
And the warrior from the sea
Love and adaptability, and sai protruding
Bring to this ritual the healing submerged in pain
Hail and welcome!

Open the astral temple of the Temple of Witchcraft, connecting to the egregore of the tradition. Open to the three realms and then call forth the Three Rays of Witchcraft.

Evocation of the Gods
Call upon the Goddess and God. In this ritual, we called upon Hecate and Zeus.

Protection Potion
Anoint each participant's wrists with protection potion, protection oil, or simple salt and water, for clearing and protection.

Great Rite
Perform the Great Rite in token with the athame and chalice.

As the sword is to the grail, the blade is to the chalice. Truth is to love. We draw upon the blessings of the gods and drink them in.

Candle Spell
Perform the candle spell as described above, lighting the candles from one central protection candle.

Meditation
Perform the meditation to find a warrior guide as described above. Ask to meet with the warrior that is correct and good for you.

Releasing Sacred Space
Release the remaining energy with a healing circle, as done in the sabbats, and direct the healing out to aid others upon their own journey before grounding it. Thank and release the Goddess and God, Hecate and Zeus. Close the connection to the Temple egregore. Close the gates to the three realms and then release the quarters.

North - Earth, Warrior from the North
To the North, I thank and release the element of earth
And the warrior of this land
Sovereignty, strength, and protection you brought
Will arm us in days to come
Hail and farewell!

West - Water Warrior from the West
To the West, I thank and release the element of water
And the warrior of the sea
Love, adaptability, and healing
Will nurture us in days to come
Hail and farewell!

South - Air, Warrior from the South
To the South, I thank and release the element of air
And the warrior of these breezes
Intellect, truth, and honesty
Will balance us in days to come
Hail and farewell!

Fire, Warrior from the East
To the East, I thank and release the element of fire
And the warrior of these flames
Will, drive, and courage
Will spark us in days to come/Hail and farewell!
Release circle in the traditional manner.

Traditional Holy Days

Though not celebrated with the larger rituals of the sabbats, the Temple keeps two types of holy days. The first are the historic holy days from the ancient Pagan world. They honor the ancient gods and have relevance to modern Witches and Pagans to remember our ancestral practices. They can be recognized at the personal altar with a simple candle lighting ceremony.

The second type of holy day is based upon important days within the modern magickal community, particular births or deaths of our honored elders of the modern Craft.

Historic Holy Days

Artemis' Day (Feb 12) – Celebration feast of the goddess Artemis, known as Diana to the Romans.

St. Patrick's Day (March 17) – Celebrating the death of St. Patrick, who drove the Druids, or "serpents" from Ireland. Rather than celebrating his "success" some celebrate his death and ultimate failure, as Pagan traditions still flourish in Ireland and elsewhere.

Parilia (April 21) – Celebration of the Roman pastoral god Pales. Also Earth Day. A day to recommit oneself to the planet.

Wesak Moon – In Buddhism, the Wesak, or more traditionally, Vesākha, celebration is usually when the Full Moon is in Scorpio and the Sun is in Taurus, usually the Full Moon in May. While October is often the time of the dead, the ancestors we typically honor during Wesak, the Mighty Dead, are the "Bodhisattvas" of the Witchcraft tradition.

Apollon Day (May 18) – Celebration of the Greco-Roman God of Light and the Sun.

Day of the Mothers/Day of Hermes Trismegistus (May 24) – Day sacred to the Celtic Triple Mothers, bringing prosperity and health as well as the feast day of Hermes Trismegistus, patron saint of alchemists and magicians.

Thor's Day (July 29) – Celebration of the Norse god of thunder.

Lights of Isis (August 12) – Celebration of Isis with candlelight throughout the night.

Feast of Hecate (August 13) – Celebratory feast day of the Greek Goddess of Witchcraft, Hecate. Known as Trivia to the Romans.

Odin's Ordeal (Aug 17 – 25) – Commemorates the sacrifice of Odin hanging upon the World Tree for nine days and nine nights to seek the mystery of the runes.

Fast of Thoth (Sept 19) – Day long fast in honor of the Egyptian god of wisdom and magick

Dionysus' Day (Oct 3) – Ritual in honor of the Greek god of wine and ecstasy, where old wine and new wine is poured together and drunk together, to heal one of illnesses old and illnesses new.

Isia (Nov 1-3) – Commemoration of the resurrection of the dismembered Osiris by the Goddess Isis.

Day of Gwynn ap Nudd (Nov 8) – The day when Gwynn ap Nudd, Celtic lord of the underworld opens his gate at Glastonbury Tor for a day.

Hecate's Night (Nov 16) – Celebration of Hecate, known as the Night of Hecate, commencing with sunset. While the Feast of Hecate in August is celebrated by the Temple community, the Night of Hecate is a solitary time for individual practitioners to honor the Mother of Witches. Some celebrate The Night of Hecate on the eve of Nov 30.

Friday the 13th – A classic unlucky day in recent Western folklore, much like superstitions about Halloween or black cats. Witches embrace it as a magickal day, for thirteen is the number of the Moon and the Witch's Coven. Friday the 13th in October 1307 is also the day the Knights Templar were arrested, and one reason it's considered unlucky. We have kinship and fidelity to those who have been persecuted by the Roman Catholic Church and accused of Witchcraft and heresy.

Elder Days

Doreen Valiente's Birthday (January 4) – Celebration of the life of the "godmother" of modern witchcraft.

Cora Anderson's Birthday (January 26) – Birthday of the co-founder of the Feri Traditions.

Robert Cochrane's Birthday (January 26) – Celebration of the birth of the magister of the Clan of Tubal Cain.

Sybil Leek's Birthday (Feb 22) – Celebration of the life of famous witch and psychic.

Scott Cunningham's Death (March 28) – Remembrance of Scott Cunningham's life and work. It was on the week of the anniversary of his death that Christopher unknowingly began his formal study of Witchcraft with Laurie Cabot at Crow Haven Corner.

Three Days of the Writing of the Book of the Law (April 8, 9, 10) – These days, in 1904, Aleister Crowley received the entirety of the Book of the Law, the foundational document of Thelema and the New Aeon, with his wife Rose Kelly. They can be celebrated with the recitations of each chapter on the appropriate day.

Victor Anderson's Birthday (May 21) - Celebration of the life of the poet and founder of the Feri Tradition.

Alex Sanders' Birthday (June 6) – Celebration and remembrance of Alex Sanders, "King" of the Alexandrian line of witches.

Gerald Gardner's Birthday (June 13) – The birth of Gerald Gardner, the father of the modern Wicca movement.

Scott Cunningham's Birthday (June 27) – Celebration of the life of a notable teacher and author.

Leo Martello's Birthday (September 26) – The birth of Italian witch and civil rights activist.

Aleister Crowley's Birthday (October 12) – The birth of the modern magician and founder of Thelema.

Dion Fortune's Birthday (Dec 6) – The birth of the modern magician who brought together Christianity, Qabalah and British Paganism. Author of the highly influential Sea Priestess.

Founders' Rituals

The Founders' Rituals are three annual rituals for the Temple, each performed by one of the Founding Members of the Temple, or by one of the Keystone Bearers of a branch temple. They embody concepts found in the Three Rays, to maintain the health and well being of the Temple as a body, as well as its individual branches.

King's Rite of Maqlu: A Red Ray Ritual

The Red Ray Ritual consists of two parts, the Maqlu Rite, and the Kingstone Rite. The Maqlu Rite is an adaption of one of the most ancient Sumerian rituals of kingship, where all ill-will directed towards the "kingdom" is transmuted and transformed in cooperation with the spirits. The Kingstone Rite calls upon the Goddess of the Land, Sovereignty, to bring the Temple in harmony with her. It centers the Temple as the *Omphalos*, or World Navel, of our work, and it opens to the Well of Souls, to invite those who are in harmony with the Temple to find us. While the Blue and Yellow Rays are community rituals, the Red Ray Ritual of Maqlu is performed in secret, only by the holder of the Red Ray energies amongst the founders, and those in the leadership asked to be present.

Cauldron of Síocháin: A Blue Ray Ritual

The Cauldron of Síocháin is the Cauldron of Peace, invoking the Blue Ray of Love and harmony with the spirits of nature and beyond. In this public ritual celebration, we acknowledge the divine within each of us, and all those ancestors before us and all those who will come after us. We drink a cup of sacred tea drawn from the copper cauldron and recite the names of our ancestors of blood, milk, and spirit, including our spiritual guides, allies and patrons beyond the veil. One by one we stand before the cauldron and recite. The purpose of this rite is to acknowledge all the help we have received and drink from the Cup of Compassion for ourselves and all others. We forgive those who have wronged us and ask forgiveness of those we have wronged. This is a ritual to forgive the past, to be in the present and create the future together in Perfect Love as embodiments of the Great Mystery.

Congress of the Bones: A Yellow Ray Ritual

The Congress of the Bones Ritual helps us commune with the creatures of flesh and blood as one of the cauldron-born. We gather together in the sacred space of ritual and we call to the Animal Teachers who hold the medicines of our flesh. We call to the Ancestors of blood, bone, milk and bread to guide us on the path, and we call to the Mighty Dead, the Hidden Company of our Timeless Tradition to initiate us in the ways of rebirth and regeneration. In vision we seek to burn with the golden flame of the gilded bones of the Mighty Ones. This ritual is often done with the greater public, or shared in forums outside of the Temple itself.

TempleFest

TempleFest is the Temple of Witchcraft's annual midsummer festival and celebration: a weekend of workshops, rituals, local vendors, and craftspeople. Started in 2010, it is a gathering of the Temple members for celebration, education, and community. Each year has a different theme and format, but the purpose of unity and community remains the same.

TempleFest was initially combined with the Temple's Litha/Midsummer ritual, then, in 2014, the date was moved from late June to early August, combining the festival with the Temple's Lammas Ritual. Since 2012, TempleFest has been associated with the Faery Court of Aroxana and Aubrey, the Temple's Fae allies, and is used as an opportunity to honor and strengthen the community's relationship with them.

Distance students can and do come to TempleFest to receive in-person consecration and blessings of solitary initiations in the Mystery School and to meet their peers, mentors, and instructors.

TempleFest 2014 design by Mark Bilokur

CHAPTER TEN: WITCHCRAFT CULTURE

Witchcraft is an art, science, and religion. Some see the three combined simply as a spiritual path, but it is also a culture. Witchcraft is the culture of Witchdom, the invisible nation beyond the veil, like Shamballa of the East, and the invisible nations scattered throughout the world. The square foot of land around each individual witch collectively makes up the body of our spiritual nation. While there is a collective culture of Witchcraft, and within it, many diverse strands, there is also a cultural ethos that the Temple of Witchcraft strives to attain.

MODERNITY AND TRADITION

Paradox is at the heart of our mystery. Only through the deep experience of seemingly diametrically opposed forces does one find the truth of reconciliation, and from that resolution, attain transformation of the soul. This is our craft of the soul, the soul body to sail deeper into the mysteries. Likewise, at the heart of our Witchcraft culture is the experience of paradox. Because of this, we don't always readily fit with other traditions of Witchcraft and Wicca.

We explore the paradox found between modernity and tradition. We have a fidelity to the past. We are seeking the regeneration of the deepest spiritual traditions of the Craft, often traditions with little written record and what is written does not always support our vision of our own roots. Do we subscribe to naïve idealism? Or do we know that our history is not always accurate? Do we shape our own future regardless of past? In the deepest mysteries, is the distant past as mutable and changeable as the distant future? All of these are possibilities, but none is fact.

Our fidelity to the past is not absolute. We don't do things in the Old Ways just because they are old. We do them because they are effective. We seek to understand why they are effective, and like the marital arts of Bruce Lee, incorporate the best of the best into our practice. As the modern age moves forward, there are advantages and disadvantages to technology, as they are advantages and disadvantages to changes in our Craft. When new ways are more effective, we seek to incorporate them into our practice. Some save us time, energy, and effort, three commodities we have in our life. Some don't. Some make us lazy when there are reasons to expend energy, effort, and time, as it's part of the technique. In the Temple, we seek to blend the best of both worlds, ancient and modern.

I don't live in ancient Greece, Rome, Egypt, or Gaul. So the practices of those times and places cannot be entirely my practices even if I have a call to those cultures. Much of what we know of those cultures is fragmentary, notes and philosophies, but not full, living practices. The text does not have the "stage directions" as it were. With education, we can put them into action, but don't know if we are doing it as the ancients did. I am a modern human, living in the modern world, or perhaps more accurately post-modern, trying to reconcile the practices of the ancient traditions in my every day life, connecting me more to my people, land and spirit, rather than cut me off from everyone and everything I know. The reconciliation is the continual resolution of paradox for this mystery, constantly unfolding and revealing new things about our life. This unfolding will hopefully help Witches be leaders in a new global cultural movement, bringing the best of ancient wisdom and modern culture together in a harmonious, holistic way.

For this reason, we tend toward the side of the occultist, the spiritual scientist trying to understand how matter and spirit work, rather than the cultural reconstructionist, though some of our membership is devoted to reconstructionist aims. Our academia is balanced by our empathy, as the mind must be balanced by the heart. Ultimately, asking ourselves does this make sense to both my head and my heart, when reconstructing or creating practices.

We recognize we are living in the Age of the Great Blessing and Great Curse, and must reconcile all this data we have before us. How do we tell a magickal human story that empowers everyone, while still giving us our purposes as Witches? Like the libraries of Alexandria, we must keep all the strands separate, yet watch the flow of how each influences the next and makes something new. It can be hard to understand the new you are creating when you are in it. Creation is a messy process. It is often only afterwards, in retrospect that it makes more sense, can be evaluated, built upon, or discarded.

Drawing from diverse cultures, we are cosmopolitan. We see Witchcraft being of the whole world, and having something to offer the whole world. With this cosmopolitan view we are are open to sharing our practices, lore, and craft. While the mysteries are secret, their essence is in the experience of them, not the symbols, words or philosophies. While rituals are important, it is in the practice of the Craft, the technique, that forges the soul body, not simply knowledge of the mysteries. We believe to preserve the mysteries is to reveal them often to the world. Those who have the eyes to see and the ears to hear will.

We reach out to the world in this Age of the Great Blessing and Great Curse. We believe, in this coming Aeon of Light, that the wisdom of the Witches must be brought to the table of the Earth, offerings potential ideas, solutions and views about the world and our place in it. We believe our destruction of the planet, is caused, at least in part, by our fundamental view of matter, nature and the globe. Traditions that see the sacred in the world can help change the overall global view, and the change in attitudes can pave the way for greater shifts of behavior, culture and science. Yet we also know that we only have a part of the wisdom needed and that we must learn from other traditions, religions, and cultures. In this age, we seek some of the legitimacy of the mainstream in terms of formally recognized institutions, accreditation, and organizations. Through these platforms, we can better work in harmony with the rest of the world's religions and organizations willing to partner with those of different backgrounds.

As we see Witchcraft as a vocation in the art, science and religion of the Craft, something fulfilled in every culture and time whether they used the word Witch or not, we see our tradition as multicultural. Part of the Great Blessing and Curse is to understand and reconcile that. This reconciliation too, leads to the deeper mysteries of the human story, and our relationship with all life throughout the ages of time upon Earth and in the starry heavens.

Our work as a Temple culturally is a mix of work in the spirit realms and work in the physical realms. We bridge these worlds in our Ministerial Church. Each of the twelve ministries has three areas of working. One is much more spiritually and mystically oriented, which may or may not involve many flesh and blood people. On the other end of the spectrum is the work that is for the education and betterment of the general public, Witches and non-Witches alike. In the vocation of the Witch, we have opportunities to serve the whole village, not just those who follow our ways. In fact often the Witch helped those who were quite different. Between the two is work that interfaces the Witches in the Temple with the outer world and the inner mystical experience. It is in this liminal place where we do most of our work.

Despite having a structure and degree system, we do not see the Mysteries as exclusive to inner orders, nor do we see the outer work of ministry as less than the more transcendent experiences of the mystery. All is life and our experience in life is at the heart of the mystery. Some of us will focus on mediating divine powers unconditionally, unseen and unattached. Others will apply that power in the work of humanity, the environment and the spirits. All have purpose and importance. The inner orders of training are truly for those who learn how to mediate and minister and find what is most appropriate for them.

Our theology, philosophy, cosmology, and mythic history seek to build bridges to reconcile these extremes. Ours is a middle way, but not static. Like lightning, it constantly arcs back and forth between the two extremes. Ours is a crooked path to walk, finding the middle way only by going to the extremes. One cannot experience spring and fall without summer or winter. The images we have of the divine are more universal, using images that repeat as archetypes across land and time. We weave together seemingly disparate myths and histories to create a new tapestry for the Temple Witch. We use modern terminology to express the balance between ancient and modern theology, with ideas such as being a panentheistic and a heuristic tradition. All of these things inform and guide our own culture within Witchdom.

WE ARE THE OTHER PEOPLE

A huge cultural understanding of our place in this world comes from a folk tale known as "The Other People." It is shared by Pagan elder Oberon Zell Ravenheart, based upon his own experience with proselytizers at his door. Oberon is the founder of The Church of All Worlds, an author, artist, and scholar in the modern Pagan movement. While the original version as he has shared it was heavier on the Bible quotes, it's the sentiment that has been adopted by the Temple of Witchcraft. Pete Pathfinder of the Aquarian Tabernacle Church (ATC) later adapted it into a "tract booklet" in 1994, with artwork from Don Lewis, imitating the religious propaganda material of traditions that tend to proselytize door to door.[1]

Most Pagans, Witches and Wiccan divorce themselves from any Christian history or theology at all, other than to state how much Jewish and Christian theologians "stole" from Pagan myths and mysteries. There is arguably a lot of truth to that sentiment. It generates an ideal of pre-Christian times, wanting to completely forget about the last two thousand years of history. While I can see why many would want to, it's not realistic. It all happened for a reason. While history is written by the victors and we might not know exactly what happened, we know that Christianity rose to dominance and influence in the world. We can't ignore it and hope it will go away. The Age of Aquarius ideal calls for more inter-faith dialogue as well as the intra-faith of the various Pagan and mystical paths. We need to sit at the table with the mainstream religions and will only do so if we can reconcile their worldview with our own, to find a story that allows for both to make sense.

The Other People story helps us with that. Essentially, door to door Christian proselytizers come knocking on the unsuspecting Pagan's doors in the comic track book, or Oberon's door in real life. They extoll the virtues of salvations from Original Sin. The Pagan tells them "But that doesn't apply to us! We've no need of salvation, because we're "the other people" and don't have your "Original Sin." The Christians protest, as the Pagan goes onward to quote from the Bible, explaining the Bible from a less orthodox point of view.

In the story of Genesis, the name of God, Elohim, is more correctly translated as "Gods" or "Pantheon." and in Genesis 1:26-28, the "Gods" create humanity, male and female, as well as the creatures of the Earth. Not until later does it reference Yahweh, one of the "gods" as making the Garden of Eden. It is comparable to a private garden or experiment. Only there is Adam and Eve. Through the advice of the Serpent, Eve is "tricked" into eating the Fruit of Knowledge of Good and Evil. It is revealed that Yahweh lied when he told Adam and Eve they would die if they ate the fruit, and the Serpent actually told the truth. The couple is cast out of the paradise of Eden and the serpent becomes cursed and feared. Eventually, Adam and Eve make a life outside of Eden and raise two brothers, Cain and Abel. Cain and Abel offer sacrifices to Yahweh. Yahweh only accepts the meat sacrifice of the shepherd Abel, and rejects the agricultural sacrifice of the farmer Cain. Cain kills Abel and is cursed as the murderer, given the "Mark of Cain." Cain goes to the land of Nod, east of Eden and eventually finds a wife, most likely somewhere near the shores of the Caspian Sea. So where did his wife and her people come from in the Land of Nod? Adam and Eve's third son, Seth, also finds a wife. Where did she come from?

So essentially this tale tells us there were "other people" in the world, not created by Yahweh, not connected to this "Original Sin" and therefore not out of harmony with their own gods and goddesses. Pagans, continually cautioned against in the rest of the Old Testament, are the children of these gods, the Other People to those of Eden. We are the Other People.

From this, many take the idea that if we do not have Original Sin, we have what radical priest Matthew Fox calls Original Blessing. We never left the Garden of our Gods. The whole world is the Garden of the Gods where we are blessed and free. Sadly, we've allowed ourselves to believe a story that is not ours. The propaganda machine of Christianity has given us a global story of banishment from the Garden, with a mindset that we are disconnected. How else do we explain the ecological conditions of the world today? How else do we explain our guilt and neurotic behaviors? How do we explain our capacity for such self destruction?

The longer the Christian theological paradigm became the dominant influence, the more we diverged from our Original Blessing and the birthright of magick. Even in a post modern, supposedly secular era, the basic coding much of the Western world has is based upon the story of banishment, sin and the sacrifice of another. The longer this went on, the more it divorced itself from the original Christian ideals of love, forgiveness and charity. Thus allowing things like the Crusades and the Burning Times, completely contrary to the teachings of Christ, to rise up in the name of Christianity. All of this theology is based upon the Old Testament of Judaism, yet the Jewish faith does not believe in Original Sin and focuses upon taking responsibility for your own actions in the world.

Much of our own work as Witches is waking up ourselves, and others, to the interconnectedness and interdependence of all things with the Earth and ultimately the stars. To hurt the land and to hurt another is to hurt oneself. By breaking the spell of Original Sin through magick, we can return to the Garden of the Gods and help others see it blooming all around us, all the time. A main component of our own Temple theology is an awakening to the consciousness of this First Time, this Motherland, this Garden of Paradise where the gods are still fully present with us if we but open our eyes and look.

Our story is not of banishment, lies and guilt, but of awakening, homecoming and reunion. In the old alchemical tradition, to evolve, things must be broken down, purified and recombined. For whatever reason, the last two thousand years has occurred to break us down and purify and temper us to return. "Dissolve and coagulate" is the motto of the the hermaphroditic lord of occultism, Baphomet. We now simply have to reunite.

Muggles, Cowans & the Garden of the Gods

Despite being the "other people" of this story, we believe in the possibility that everyone is "other." We all have a path to walk. We all have a story to tell. We all have magick in our blood to share with the world, no matter what religion, tradition or political party we might identify with at this time.

In the past, there have been efforts to make Witchcraft exclusionary, which are not all bad. The path of the Witch is not for everyone. It's not everyone's calling. We are currently in a magickal culture where someone with a book and little practice can feel justified calling themselves a Witch with no fidelity to any form of Witchcraft. Sadly, such people are often the most vocal in the community, creating the most confusion among new seekers and the general public.

In an effort to differentiate between Witches, Pagans, and those who are not, various terms have been used. Some are simply meant to be descriptive, while others can come across as derogatory. Sometimes they are used in the Pagan community with no ill spirit, but it's important to think about whatever words we use.

Due to the popularity of the *Harry Potter* series by J.K. Rowling, embraced by Witches, Wiccans, and Pagans despite the author not being particular "pro" Pagan in her own beliefs and sentiments publicly, the term "muggle" has become commonplace. In the Harry Potter world, a muggle is a non-magickal person, someone who doesn't know about the secret wizarding world behind the "ordinary" façade. While the heroes of the series don't use it in a derogatory manner, the villains certainly do, with the term "half-blood," a half muggle and half magickal personal as a "mud-blood."

In earlier times, and still in initiatory British Traditional Wicca, the term cowan was used for non-Witches. It was used mostly to mean the same thing, though technically a cowan was an unaffiliated mason, not a member of a lodge. It implied that a person could perform aspects of the "craft" but were not officially sanctioned. From this perspective, uninitiated cunning women and men of the European villages would most likely be akin to cowans, though I still consider them my spiritual ancestors. With the rise of Wicca, it became a term for "ordinary" people who did not identify as a Witch or Wiccan, or even Pagan.

Though less popular than muggle, I prefer this term. It implies that non-Witches, and some would say non-initiated Witches in a formal BTW line, can still practice as they will, but are not recognized by the greater order of Witches.

I'd like to think we are all part of the Greater Garden of the Gods —free to see and experience divinity as we would. Some come to the path of the Witch to learn what we have to share and teach. It's one step of many on their journey, often their healing journey. As healers, we take people in and teach them what we can. We should be unattached to the result. Will they be High Priestesses or High Priests of the Craft for the rest of their lives? Who knows? They might think so though our intuition tells us otherwise. They are here now, learning, fulfilling their obligations, so go with the flow of spirit. Some of the most amazing ministers in the Temple are people I did not necessarily think at the start would finish the program, and many I had high hopes for in the long term are nowhere to be found today.

While there are non-Witches, those who are not called to this path in this lifetime or perhaps any other, it doesn't mean such individuals don't have their own magick and spirituality. Such practitioners often have something to teach and show Witches. If we are truly wise, we will watch, listen and learn.

We don't seek to proselytize or convert others. We are open and share our ways, if they interest people, we are often willing to teach. We are not required to teach anyone we don't feel comfortable teaching and, like many occult traditions, we often make sure the student is ready by providing tasks that could seem like obstacles to the lazy. In older times, one was required to ask three times before getting a "yes," to show the student could persevere. While we might not require three attempts, we have our own ways to make sure the student is ready for more serious training.

WISDOM SAYINGS

The Alexandrian Book of Shadows has a section known as Various Aphorism, containing bits of folkloric wisdom. They are terse statements or observations that are meant to help Witches on their way. The Temple of Witchcraft draws upon aphorism, or wisdom sayings, from both ancient and modern sources relevant to our Craft. None are doctrine, but simply ideas to ponder and see if their wisdom will be true for you.

Know Thyself – Temple of Delphi

A driving thirst for knowledge is the forerunner of wisdom. – Robert Cochrane

'Tis an Ill Wind that blows no minds.

A candle loses nothing by lighting another candle. – James Keller

Just because something is old, it does not necessarily make it more valuable, and just because something is new, does not mean it has no validity.

I believe what I will and will what I believe. – Austin Osman Spare

Fantasy is the Ass that carries the Ark. — Gareth Knight

Keep your silence amidst the noise of the world for there is peace in that silence. – A. Witch

If you would walk the witch's way, observe with care the child at play. – Lady Circe

Witchcraft is not a religion of guilt.

You are free to come and go as your conscience dictates. — Alex Sanders

There are no rules, just consequences.

We are all sorcerers, and live in a wonderland of marvel and beauty if we did but know it. — Charles Godfrey Leland

Every thought, every word and every deed becomes an expression of our magick, as our life becomes one entire spell.

All the wonders of magic are performed by will, imagination and faith. – Paracelsus

The intuitive mind is a sacred gift; the rational mind is a faithful servant. We have created a society that honors the servant and has forgotten the gift. – Albert Einstein

The way you look at the world is the way the world looks back at you.

Witches Don't Believe, We know.

All Desire is Sacred.

Fairly take and fairly give. – The Wiccan Rede

Speak little, listen much. – The Wiccan Rede

Great Oaks from Little Acorns Grow.

To Give you must be able to receive. To receive you must be able to give.

Are you thinking like a witch? – Adam Sartwell

Let food be your medicine and medicine be your food. – Hippocrates

Within the heart of God is the heart of a mother. – Scottish saying

Divination is not supernatural. It is common sense. – Huichol saying

Just because you can do something, doesn't mean you should do it.

The stars may impel but they cannot compel! – occult saying

Work without Lust of Result. – occult saying

Those who do not enact Sacred Drama in ritual are destined to enact out drama in daily life.

When you desire something, work on yourself rather than on other people. – Nancy B. Watson

My gods have grown with me hence I never outgrow them. – Austin Osman Spare

The goal of life is living in agreement with nature. – Zeno

The Craft is a scavenger religion believing that if it works, use it. – Maxine Sanders

If you call upon the Gods and they answer, who is there to oppose or to challenge the integrity of your Path. – Andrew Chumbley

It is not good for all your wishes to be fulfilled. Through sickness you recognize the value of good health. Through evil the value of good, through hunger, satisfaction, through exertion the value of rest. – Heraclitus

May the Lady and Lord Grant You All you desire, and protect you from what you want.

Thoughts are things. – occult saying

There are no mistakes in nature. There are no spare parts to the universe. Everything has a purpose, even if we don't understand or agree with it.

Be True to your nature, don't be trapped by your nature.

Those who seek only the heavens never grow deep. Seek wisdom in the dark, wet places and you'll find the light of stars.

For a tree's branches to reach to heaven, its roots must reach to hell. – Alchemical Saying

All things contain poison and nothing is without poison. – Paracelsus the Wise

You cannot move from where you are not. – Starhawk

Neither coddle nor punish weakness. – Victor H. Anderson

To truly live, you must die before you die. – Sufic saying

Evil can be defined as misplaced force. – Dion Fortune

Life is too wonderful to suffer misery for long. – Maxine Sanders

Everything in this world casts a shadow.

My fate is in the Lap of the Goddess. – traditional saying

What's Fair is Foul and What is Foul is Fair.

Effectiveness is the measure of Truth. – both Serge Khalili King and Aleister Crowley

Great minds contain no opinions, merely ideas. – Austin Osman Spare

Look for the threads of truth found in many lands and many times Weave your own tapestry with these threads.

Truth is most oft found twixt the horns. – old Witch saying

Who initiated the first witch? – Doreen Valiente

A Witch is born, and not made; or if one is to be made, then tears must be spilt before the moon can be drawn. For the Lady chooses whom she wills to be Her Lover, and those She loves the most, She rends apart before making them Wise. – Robert Cochrane

An initiate owns nothing, but has use of everything. – Dion Fortune

To heal, you must know how to hex. To hex, you must know how to heal. They are two sides of the same coin. – Craft saying

We must be the change we wish to see in the world. – Ghandi

All of us have a bit of witch in us. – Dona Mercedes

All gods are one God and all goddesses are one Goddess, and there is one initiator. – Dion Fortune

Life Feeds Life.

If any Wiccan truly labors, just payment becomes a personal right. – Lady Galadriel

History tells us outer truth and inner lies, while myths tells us outer lies and inner truth.

Let all things be as they were since the beginning of time. – Craft saying

When the student has learned all there is to be learnt they discover that there is nothing to be learnt. – Druidic saying

Who would be a leader must first be a bridge. – old Welsh saying

Power answers power. Love answers love. Truth answers truth. — traditional saying

All times are the same time. The initiation of a sorcerer reveals this. That is why they say a true initiation never ends. – Grant Morrison

It is told that the Buddha, going out to look at life, was greatly daunted by death. "They all eat one another!" he cried, and called it evil. This process I examined, changed the verb, said, "They all feed one another," and called it good. – Charlotte Perkins Gilman

After all the traditions have been put aside, all the labels stripped, I find that we are all Witches under the skin. – Leo Martello

We sacrifice the ordinary in exchange for the extraordinary. – Maxine Sanders

In the final analysis a Witch is someone whose entire being is permeated with the Craft of the Wise. – Leo Martello

A braided rope is stronger than a single strand.

The Witch admits to rebellion, but denies anarchism, maintaining that he has a truer sense of the cosmic order than most of his critics. – Stewart Farrar

To be born is to die in the spirit world, and to die is to be reborn in the spirit world.

You can't honor that which you know nothing about. – Joe Hughes

Become thyself, in order to know the cosmos and the gods. – A Pythia at Delphi

Preserve the mysteries. Reveal them often.

Along with the wisdom sayings or aphorism, we also have some shared cultural sayings in Witchcraft, Wicca and Neopaganism. Though most see them from a surface perspective, each has a deeper meaning and mystery to it.

Blessed Be

Used as a greeting, blessing and farewell by many Witches, it's deeper teaching is in the blessing of self, others and the world. While everything is inherently holy to the Witch, the act of blessing is to engage in relationship with something or someone, to encourage the best virtues possible. The act of blessing all things puts us into right relationship with ourselves, with each other and all of nature.

Merry Meet, Merry Part and Merry Meet Again

A more ritualized form of greeting and farewell, particularly used at the end of circle gatherings. It indicates that people come together, then leave in peace to come together again. The deeper meaning refers to the joy and peace within the heart in gathering with community. One comes together in the spirit of merriment and leaves the same way, in that we have gathered not only in this lifetime, but in many lifetimes, and will continue to do so. Faery teacher Orion Foxwood has taught about the relationship between merry and "faery" and the use of the word for enchantment. By enchantment, or magick, we have met, parted and will meet again, indicating a great force—as faeries are considered agents of "fate" and it is by fate we gather. The appropriate people come together and part as needed.

May You Never Hunger, May You Never Thirst

Drawn from novel *Stranger in a Strange Land* by author Robert A. Heinlein, and popularized by the work of the Neopagan Church of All Worlds, the phrase is to indicate a blessing during sacrament, so one will not hunger or thirst. The deeper meaning refers to spiritual hunger and thirst, beyond the physical.

By Seed and Root, by Stem and Bud, by Leaf and Flower and Fruit

A phrase used in rituals of blessing to show the cycle of life in the green realm of nature. We start as seed that forms a root. Stems grow upward forming leaves and buds, leading to flower and fruit, which then contain the new seed. The cycle of life is continuous, though its form changes.

The Good Neighbors

A name for the Faery Races is simply to call them "the Good Neighbors." They may also be called "the Kind Folk" or "the People of Peace." In days past, you would not call them by their direct name, for that would be considered insulting. Today, we can think of it as addressing someone in our life as "human." We wouldn't do that, so why do it to our friends in the other orders of being? Yet with so little education on the other entities in our society, sometimes we have to say things like faery to make our meaning clear.

More importantly, the sentiment of the good neighbors, for those races and for humanity and specifically Witches, is essential. We do not live alone in the world, with many seen and unseen around us. All should be striving to live in peace and harmony, to be "good neighbors" to each other. This ties into the mysticism of Jesus Christ, "love thy neighbor as thyself." If we live in love of our neighbors, we'll create a society of humans, animals, angels, faery, gods, and spirits that will be unlike any other.

May the Circle be Open but Never Broken

A recognition that our ritual circles are opened, meaning the rite has ended, but the circle is not broken or dismantled. The opening casts the ritual space across space and time, so all the universe is our sacred space, touched by our work in the magick circle. Our circle's edge touches and crosses the edge of all other circles, across time and space, from the beginning to the end of all Witches.

SPIRITUAL VIRTUES

There is no one universally accepted code of virtue in modern Witchcraft, nor one required or demanded of members of the Temple of Witchcraft. We look to our lore for guidance, not dogma. One popular set of virtues has arisen through the deconstruction of the Charge of the Goddess as written by Doreen Valiente. "Cultivate the traits of beauty, strength, power, compassion, honor, humility, mirth and reverence." These eight traits have become associated with the eight holidays of the Wheel of the Year.

Beauty	Imbolc
Strength	Lammas

Power	Litha
Compassion	Yule
Honor	Ostara
Humility	Mabon
Mirth	Beltane
Reverence	Samhain

For those Temple members inspired more by Germanic Paganism, often considered Heathenry, the Nine Noble Virtues of *The Poetic Edda*, codified by John Yeowell and John Gibbs-Bailey in the 1970s serve as an ethical code. They do seem to capture many of the virtues of the Northern Pagan Traditions.

- Courage
- Truth
- Honor
- Fidelity
- Discipline
- Hospitality
- Self Reliance
- Industriousness

Founder Steve Kenson, while writing for the Role Playing Game *Mage: The Ascension* in a supplemental book known as *Dark Ages: Mages Grimoire*, created a list of Pagan Virtues for the Old Faith, inspired by his own understanding of ancient and modern Pagan traditions.

Foundations of the Temple

These four echo and instill the essence of the Eight Wiccan Virtues and the Nine Noble Virtues, associated with the four elements.

Vitality – Earth: Celebration of life force, of participation in the world, enjoyment of earthly pleasures and the experience of the cycles and seasons of life. Those who celebrate life must therefore be able to embrace death as a part of the cycle of life.

Courage – Fire: Courage is the ability to do what needs to be done, despite danger. Courage is not foolhardiness, but the virtue of doing what is necessary, even when what is necessary is not easy. Courage is celebrated in Pagan society, while its opposite, cowardice, is a stigma.

Honor – Air: Honor is the action of living by a code of ethics, of being trustworthy and dedicated. Honor is almost a tangible commodity. It is better to die with honor than to live without it. A key concept of honor in the Pagan societies and in magickal cultures is the oath, your word being your bond, which must be honored.

Generosity – Water: The ability to freely give to others is the last virtue. Those who have more than others, and share it, are looked upon well by humans and the gods. Hospitality to strangers and beggars in particularly is considered a Pagan virtue, as many myths tell of the gods disguised as beggars or travelers.

The work of popular American author Scott Cunningham is beloved by those in the Temple. His thirteen Goals of the Witch have been corresponded with the zodiac lessons of the Seminary in the Temple. The thirteen goals are also aligned with the traditional thirteen powers of the Witch, or Gifts from the Goddess, as cited in *Aradia, or The Gospel of the Witches*.

Sign	Thirteen Goals of the Witch	Thirteen Gifts of the Goddess
Aries	Know yourself	To use the power to bless friends and curse enemies
Taurus	Exercise the body	To bring forth beauty, inner and outer

Gemini	Learn	To understand the secret signs of the hands, stars, cards and omens
Cancer	Breathe and eat correctly	To commune with animals and wild creatures
Leo	Know your Craft	To banish people, things and even misfortune
Virgo	Attune with the cycles of the Earth	To cure disease and wounds of body, mind, heart and soul
Libra	Achieve balance	To weave spells of love, romance and seduction
Scorpio	Celebrate life	To sense, conjure, converse and command spirits
Sagittarius	Apply knowledge with wisdom	To conjure good fortune
Capricorn	Keep your words in good order	To know and find hidden treasures and truths
Aquarius	Keep your thoughts in good order	To understand the Voice of the Wind
Pisces	Meditate	To predict and control the weather
Spirit	Honor the Goddess and God	To possess the knowledge of transformation

Our Ministerial Code

The Temple has a Spiritual Code proposed for all ministers, ordained or not, and it is the guideline and ethos for our membership. These eight points are core ideals in the Temple we are all working towards. Those who do not agree with basic ethos of this code may not be suitable for membership in the Temple.

Responsibility

We take responsibility for our words, thoughts and deeds, observing the balance of nature and spirit, and striving to live the essence of the Wiccan Rede in "harming none" whenever and wherever possible.

Community

We recognize the value of community, working to develop and nurture our community and tradition. While being leaders, we also recognize we are truly called to serve. We honor our obligations to our spiritual community but are also mindful of responsibilities to family, friends, local community, and country.

Spirituality

We actively work on our own spiritual evolution, education, and healing, exploring new mysteries while grounding them in the wisdom of Witchcraft. We maintain a spiritual practice that nourishes us on a physical, mental, emotional, and spiritual level, keeping a healthy balance where we can be of service.

Reverence

We honor the Divine as both Goddess and God, immanent in the Earth and Universe, transcending beyond the bounds of space and time. We strive to honor and protect the world, and our immediate environment. We work in service and partnership with the Divine.

Tolerance

We respect other views of Witchcraft, Wicca, Paganism, Magick, and Spirituality, even when we do not necessarily agree with them. Clear and honest dialogue is encouraged, even when the result is to agree to disagree.

Boundaries

We maintain appropriate boundaries, treating others with respect while acknowledging our own vulnerability and personal issues. Whenever there is a personal conflict of interest with a student, client, or other Temple member, refer those seeking aid to another Ministerial Member within the Temple, or to a qualified minister outside of the Temple who can provide appropriate aid.

Mediation

When disputes occur within the Temple or the larger community, we seek a peaceful resolution for all parties involved. Whenever possible, we seek mediation to settle the disputes fairly and equitably, calling upon our sisters and brothers in the Libra Ministry.

Empowerment

We seek to claim our own power as Witches, meaning that we take action, work for beneficial change, and own the outcome of our choices. We also seek to empower others, preferring to teach them to do for themselves and to own the outcome of their choices- rather than doing things for them, whenever possible.

The Spiritual Code has been corresponded with many different magickal systems that are used in the Temple. The first is the seven fold path. In the training of High Priestesses and High Priests in the Seminary, we pass through the seven gates of the underworld. Each gate corresponds with a chakra, planet and alchemical operation, and now a point within the Ministerial Spiritual Code:

Gate	Planet	Chakra	Alchemy	Code
Seventh Gate	Saturn	Root	Calcination	Responsibility
Sixth Gate	Jupiter	Belly	Dissolution	Community
Fifth Gate	Mars	Solar Plexus	Separation	Boundaries
Fourth Gate	Venus	Heart	Conjunction	Mediation
Third Gate	Mercury	Throat	Fermentation	Tolerance
Second Gate	Moon	Brow	Distillation	Spirituality
First Gate	Sun	Crown	Coagulation	Reverence

The union of all seven creates true empowerment.

Another method of correspondence is to align the eight key words of the Spiritual Code to the eight spokes of the Wheel of the Year. The cycle of the year give us a chance to contemplate each in their own turn of the Wheel.

Sabbat	**Astrology**	**Godform**	**Spiritual Code**
Yule	Sagittarius-Capricorn	Goat Horned God	Reverence
Imbolc	Aquarius	Jack Frost	Spirituality
Ostara	Aries-Pisces	Ram Horned God	Tolerance
Beltane	Taurus	Jack of the Green	Responsibility
Litha	Gemini-Cancer	Bull Horned God	Empowerment
Lammas	Leo	Jack Corn	Community
Mabon	Virgo-Libra	Stag Horned God	Mediation
Samhain	Scorpio	Jack of Lantern	Boundaries

Belenus by Derek O'Sullivan

A strong part of our ethos in regard to the spiritual code is to use it as a guide in the application of feeding and starving various thought forms, energies and behaviors. Similar to the Cherokee parable known as "The Wolves Within" or "The Two Wolves," we look at the same pattern in plant imagery rather than animal imagery. In the Cherokee tale, a grandfather is talking to his grandson about a "terrible fight going on inside me." It's a "terrible fight between two wolves. One is evil. He is anger, fear and hate. He cannot think." He then goes on to describe the other wolf. "He is good and does no harm. He is in balance with all things around him. Both fight inside me, seeking to dominate my spirit." he goes onto explain to the boy, and in fact, everybody has the same fight going on within, with two wolves. The boy asks his grandfather, "Which wolf will win?" His grandfather says, "The one you feed."

In Witchcraft, we look at feeding a plant or starving a plant. Those you give water (emotion), light (energy) and good soil (time and space) to, will grow. Those you deny water, light and soil, will wither. If you seek to grow and encourage someone's behavior, a thought, an idea or a circumstance, give it what it needs to grow. If you wish to discourage something, particularly unhelpful behavior and actions of others when they do not support the ethos of the spirit code of a community, you deny feeding it more emotion, energy, time and space. It's a basic magickal concept, but one that is applied regularly in the growing of our "community garden."

Ultimately be it the metaphor of wolves, plants, spiritual virtues, or ministerial codes, we have an ethos of interdependence. True separation is an illusion. All things are connected, while at times nature seems to be in competition with itself. Here we see illustrated the Darwinian "survival of the fittest" in action. As survival becomes less of an immediate concern with the growing ingenuity of of our species, we can focus upon the aspect of interconnection, and be keenly aware of the effect our actions have upon all. We can take a role, as we advance from a deeper, lower level of consciousness, at what is known as the root chakra, and not simply ascend, but expand, to not forget survival, but to also include empathy, compassion, communication, vision and spirit to our role as guides and caretakers of each other and the world. If, in our interdependent Gaian model of the world, everything is like an organ within the body of Mother Earth, who is an organ within a Solar Being, who is a cell within the great Star Goddess who weaves the fates, then what, as a species, are we? Trees and forests are the lungs. Rivers are the blood of the Earth. Mountains are the bones. Fungus and insects are part of the digestive system of nature. By our current behavior, we must either be a cancer upon the Earth, or part of the immune, nervous, or endocrine system. Which do you choose to be?

As a community, modern Witches usually accept those who are on the edge of society, the unusual, those rejected by most others. As with Adam's story on the Feast of Hecate, we stand for those who are not claimed by others, yet we still maintain our spiritual code. If one's public behavior in the community is not acceptable to the norm, to the established acceptable behaviors and similar values, and one will not choose to work in cooperation in the community, it can indicate such an individual is not able to be in a greater community at this time. That's a choice made by unacceptable behavior.

While the ministerial code covers a broad range of ideas and values, it helps us unify an otherwise diverse community. Some of us in the Pagan/Wiccan/Witchcraft communities center our values differently, but shared values and common cause regardless of the origin of the values can bring us together. Depending on our ministerial work and focus, our values might originate from different world-views. Some of us minister from a very human-centric point of view. Our work is around social service and social justice. Others follow a similar vein, but for all of creation, and particularly express their values in a geocentric, or biosphere-centric view, valuing the Earth as an entity first and foremost. Those who look to gods beyond those found manifested in nature might be focused upon the work and values of the gods, spirits and deities, though not necessarily be rooted in environmental issues. They are often looking to develop the tradition, religion and culture of the magickal community. Many are true occultists at heart, exploring consciousness and valuing the development of consciousness through technique and philosophy to understand how the universe works. Many priest/ess, like myself, don't see these things as mutually exclusive, and our broad range of shared community values and goals welcomes any of these viewpoints from a minister.

Secrecy, Sacredness & the Mysteries

Witchcraft was nurtured in a culture of secrecy. At one time, that served us. Our ancestors, real or mythic, were persecuted for their Craft, not only in the Christian era, but as well as the late Greek and Roman period. The worst of it was from the Christian persecutions of Europe, as well as their later Christian misunderstanding and persecution of indigenous cultures as they explored the "New World." This has been characterized in our lore as the Burning Times. Secrecy saved Witches and would-be, could-be Witches of days past. Our direct spiritual ancestors only became public after the repeal of the Witchcraft act in the United Kingdom, making themselves known to the public in the 1950's. Many Witches of that time thought that was a mistake and advocated secrecy. Many still do. If it was not for the more outlandish of these spiritual ancestors, our movement of popular books and public organizations would never have occurred. Their magickal desire, their Will, to make sure Witchcraft would not die out was fulfilled.

Today, the culture of secrecy does not serve us. It can lead to further misunderstandings with the public and with each other. Secrecy can breed unhealthy cults of personality, while transparency and accountability helps us join the table of world religions and mature as a culture on our own. Many believe that secrecy equates with sacred. Our oaths of secrecy were not just for safety, but were to preserve the mysteries. Certain things should not be revealed to the profane. In the Temple we believe that certain things can never be revealed to the profane, for it can hide in plain sight before them. Words do not make the rite, but the experience of it directly. In the experience the mystery is found.

Some say that to reveal too much technique, in books or lectures, is dangerous, as one who is not properly prepared can use it, and by accident or intent, cause harm. Yet those who are prone to harm in either way are going to find the tools to harm from a simple high school education. The tenets of biology, chemistry and physics can be deadly. The use of the well placed word, written or oral, can change worlds and not always the way you intend. Math skills can be used to solve equations or embezzle. Yet we still make this information available to all who seek it. The door to the mysteries should also be accessible in some way to the seeker. Some are not fit for higher education, just as some are rejected from academia, but a basic education can be presented. Part of the reason for founding the Temple of Witchcraft and moving away from the traditional coven structure, is that the number of sincere seekers now outstrips the openings available in solid covens. Not everyone who completes all of the degrees of their education should serve in the capacity of coven leader, but that has been the model. Today we seek new ways of service, to preserve the mysteries through revelation, and to develop the culture through transparency and accountability.

Social Service

An essential part of the Temple structure is the ministerial church, with its twelve ministries. A core concept in the identity of the Witch is the symbiotic relationship to the village, to the community. In this day and age, we are challenged to integrate this relationship in new ways. In some circumstances, the "villagers" come to the Witch at the edge of the village. In others, the Witch must go to the villagers. We try to balance both the outer work of service to the community with the inner work of the the mystical experience. These are often considered the Lesser and Great Mysteries, though you cannot truly have one without the other.

Part of the ways we work in social service include:

Public Rituals

We provide public rituals not only for religious reasons, but to be visible in the community. It allows those who are seeking and curious a safe opportunity to experience and see if the Craft is right for them. On a deeper mystery level, we believe that we must turn the Wheel of the Year to keep the cycles, seasons and cosmos in balance. The large human population verses the relatively tiny portion of people maintaining these customs and mediating the flow of power between the worlds can unbalance us. As we, and others, do this, we can begin to address this imbalance.

Training of Practitioners

Many of those who study within the Temple go on to provide professional service to the community, including spiritual counsel through divination, teaching, house blessings, handfastings (weddings) and other rites of passage, spiritual healing through energy work, ritual and shamanism, environmental healers, mediums, death walkers, and banishment/exorcisms.

Mentorship

In an ongoing effort to better prepare practitioners, teachers and mentors, the Mystery School has a mentorship program for current advanced students and graduates to mentor younger students. By reviewing their homework and building relationships they help the students develop a strong magickal foundation, by allowing them to ask questions and have discussions with those more experienced.

Information

Beyond the books, recordings, and classes, we provide several sources of information for the Temple community and the wider community at large. We release a free quarterly newsletter called *The Temple Bell* (now available online via our website). Filled with articles, art work and poetry, it also provides an update on Temple activities, finances and volunteer positions.

We also produce a semi-regular free podcast hosted by Temple co-founder Adam Sartwell called *Voices from the Temple*. In it, he both communicates the current activities of the Temple along with interviews with members in the community, and with authors and teachers outside of the community.

Lastly, we publish books that serve as community fundraisers for the Temple, including this book. Most are anthologies allowing others an opportunity to see their work in print, as well as explore, deepen and share their own experiences and research.

Community Collections

From the beginning of our work we have made community collections of foods, toys, and animal shelter donations a part of our "harvests." We partner with local charities to distribute them to the greater communities around us.

Volunteerism

The entire purpose of the Ministerial Church within the Temple is to provide an outlet for community members and students to explore areas of service and possibly build their own ministries with support. All are encouraged to volunteer to the level that is appropriate for their health, age, time and talent.

Work Study Scholarships

We provide a range of options for those seeking education that might be beyond their financial means. We have scholarships and work study volunteer opportunities for those who give of their time in the Temple, or in local communities.

Mediation

A service provided to help facilitate communication within the Temple coming from our Libra ministry. Libra offers mediation service between conflicting parties. It is a part of our ministerial code. While not all situations can benefit from, or be resolved by meditation, and not all parties are open to it, the spirit of win-win conflict resolution and the ability to provide that in serious situations by trained mediators is a part of our social work within the overall Pagan community.

Inter-Faith and Intra-Faith Work

Our definition of what constitutes a Witch and Witchcraft is wide and inclusive. We welcome work with many different Pagan, Heathen, nature based and mystery based traditions, and seek common ground with traditions beyond. We support the ethical, humane, and healing work of many traditions through open dialogue and appreciate the support we have received from these traditions.

Pilgrimages

As part of the Sagittarius ministry, the Temple of Witchcraft sponsors affordable pilgrimages for members and guests to sacred sites. We've had successful retreats to Glastonbury in 2011 (including events at Stonehenge, Avebury Circle and Cadbury Castle) and Wales in 2013, with planned retreats to Scotland and Ireland as well as a return visit to Glastonbury.

New Moon Healing List

Every New Moon the Virgo ministry puts out an updated healing list of those who are seeking healing and blessing of physical, emotional, mental or spiritual ailments. Like a prayer list in other traditions, the use of the list through each cycle of the Moon gives serious practitioners in the Temple a chance to work with the monthly group, often adding their own cases to their own personal healing list as an extension. Interested people can visit the Temple of Witchcraft's website to email the healing coordinator to be placed in the list, and receive a confirmation after the first time, before the dark Moon, to confirm remaining on, or being removed, from the monthly list.

Bereavement Circle

The Scorpio ministry offers regular bereavement groups in a facilitated safe space to share grief over the loss of a loved one and receive community support to process the loss and continue with life while honoring the loved one. We also maintain ancestral altars for our Beloved Dead and Mighty Dead.

In times past, the followers of the old gods would leave offerings, plates of food, at crossroads or at city gates. Onions, garlic, and pomegranates were common. Such offerings might be dedicated to Hecate, eventually leading to the building of a Hekation, a pole with three masks at a three ways crossroad, or a small pile of stones, a Herm, representative of Hermes, god of magick and travelers. There has been a modern revival of this practice, Herms and food offerings to both of these deities, at the Dark Moon. Travelers, vagrants and wild animals, in need of support and food, would be the agents of the gods to claim such offerings, and some see this as a form of ancient world social service. In the modern age, we continue these traditions of spirit, while also directing our resources towards longer reaching solutions and cooperative efforts. While we do not neglect the magick of ritual offerings, our formal social service is a way we seek to extend the ethos of this ancient practice of offering.

CUSTOMS AND VIEWS

As a relatively new expression of Witchcraft, we are still establishing the customs and views of our culture. Nothing is set in stone. Our work is a collection of techniques. There is no requirement of belief, just an openness to experience. In those shared experiences, the culture of Witchcraft can grow. Because of our view on the paradox of tradition and modernity, we have some views that some would consider unusual in terms of Witchcraft. There is an aesthetic that develops in any Temple, and here are some developments of our own particular expression of Witchdom.

Though the modern Witchcraft movement has undoubtedly grown out of what is considered to be the British Traditional Wicca and Modern Eclectic Wicca movements, we do not place the same emphasis on gender, fertility or heterosexuality as many (but not all) who identify as Wiccan do. While we see Fertility as a mystery tradition, it is but one branch of our five fold mystery training. We are welcoming of all orientations and gender identities, and see the sacred in all those expressions of humanity and divinity. We are not an exclusive GLBTQ tradition, but one that is inclusive of heterosexuality, homosexuality, bisexuality, and pansexuality. At heart, we believe we each have a unique expression of the Principles of Polarity and Gender, and no one model fits all.

We have no rule around the use, or lack of use, of Craft Names. Some choose to take magickal names upon initiation. Some come to us with magickal names or have multiple names. Others choose to embrace their birth name. All are valid options. None are required. We do teach in our mysteries that there is power in the secret name between you and the gods, what the Egyptians call the Ren, but none should divulge that publicly. We do not use the titles of Lady or Lord for the High Priestesses and High Priests of the tradition. We see the Lady and Lord as the Great Goddess and Great God, and while we are aligned with them, we do not take such titles. If someone has been initiated into a tradition that does, we can respect that in the context of the tradition, but generally in almost all settings we simply refer to ourselves and others in social settings by our chosen, preferred first name. When in doubt, ask someone what they want to be called, and if you are not sure, we usually then focus upon legal birth names.

We are considered a "robed" tradition, in that we tend to dress up and adorn the body for rituals. Though there is no particular style requirement, we encourage people to adopt magickal dress. While both the everyday and the high ritual are spiritual, one can do ceremony in any clothes, or none at all, the developing culture encourages black as the color of ministers, priests, and priestesses. Black is of the mysteries, the darkness of the beginning and to which we return. Black absorbs all light frequencies, and draws information and power to us. Particular rituals can be adorned with specific colors, based upon the colors associated with the sabbats, planets, signs, and elements, and particular roles within a ritual might emphasize a color, but black tends to be the dominant color. We are not a skyclad tradition, meaning we do not require ritual or recreational nudity. While some specific rituals might call for it, none in a group setting are mandatory for the advancement of education or to take a leadership role.

Likewise, while anyone is free to wear anything they would like, certain accoutrements have become cultural symbols in the community.

Cord

Using a five fold system of training, we have five (some use six) cords to denote completions of a degree. The cords are loosely braided together until graduations from the fifth level. They are used as a cingulum, a tool that can both measure sacred space and be used as belt around a robe. The starting length is usually nine to thirteen feet, keeping in mind the cord length shortens with braiding. The colors are red (first degree/Witchcraft I), green (second degree/Witchcraft II), blue (third degree/Witchcraft III), yellow (fourth degree/Witchcraft IV) and black, white, violet, silver or gold (fifth degree/Witchcraft V). Those in the mystery school and graduates of the mystery school are considered "cord bearers" in the tradition.

Pentacle Pendant

In first degree initiation, one is encouraged to acquire a pentacle pendant to wear as a sign of a Witch and initiate. Many who have passed the first degree still wear a pentacle, myself included. Many who are not members of the Mystery School wear it as a sign of their path.

Pentacle Ring

Harkening back to the traditions of Pythagoras, when initiates of his mystery school would wear a ring with the pentalpha upon it, we today as Witches wear a pentacle or pentagram ring as a sign of a second degree Priestess or Priest.

Witch Bag

Some Witches will openly wear their Witch Bag, a medicine bag for tools and fetishes connecting them to their spirit allies in the shamanic traditions. Creation of such a tool is a part of our Witchcraft III work. It is often like a portable altar within a small bag. Some can easily be worn on the belt, while others are larger.

Bracelet

A bracelet is sometime worn in the fourth or more usually the fifth degree, to denote the fifth sacred tool of Inanna, the ring of power. It relates to the Temple of the Solar Plexus, and is symbolic of the sending and receiving of power, as well as the mysteries of the Left and Right Hand Paths of magick. Because of this, some make the bracelet a protective charm in function, sending and receiving energy as needed.

Breastplate

Another tool of the fifth degree teachings is the breastplate. In this case, not a true girdle or armor, but a talisman worn at the heart level, with twelve small stones, one for each of the twelve signs of the zodiac as experienced in the High Priest/ess training. It is often small and worn under the cloths. While HP/S are free to use whatever stones they feel correspond with the twelve signs, as there is a lot of discrepancies in different birthstone charts from different cultures and time periods, here is a Modern Witch's Birthstone chart used in the Temple, with some of the more popular healing and magick stones used in our practice:

Aries	Ruby/Garnet/Diamond
Taurus	Emerald/Rose Quartz

Gemini	Agate/Carnelian
Cancer	Moonstone/Pearl/Beryl
Leo	Citrine/Topaz/Diamond/Amber
Virgo	Agate/Sapphire
Libra	Peridot/Jade
Scorpio	Diamond/Obsidian/Jet
Sagittarius	Sapphire/Lapis/Turquoise
Capricorn	Onyx/Garnet/Jet
Aquarius	Opal/Aquamarine
Pisces	Amethyst/Aquamarine

Along with the zodiac stones, moldavite is another popular stone in the Temple, referencing both the celestial and terrestrial nature of our mysteries. It is a powerful tektite, some associate it with the emerald heart of the Earth, the Holy Grail, the emerald from the crown of Lumiel, and the Theosophical descent of Sanat Kumara from Venus upon the Earth as a Lord of Flame. Moldavite's greatest gift is to speed the spiritual evolution and healing process in people, bringing to light their highest good and true will, helping manifest "heaven upon Earth."

Amber & Jet Choker

Upon graduation from the Seminary, graduates are given an amber and jet choker necklace, designed upon their own measure. It is a symbol of duty and devotion to the Goddess and God. Both stones are actually fossilized organic plant matter, and traditionally a sign of a High Priestess in British Traditional Wicca. Upon guidance, I began using them personally, then with further guidance, giving them to graduates. Amber is considered solar and healing, though amber is also sacred to the Lady Freya. Jet is considered feminine and protective, but is also sacred to the gods and goddesses of the underworld. Together, they are like the living and dead, amber and jet, holding hands in a circle, showing us the intimate connection between Witches who are living and those who dwell among the Mighty Dead. We all form the circle in partnership together.

Stole

Various stoles can be created and used by Ministerial members and ordained ministers. Stoles with the sigil of a ministry denotes a Lead Minister within the Temple. Others stoles might be used for handfastings, funerals or exorcisms, as needed by the minister.

Key

While the skeleton key is a sign of connection and devotion to Hecate as the opener of gates and doors as well as a symbol of protection, in the Temple, ordained ministers are given a key at their ordination consecration, as a symbol of having the full trust and faith of the Temple leadership to "come and go freely" in their ministry within the Temple. Keys offered to Hecate in the Feast of Hecate ritual are saved and then given to ministers to wear after ordination. Some are used as jewelry, while others are placed within the Witch Bag. Do not assume anyone who wears a key at Temple events are ordained ministers. Many are simply devoted to the Queen of Witches or wearing it as a magickal charm. Those who are ordained in the Temple are considered "key bearers" in our order.

Crystal Skull

Ordained ministers approved to officially teach in the Mystery School are given the gift of a crystal skull, to help maintain communion with the spirit allies of the Temple, most specifically the enlightened ancestors of the Mighty Dead. The tradition draws its origin from my time in training in the Shamballa Reiki traditions. Crystal skulls were used by Master-Teachers as allies to help clear students and hold the space. Their creation was believed to be guided by "those upstairs," the Theosophical ascended masters. Other traditions of Witchcraft use skulls, real or fashioned from wood, clay, glass, or plaster, to facilitate ancestral contact. I was able to obtain a roughly life-sized crystal skull from Brazil that worked with me in both Reiki and other traditions and, upon establishment of the Temple proper, wanted to be included in the Temple of Witchcraft community. Though I wanted a very occult or mystical name, the consciousness of the skull insists its name is "Brad" which I later found out also means "broad or wide." Brad suggested that he opens and widens the way for those who walk the path. New skulls given to students spend an amount of time "incubating" in Brad's presence, attuning them to the work of the Temple.

All of these are magickal tools, not simply objects trying to convey a status. Each one has a magickal purpose and function, and serves as a reminder and rededication to our Craft every time we use it. Some perform specific prayers with each piece, but no prayer by rote is required. People should move as their heart, mind and will dictates.

While the Temple is not a political organization—there is no one description that would fit all members with perhaps the exception of Witch—our views collectively tend to focus on the interconnectivity of all people, and all things, seen and unseen. We believe there are no spare parts to the universe—everyone and everything can attune to their greatest self and play a role. Polarities must work in cooperation, not conflict, to move the fulcrum of the universe towards change.

We hearken to the regeneration of the Garden of the Gods, a time of acknowledged interconnection to all, tempered by Will, Love and Wisdom, guided by Power, Trust and Knowledge. Establishing that Garden within us is the personal Great Work, and establishing it all around us, where all have the freedom to be as their True Will, Perfect Love and Divine Wisdom dictates, is the communal Great Work. This naturally lends itself to cooperative models, as marked by the Aquarian Age. We explore lateral models of leadership, without wholeheartedly dismissing vertical ones. All axes exist in the third dimension of space and time. We see justice for society, the environment and the individual, and work to support others and their communities while taking care of our own needs, believing the two are not mutually exclusive. We seek the ideals of revolutionary thought and change in harmony with the turning Aeon, but realize that lasting change can come more slowly than we hope or predict.

Exchange & Support

As a modern Craft tradition both in the public eye and with very public long term goals, we believe in the concepts of balanced exchange. Sometimes this manifests as time and volunteerism, other times in financial exchange, which can be controversial to some Pagans and Witches. Many assume that if one is involved in a religious non-profit, then everything should be free. There is an assumption of unlimited assets and resources, akin to large institutions such as the Catholic Church. Yet such institutions have had both two thousand years to amass such resources, with a large and dependable congregation making weekly donations. Other religions have mandatory tithing of a certain percentage of income to gain the necessary resources.

Pagan and Witchcraft groups are small, independent and often attract those who do not have the financial resources to donate weekly or tithe. Many who flee these dominant religions still feel that all religion should be "free," and technically, no one needs to buy anything to practice their personal version of the Craft. Communities come together for mutual goals and, in our current society of currency exchange, if we want religious services, including mediation, counseling, large festivals, training, prison ministry, and hospital visits, we need to find ways to manifest those services within our community. Currently most Pagan clergy hold down traditional jobs while working to fulfill the needs of their community without a network of support

The original stipulations against payment for the Craft come from the British Traditional Wicca Book of Shadows, specifically the *ardanes,* or laws, found in the Gardnerian Book of Shadows. Such organizations were limited to thirteen members, and a paired duo of High Priestess and High Priestess to share the responsibilities of the coven. No one person was ministering to a larger group. Originally in Wicca, there was no congregation. Everyone was their own priest or priestess. While this is still true in theory, in many other forms of Paganism, Witchcraft, and Magick, we have a growing population that identifies as Pagan, wishes to take part in community, but does not want to join a coven, undergo formal training or initiation, or partake in solitary or small group rituals. They have come to enjoy and expect larger public rituals for community connection and religious experience. As this demographic grows, there are now more expectations for the organizers of such rituals and festivals to also fulfill the role played by clergy in other religions, yet the resources are usually not there for these ministers to work full-time for their community. The Temple of Witchcraft was founded as a legal organization to address some of these challenges in our own community.

While the ardanes prohibiting money exchanging in British Traditional Wicca might be appropriate for that time and tradition, it might be preventing us from larger community goals of retreats, land, buildings, and more intentional communities. I don't think Gerald Gardner ever envisioned Wicca as being a part of large festivals and public gatherings, despite his desire to publicize and promote the Craft. Most involved in the early British Occults and Wiccan movements were part of the British middle and upper class, with funds to travel the world, research, and write. While some worked, their daily life was not the same work week we recognize today in America. Subsequent elders in the movement without the same resources, yet saddled with the same laws, such as Alex Sanders, often lived impoverished lives due to their full-time dedication to the Craft and the lack of compensation for their time and work.

British Traditional Wicca was exclusively a minister tradition to train clergy for the clergy, usually not performing acts for the general public. That ethos most likely began with the healing clinics put on by Alex and Maxine Sanders and certainly grew with the introduction of British Traditional Wicca into America. One high ranking British priestess at the core of the movement told me that the Craft in her day had certain standards, and looking around an American festival with me, she said more than half the people gathered would not pass her standards to be trained or initiated. People would be turned away for both physical and psychological handicaps. The Celtic concept of the "perfect king" unblemished was taken seriously, so some missing a limb, or even the limited use of the limb would be deemed unfit in this life. Anyone with any of the modern mental and biochemical illnesses, even if controlled by medication, would be deemed unfit. This priestess also told me those who marked their bodies, as with tattoos, despite ancient tribal associations, would not be acceptable for the Craft in her day, but she allows them now as times have changed.

Homosexuals and transsexuals, until fairly recently, were considered unfit, or at the very least had to "act straight" in circle to be considered eligible. Some lines of British Traditional Wicca still consider homosexuals and transsexuals unfit and unwelcome, focusing on the literal definition of the fertility mysteries, despite Gardner having no children of his own. Many do not recognize same gender initiations, homosexual or otherwise, even though Wiccan founder Alex Sanders was known to initiate in this way in the later years of his life. Anyone obese and unfit, defined as someone who could not climb or hike with the normal pace of the group, would also be declared unsuitable, a particular difficulty for the modern American Wicca movement. Anyone could worship the Goddess and God, but they would not be Wiccan, and would not be initiated. British Traditional Wicca, while embracing of many aspects shunned by Christian society, certainly was not a tradition for all people. Like the ancient mystery schools, it turned away more people than it accepted, and the clergy were not expected to then minister to those who were turned away.

Prior to the revival of Witchcraft through the work of Gerald Gardner, one strong archetype of the Witch was as cunning man or cunning woman of the village. Modern Paganism has latched onto this image, in contrast with the Christian image of the diabolical Witch. The Cunning Man would always require compensation for services—be it advice, divination, spells, or charms. Mainstream religious events in the post-Christian era would be handled by the priest from the Church, and weekly donations would be made for those services when needed, but the Witch would be paid on a case by case basis. The exchange was for service. Perhaps it was not always coin, but bread, chickens, milk, or cheese, as the currency of exchange. It was the same in the ancient world. Ancient Pagan priestesses and priests expected payment in the form of donations (and unlike today, were taxed by the state for their Temple) and the rural Witch of the crossroads got other forms of payment, but in each case there was compensation.

My own original experience in the Craft was very professional and required compensation. I took formal classes in Witchcraft by a professional teacher, an expert in her field, and was charged for those classes. There was a clear agreement. This is the class. These are the times. These are the topics. This is what you should learn by the time you leave. This is the price. With that agreement in mind, the obligations on both sides were fulfilled. Unlike some British Traditional Wiccan coven structures that have messy, unconscious family dynamics involved, the teacher did not play the role of a family member. No loyalty or oath was demanded from me any more than from my college professors and music teachers. I was paying fairly for a service and got what I was promised. Even joining a tradition, the ideal was to uphold the values of the tradition and do its work, not blind or unthinking loyalty to an individual founder or teacher. Initiation meant adulthood and equality, and the ability to disagree.

This does not mean that free resources are not available in our community. While the Temple of Witchcraft does offer many free, or open donation programs, there are great resources available online, and surprisingly many books available through inter-library loan programs. Forums, message boards, personal peer and mentor relationships can develop through the internet. Many podcasts, online radio shows and educational platforms offer free or discounted materials. In truth, anyone with an open heart, mind and an understanding of the basics can commune directly with the spirits and nature, to receive a balanced education the path. Yet this is different from expecting participation in established community or creating community, without investing time, resources, and support. Sometimes the first stage of the work is finding the appropriate community whose goals align with your own, willing to support your development on the path. There are many expressions of Pagan, Wiccan and Witchcraft community, and not all are alike.

The Temple of Witchcraft community models the structure of fair and equal exchange. We are always looking for ways to fairly compensate those who are working as professionals in our community, as part of the "fairly take and fairly give" of the Wiccan Rede. While we have many scholarship and work study volunteer programs for many events to aid those in genuine need, generally our process is one of fair payment in the currency of the land. Like the old Strega traditions, "Something must be given to be received and something must be received to be given."

We believe the next step is professional paid clergy, and while none of our clergy makes a full-time salary at this time, they make a percentage of what they bring in as independent contractors. Our expenses are covered and professionals with expertise are compensated for that expertise. This includes teachers, celebrants, and spiritual counselors who use esoteric healing and divination. If the service does not have an exchange mechanism and is offered freely, then the minister is not compensated. All Board of Directors, Council Lead Ministers, and Deputy Ministers are strictly unpaid volunteer positions in the Temple.

We take a professional business approach, working with those experienced in mainstream business, finance, leadership, and real estate, to make effective goals and the plans to reach them. While we believe in the power of magick, we also believe intention must be followed by real world action. This system encourages ministers to gain the training they need, in and outside of the Temple, to deepen their professional skills while also building collective Temple resources. These resources can then be used towards our long term community goals of permanent spaces, sanctuaries, and structures, with appropriate social and spiritual services, across America and the world.

Thickening the Witch Blood

A controversial thought amongst traditional and modern Witches is the concept of the "Witchblood." Some think of it as a literal genetic connection. One is or isn't, based upon some seemingly nebulous genetic factor. Witchcraft had to be somewhere in your family tree. Others see it as a spiritual component, with legends of the first Witches as the children of divinities, angels, or faeries. Many teachers of the blood think that we all have the potential of the blood. We are all from a Pagan ancestry if you go back far enough, even apparent monotheists such as the Hebrews. We simply have to awaken the light within the blood and let it shine. Our practices that are of an initiatory nature are what wake up the light within our blood.

After a public invocation of the Horned Witch God through temple founder Steve Kenson, we were given indication from the God to "thicken" the Witchblood. Many seek the title of Witch, but do not treat it as a vocation, a school for the soul, or a society with standards and practices. While anyone can call themselves a Witch, not everyone is. Many are simply seeking and don't know how to go deep into the mysteries, so we seek to help thicken the blood as instructed by the God, by making practitioners as conscious and deep in their practices as possible. This practice is what distills our essence within, and those who are not truly called to the Craft will be able to see Witchcraft as one stop on a larger healing or questing journey. Hopefully we can instruct such people, but our groves and temples are not where they will put down their roots. We wish them well and nurture them with our ways when they are in the garden, but also wish them well when they leave, making room for others.

One of the most important aspects of the Temple culture is another paradox, for the real experience is found in the paradox. This is the paradox between structure and fluidity. We seek to have a container in which people can understand, heal, and express themselves safely, but a dynamic that will allow the container to organically grow and change. We don't want anything to remain static, we want development in a balanced and reasoned manner. While we have structure, for every guideline or rule we have, we also have the potential to make an exception, adapt, or change it as circumstances arise. Magick is ultimately an act of communication, so a key teaching within the Temple is communication. Sometimes it is easy and clear. Other times it is difficult, but at all times it is essential to the well being of any community, and in particular a magickal community.

We encourage those in the Temple to stand between, asking their questions and seeking their own answers, finding their own truths. Teachers and community can point the way, but there is no one way that is right for all. For things to grow and develop, one must have a fidelity to the past foundations while having a willingness to build upon those foundations and remove the parts that no longer serve. Two reminders of this self-seeking have come up in the Temple culture. Our first Dean of Students, Rama Danu, mishearing me, thought my answer to a question she posed was "Ask the salt." She created a divination system with a symbol for "salt" and the earthy knowledge of this common crystal. That phrase, along with my often typical answer to any question, "Have you meditated on that?" have become common refrains in the Temple.

The ethos of seeking your own truth is encoded in the fourth degree teachings of the Temple Mystery School. In the tradition of occultists before us, seekers are encouraged to create their own "Reality Map" or magickal model and system, based upon their own experiences, understanding, and interests. While the Qabalistic Tree of Life is used as the model for a primary reality map, creativity is encouraged in the completion of the degree. Such a model of the universe is said to be the initiatory work of a Major Adept in the original Golden Dawn system of magick, but here we get some practice with the idea before ever claiming such a title. Just as the founders and leaders of the Temple have developed their own teachings and systems, even if only for personal practice, individuals within the Temple are encouraged to do the same. Systems, lore, and paradigm are always stressed over dogma and orthodoxies.

The Temple of Witchcraft is an open-ended system. We do not claim to have all the answers or a patent on the mysteries. We readily accept tested and true wisdom from different traditions, cultures and points of view as a corroboration and compliment to what we are already doing. We are ready to share our experiences and techniques in the Age of Light and encourage people to use them as they are guided.

We see our own additions to the Craft as a whole as part of its revivification and welcome the influx of new energies, ideas and experiences when we need them. Without this rejuvenation, a system and tradition grows slow and stagnant, calcifies and will become useless. We must work with the only constant in the universe, beautifully embodied in the turning of the Wheel, and that constant is change. One only needs to look at the Catholic Church in its current form as an example of such calcification. Their attempt at revivification with Vatican II council was too little too late. The magick flows away and into other expressions of the Christian tradition, often the more mystical.

We are advocates of what the magician and mystic Dion Fortune referred to as "the three fold way." When looking at divinity, we can't hope to understand it from just one perspective. A grounded, educated, and experienced triple perspective gives a clearer view. One could maintain a core practice but be informed by other systems of practice. Dion herself was a Hermetic mage, but also deeply devoted to her Christianity. She saw British Paganism, particularly the period of King Arthur, as a bridge between these two, modeling her own triple way. In my own practice, while my root has always been Witchcraft, I've delved deeply into what I consider occultism, including Hermetic Magick, Qabalah, and Alchemy. For my third path, what began as a journey into lightwork and ascension practices of the New Age, led me to Theosophy and the mysteries of India and Tibet, particularly expressed in the practice of yoga.

We encourage members to take a break from Temple studies, or after graduation, seek out other traditions, trainings, and teachers and explore. Sometimes the experience will lead you away, as your heart and will call you elsewhere and we are happy to be a stop on your journey. Many come to us for healing tools, and then turn their attention elsewhere. As a tradition of healing, we consider this a great service and honor. For others, the experience away enriches their understanding and appreciation of Witchcraft, and the Temple community. They are then more effective in their work with us. I know my own depth of Craft practice was greatly benefited from the synthesis of other views and philosophies.

Being at heart a scavenger religion, with the totems of crows, ravens, vultures, owls, wolves, coyotes, jackals, and bears guiding us, we seek to integrate the wisdom that others might leave behind, and find beauty and wisdom in the strangest places. We don't simply collect it, but we integrate it into the Great Work of the Witch.

Our gods are the gods of the crossroads, the gateways, the in-between places. We connect the seen and unseen. We connect the known and unknown. We are found in the heart of paradox and we are here to serve a particular purpose in the evolution of the Earth and all her children. Rise up and lead with magick in your heart, mind, body and souls. Blessed be.

[1] ATC. *The Other People.* Pathfinder Press Publications. Kelmscot, WA: 1994.

APPENDIX ONE: BIRTH CHART OF THE TEMPLE

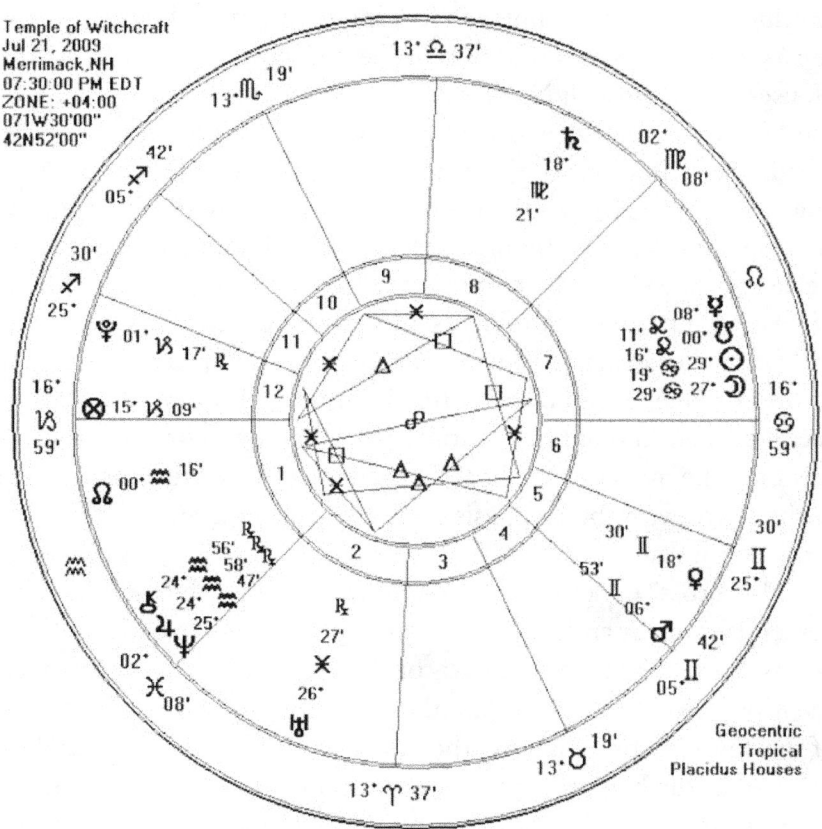

Birth Chart of the Temple of Witchcraft

The official Birth Chart of the Temple, the signing of the founding documents, occurred on July 21st, 2009, at roughly 7:30 PM in Merrimack, New Hampshire. This yields an organization with the energies of Cancer Sun Sign, Cancer Moon Sign and Capricorn Rising Sign, also known as the Ascendant. With this primary triad of the organization's natal chart, there is already a strong connection to the Goddess of the Moon through Cancer, and the Horned God, through Capricorn rising.

In terms of the balance of the astrological mandala, there is an emphasis of energy on the Western Hemisphere, Houses Four through Nine, indicating our relationships and interactions with others are of great importance, from individual relationships, to relating with the entire human race, and in our case, the races of spirits with whom we work. Out of the quadrants, the third quadrant, Houses Seven through Nine, is emphasized, with both the Sun and the Moon present. Objective and public relationships are a key trait of this chart. In terms of the elements, due to the influence of the Sun and Moon, water is dominant, though there are many planets in air signs. Emotion and thought are key words for our work. Fire is the weakest of the elements in the chart. According to the philosophies of Eastern influenced astrologers, including Christopher's teacher and the former co-owner of Unicorn Books, Jan Brink, places of "lack" in terms of elements and houses often indicate past life work accomplished, and not necessarily a place of growth or challenge in this life. The modes of cardinal, fixed, and mutable are fairly balanced in the chart, with the emphasis on cardinal signs, again due to the influence of Cancer.

The "cross" or "tree" of the chart, the union of the ascendant, descendant, nadir and midheaven, or east, west, north and south points respectively, create an axis of the Horned God (Capricorn) and the Moon Goddess (Cancer) on the east-west line, with the mysteries of the Taurus/Scorpio axis on the north-south line. There we find the energies of the holidays of Beltane and Samhain, key turning points in our tradition of life and death, as well as the Bull God ruled by the Lady of Love, Pleasure and Flowery Enchantments with the Guardian of the powers of Sex and Death. Around the wheel of Houses, we have Aquarius and Leo intercepted by the First and Seventh house, showing the areas of greatest karmic work – aquarian ideals of community to better know ourselves, creativity and artistic expression to better know others, and a repeat of the signs Gemini ruling the Fifth and Sixth House, and Sagittarius, ruling the Eleventh and Twelfth House, where communication, education and philosophy are emphasized.

The three outer planets (Uranus, Neptune and Pluto), along with Jupiter, Chiron and the North Node of the Moon are all retrograde, showing that deep reflection upon the past is a part of the greater spiritual mission, while most of the personal planets are direct, demonstrating a power to get things done in the world.

A deeper and more detailed analysis of the forces invoked in the "birth" of our Temple can be done by experienced astrologers, this snapshot gives members an understanding of the mission, powers and challenges in the Temple's astrological mandala. Like any relationship, our own personal birth charts interact with that of the group consciousness of the Temple. Use this information to better understand your own relationship and role in the Temple if you choose to participate in our Work.

Special thanks to Karen Laporte for astrological consultation.

Appendix Two: Articles of Incorporation

Temple of Witchcraft – Articles of Agreement

THE UNDERSIGNED, BEING PERSONS OF LAWFUL AGE, ASSOCIATE UNDER THE PROVISIONS OF THE NEW HAMPSHIRE REVISED STATUTES ANNOTATED, CHAPTER 292 BY THE FOLLOWING ARTICLES:

Article I

The name of the corporation shall be:

The exact name of the incorporated religious organization is "The Temple of Witchcraft," a nonprofit corporation, herein after known as the "Organization" within this document.

Article II

The object for which this corporation is established is:

The mission and purpose of the Organization shall be to aid the training of practitioners and clergy in the religious and spiritual traditions of Witchcraft, Wicca, Paganism, Heathenism and other Earth based traditions. We shall encourage, publish and teach these traditions and the arts associated with them. Further our organization shall provide a place where both public and private events may occur in accordance with our mission. Such events that will be included in our mission shall be educational workshops, classes, seasonal and astrological celebrations, rites of passage, spiritual guidance, interfaith outreach and community building events. Our focus shall be on the Spiritual Arts and Sciences, along with the personal and community development that occurs through such arts and sciences. The study of the aforementioned traditions includes; the study of mythology, culture, healing and mysticism.

The Temple of Witchcraft, as an organization wishes to incorporate as a religious, educational, cultural, nonprofit, which shall be organized exclusively for charitable, religious, educational purposes, including, for such purposes, the making of distributions to organizations that qualify as exempt organizations under section 501(c)(3) of the Internal Revenue Code, or the corresponding section of any future federal tax code.

We shall provide these services through our organization and from time to time with other spiritually based organizations that share our similar philosophies. Our aim is the regeneration and advancement of the rich cultural, philosophical and religious heritage drawn from the related traditions of Witchcraft and Earth-based spiritual paths. We will also strive to provide to the public and the media accurate and concise information about Witchcraft and related Earth-based traditions.

Our organizational direction shall be guided by a Board of Directors who wish to contribute to the education, growth and evolution of our Community. To better serve the community, we seek to incorporate as a nonprofit religious, educational and cultural organization in the State of New Hampshire.

Article III

The provisions for establishing membership and participation in the corporation are:

Membership classes will be divided into four classes, defined as General, Honored, Ministerial and Founder. There are no set membership fees; therefore the classes of membership are divided by levels of training in the Organization and not by membership dues paid. General members are those who attend at least three public Organization functions, including rituals, workshops or other gatherings of the Organization. Honored members must make a commitment to formal training in the Organization by enrolling in and completing classes within the training program of the Organization. Ministerial members must complete all the required courses of Honored Membership, specifically Level Programs One through Four and must be currently enrolled in or be a graduate of the seminary of the Organization. Founder members will be named by the Incorporators upon incorporation and Founder members, or the successors of the three original founders, will help oversee the organization. Only Ministerial and Founding members may serve on the Board of Directors of the Organization. Only members upon the Board of Directors shall be voting members.

Article IV

Provisions for Dissolution:

The provisions for disposition of the corporate assets in the event of dissolution of the corporation including the prioritization of rights of shareholders and members to corporate assets are:

Upon the dissolution of the Organization, the Board of Directors shall, after paying or making provision for or the payment of all liabilities of the Organization, distribute the assets for one or more exemption exclusively for the purpose of the Organization in such manner or to such organization or organizations organized and operated exclusively for charitable, educations, religious or scientific purposes as shall at any time qualify as an exempt organization or organizations under Section 501(c)(3) of the Internal Revenue Code of 1986, or corresponding section of any future federal tax code, or shall be distributed to the federal government or to a state or local government, for a public purpose.

Article V

The address at which the business of this corporation is to be carried on is:

The information found in Article V is not a permanent part of the Articles of Agreement.

The address of the principle office of the Organization in New Hampshire is:

Temple of Witchcraft, 49 North Policy Street, Salem, NH 03079

Article VI

Capitol Stock

The amount of capital stock, if any, or the number of shares or membership certificates, if any, and provisions for retirement, reacquisition and redemption of those shares or certificates are:

The Organization shall have no capital stock and shall have no authority to issue shares.

Article VII

Board of Directors

Signatures and post office address of each of the persons associating together to form the corporation:

The affairs of the Organization shall be managed by the Board of Directors. The initial members shall consist of the five (5) incorporators and such other persons as may be chosen by them, all in a manner not inconsistent with these Articles of Agreement, the Code and with the provisions of N.H. RSA 292, as amended.

Article VIII

Provision eliminating or limiting the personal liability of a director, an officer or both, to the corporation or its shareholders for monetary damages for breach of fiduciary duty as a director, an officer or both is:

The Directors and Officer(s) of the Organization shall not be held personally liable for any debt, liability or obligation of the Organization. To the fullest extent now or hereafter permitted by law, no Director or Officer(s) shall be personally liable to the Organization or its members for any monetary damages for breach of their fiduciary duties as an officer(s), so long as those officer(s) and director(s) do not breach their duty of loyalty, act in bad faith, intentionally violate the law, or derive improper personal benefits from the activities of the Organization.

Article IX

General Provisions

1. No part of the net earnings of the Organization shall inure to the benefit of, or be distributable to its members, trustees, officers or other private persons, except that the Organization shall be authorized and empowered to pay reasonable compensation for services rendered and to make payment and distribution in furtherance of the purposes set forth in Article II hereof.

2. No substantial part of the activities of the Organization shall be the carrying on of propaganda, or otherwise attempting to influence legislation, and the Organization shall not participate in, or intervene in (including the publishing or distribution of statements) any political campaign on behalf of any candidate for public office.

3. Notwithstanding any other provisions of these Articles, the Organization shall not carry on any other activities not permitted to be carried on (a) by a corporation exempt from federal income tax under section 501(c)(3) of the Code, or corresponding section of any future federal tax code, or (b) by a corporation, contributions to which are deductible under section 170(c)(2) of the Code, or corresponding section of any future federal tax code.

Article X
Amendments

These Article of Agreement for the Organization may be amended or repealed at any meeting of the Board by a majority vote of the Board; provided however, that written notice of the proposed change shall be specified in the notice of the meeting, and provided further that no such action shall be taken, or if taken, shall be a valid act of the Organization, if that action would in any way adversely affect the Organization's qualification under Section 501(c)(3) of the Code.

Article XI
Incorporators

The signatures and post office addresses of each of the persons associating together to form the Organization are set forth below.

Christopher Penczak
Stephen Kenson
Adam Sartwell
Michelle Wright
Jocelyn Van Bokkelen
Mary Hurley

APPENDIX THREE: TEMPLE BY-LAWS

By-Laws of the Temple of Witchcraft

Article I: Name

The exact name of the incorporated religious/educational/cultural organization is "The Temple of Witchcraft," herein known as the "Organization". It shall be a non-profit corporation organized pursuant to NH RSA Chapter 292.

Article II: Offices

The principal office of the Organization shall be located in the State of New Hampshire. The Organization may have such other offices, either in or outside of the State of New Hampshire, as the Board of Directors may designate or as the business of the Organization may from time to time require.

Article III: Incorporators

Section 1. Meeting of Incorporators

There shall be a meeting of the Incorporators, upon filing the Articles of Agreement with the State of New Hampshire. The Incorporators shall act to appoint a Board of Directors for the Organization.

Section 2. Notice of Meeting

Written or printed notice stating the place, day and time of the meeting and, in the case of special meetings, the purpose or purposes for which the meeting is called shall be delivered not less than five (5) nor more than thirty (30) days before the date of the meeting, either personally or by postal or electronic mail by or at the direction of the President, the Secretary, or the Officer or persons calling the meeting, to each Incorporator.

Article IV: Membership

The Organization shall have four classes of membership, defined as General, Honored, Ministerial, and Founder:

Section 1. General Requirements

There are no set membership fees; therefore the classes of members are divided by where they are in their training in the Organization and not by membership dues paid.

All members of the Organization are required to follow and agree to all requirements set forth by the classifications of membership in addition to their specific duties.

All members of the Organization should have read the articles of agreement and By-Laws as established by the Organization and agree to further support the Organization's mission and policies. This includes all other written or published documents put out by the Organization and its Directors.

- Membership must fall under one of these four categories: General, Honored, Ministerial or Founder.
- Members must be no less than eighteen (18) years of age, or have written consent of a parent or legal guardian. This membership is open to anyone who identifies with practicing an Earth-based spiritual tradition or seeks to know more about and explore such traditions.

Section 2. General Membership

General members are those who attend at least three public Organization functions, including rituals, workshops or other gatherings of the Organization.

General members need not make a specific commitment to formal education by the Organization and need not be a part of any of the Organization's training program.

General members are welcome to attend any public event but shall not attend private events of the Organization without being a member of one of the following membership classes: Honored, Ministerial, Founder.

General members are non-voting members.

Section 3. Honored Membership

Honored members must make a commitment to formal education by the Organization by enrolling in and completing classes within the educational program of the Organization.

Honored members must currently be enrolled in one or more courses or training programs with the Organization, or must be graduates of any of the training programs, or must be given an honorary certificate or degree for Honored Membership by the Board in recognition of previous training, experience, or community service.

Honored members may serve on committees associated with the ministries of the Organization.

Honored members are non-voting members

Section 4. Ministerial Membership

Ministerial members must complete all the required courses of Honored Membership, specifically Degree Programs One through Four and must be currently enrolled in or be a graduate of the seminary of the Organization.

Ministerial members shall support the Organization through donations, time, and energy which shall be devoted to furthering the Organization and its purpose.

Ministerial members may serve on or lead any of the committees associated with the ministries of the Organization.

Under special circumstances the Organization at its discretion, may give an honorary certificate or degree for Ministerial Membership in recognition of previous training, experience, or community service.

Ministerial members may serve on the Board of Directors.

Ministerial members are non-voting members.

Section 5. Founder Membership

Founder members (hereinafter "Founders") are the three founders of the Organization or their successors.

There shall be no more or less than three (3) Founders of the Organization. Membership as a Founder is for life or until the Founder chooses to retire or is removed for a material breach of their fiduciary duties.

Foundations of the Temple

Upon the death, retirement or removal of a Founder, membership shall be limited to the remaining Founders unless and until the surviving Founder(s) unanimously agree to nominate and appoint a successor. If, for some reason, all of the Founders are unable to serve and cannot nominate their successors, the Board shall appoint new Founders by unanimous vote.

Founders may serve on or chair any of the committees associated with ministries of the Organization.

Founders may serve on the Board of Directors.

Section 6. Resignation from the Organization

Members of the General Membership may resign at any time with or without documentation of their intent to resign. Any member in the classification of Honored, Ministerial, Founder who is in good standing may resign the Organization at any time provided the member submits a letter of resignation to the Secretary of the Board which should include resignation from any titles, offices, or positions of authority. The resignation shall be effective 30 days from the date of submission.

No membership fees, class tuitions or donations will be returned, reimbursed or prorated at any time for any reason. Any members who resign in good standing may reapply for membership at any time by submitting a letter to the Board stating their intention to rejoin the Organization. Application for membership must be approved by the Board, but acceptance does not include reinstatement in any previous titles, offices or positions or authority.

Section 7. Refusal and Termination of Membership

The Board may refuse membership to any individual it deems is not suitable to the nature, spirit, and purpose of the Organization by a majority vote. Members who have been previously denied, revoked, or terminated by the Board may reapply after ninety (90) days, but will be subject to the approval of the majority of the Board. The Board may determine which members will or will not be reinstated by its own discretion and authority. The Board and the Founders reserve the right to deny any member who has been previously removed from the Organization by majority vote of the Board.

Article V: Board of Directors

Section 1. General

The Board of Directors (hereinafter "the Board") shall consist of at least five (5) and not more than seven (7) officers. Those officers shall include: The President, Vice President, Secretary, Treasurer, and Board Advisor. The Organization's incorporators shall select and appoint the initial Board by unanimous vote. When the term of any Director is about to expire, the vacancy shall be filed by a 2/3 majority vote of the Board at the annual meeting after consultation with an ad hoc nominating committee of no less than three Honored or Ministerial Members in good standing chosen by the Board to recommend the nominated parties. The individual officers of the existing Board shall continue to serve until the remaining officers appoint a successor or until an officer is unable or unwilling to serve or is removed from office. Officers shall serve a term of two years, at which time re-elections will take place.

Section 2. Control and Power

The Board shall have the control and power to manage the activities, property and affairs of the Organization and shall determine the manner in which the funds of the Organization, both principle and income, shall be applied, within the limitations of the Organization's Articles of Agreement, these By-Laws, the Code and Chapter 292 of the New Hampshire Revised Statues Annotated. Prior to taking any action that is considered outside of (normal care) of the Organization the Board will submit all plans for final approval to the Founders. The Founders shall have the right to approve or deny the Board's proposal. If the Founders reject the Board's proposal, the board may revise their proposal and resubmit it to the Founders for review, at which time the Founders may again approve or deny the proposal.

Section 3. Meetings

The annual meeting of the Board shall be held at such place and time as determined by the Board in the month of November. Regular and special meetings of the Board, shall be called by the President or at the request of two-thirds (2/3) of the membership of the Board and shall be held at such time and place as may be set forth in the notice thereof, provided that at least five (5) days advance notice, in writing, by post or electronic delivery of every meeting shall be given to each officer.

Special meetings of the Board and chairs of the committees may be called from time to time by the Board of Directors as deemed necessary. In this case the Board will notify the committee chairs at least five (5) days in advance of the meeting by means of electronic delivery, in writing. Such notices shall be sent to the addresses shown on the records of the Organization. Any committee chair may waive notice of a meeting by an instrument in writing filed with the records of the meeting or attendance at the meeting without protest.

At all meetings of the Board, a majority of the officers shall constitute a quorum for the transaction of business. At any meeting at which a quorum is not present, the officers present may adjourn the meeting, without notice other than announcement, until such a time as a quorum can be present or available.

Section 4. Committees

Committees may be formed and disbanded at the discretion the Board to further the Organization and its purpose. The Board may designate one (1) or more standing committees by resolution(s) passed by a majority of the Board. Such committee(s) shall consist of one (1) or more Honored or Ministerial Members or officers or Founders and shall have such powers and duties as the Board deems necessary to carry out the functions of the specified committee. Ad hoc committees will disband after they have completed their intended purpose or when the Board votes to disband the committee. Committees will function directly at the discretion of the Board of Directors and may not act as a separate entity for the Organization nor act as a promoting representative of the Organization.

Section 5. Removal

If an Officer is determined by the Board and/or Founders to be unwilling, unable or otherwise unfit to perform the functions of their position, the Board shall convene to discuss the action to be taken against said Officer in question. Should the Board decide by 2/3rd majority vote to remove said Officer from their position on the

Board, the Board must submit its decision to the Founders for their approval. If the Founders approve of the removal, the said Officer shall be removed from the Board and return to having a full member status unless the Board and /or Founders terminate the membership as well as removing the Officer from the Board. An Officer may also be removed by a unanimous vote of the Founders should the Founders determine the Officer be unwilling, unable or otherwise unfit to perform their assigned duties.

Section 6. Resignation

Any officer may resign at any time by giving written notice to the President or the Secretary of the Board. Any such notice shall take effect as of the date of the receipt of such notice or at any later time specified herein. Resignation from the Board does not automatically imply the officer will also be terminating membership in the Organization. A separate notification must be filed if termination of membership is also the intention of the Officer resigning. Any Ministerial Member in good standing who has served on the Board in the past can be nominated in the future to a Board position.

Section 7. Vacancies

If the position of any Officer shall become vacant by reason of death, resignation, disability, retirement, disqualification, removal from office or for other cause, a Founder shall fill the vacancy until such a time as a replacement can be found for the said position or until the position's term has expired. The remaining Officers of the Board, even if less than a quorum, shall elect a successor(s) for the unexpired term of the Officer. A special meeting may be called for this purpose if the Board deems it necessary or if the Board is below quorum due to the leave of said officer(s). Any Officer may nominate a replacement. That replacement shall take office, so long as there is a majority vote of the Board and approval of the Founders to ratify.

Section 8. Compensation and Reimbursement

No part of the net earnings of the Organization shall inure to the benefit of, or be distributable to its Trustees, Directors, Officers, Members, or other private persons or organizations, except that the Board shall be authorized and empowered to pay reasonable compensation for services rendered, reimburse those Trustees, officers and members who have spent personal funds for purchases authorized by the Board and to make payments and distributions in furtherance of the purposes of the Organization. The Board shall hire and fix the compensation of any and all employees that they, at their discretion, determine to be necessary for the conduct of the business of the Organization. Applications for any position shall be brought before the Board. If deemed necessary, the Board shall conduct interviews for such positions and approve of individuals by a majority vote. The Organization is an equal opportunity employer. Qualified applicants are considered for employment without regard to age, race, color, religion, sex, national origin, sexual orientation, disability, or veteran status.

Article VI: Officers

Section 1. General Board Requirements

The Organization shall have as executive officers a President, Vice President, a Secretary, a Treasurer, and a Board Advisor each of whom shall be appointed by the Incorporators and shall serve an initial term of two years, but may serve an unlimited number of terms. Executive officers must be members of the Ministry Class of membership or be an Honorary Ministry Member in good standing of the Organization. The initial Board of Directors will serve a five (5) year term in order to establish the Organization.

Section 1. The Founders

The Founders (3) serve an indefinite term of office. The Founders may only be replaced once a Founder has died, stepped down or been removed from his/her position. The Founders will be appointed by the Incorporators during the Board Selection Process. The Founders serve the purpose of overseeing the activities of the Organization and the Board of Directors. They will hold the original vision and purpose of the Organization and aid the Board of Directors in furthering its growth. The Founders are Ministry Members and may serve on the Board in addition to serving in their position as Founders. The Founders do not have a vote during any meeting of the Board of Directors, unless they hold a specified seat in the Board. They will oversee the Board of Directors and give them guidance as to the direction of the Organization and its activities.

Section 2. President

The Board shall elect the President. The President shall preside over meetings of the Board of Directors and shall be responsible for the agenda and general conduct of such meetings. The President will represent the Organization at local, civic, and community activities that require the Organization's presence. The President shall be responsible for overseeing the Organization's activities, the activities of the Board of Directors and the Organization as a whole. This person should be focused on the purpose, goal and overall vision of the Organization. The President should possess good people skills, the ability to speak in public, demonstrate a clear mindedness and organizational skills, and be able to conduct the business of meetings. The President should be an upstanding leader in the Organization and its community. Persons who hold this office are required to be a Ministerial member and may or may not also hold the position of Founder.

Section 3. Vice President

The Board shall elect the Vice President. The Vice President shall preside over meetings in which the President cannot be present, so long as a quorum can be met. The Vice President shall assist the President in the representation of the Organization at local, civic and community activities. The Vice President shall assist in the activities of the Board of the Directors and the Organization as a whole. This person should be focused on the purpose, goal and overall vision of the Organization. The Vice President should possess good people skills, the ability to speak in public, demonstrate a clear mindedness and organizational skills, and be able to conduct the business of meetings. In addition to these skills they should be able to oversee the committees of the ministry, and other classes, events, seminars, fundraising events and celebrations. The Vice President shall be an upstanding leader in the Organization and its community. Persons who hold this office are required to be a Ministerial member and may or may not also hold the position of Founder.

Section 4. Secretary

The Secretary of the Organization shall be elected by the Board and shall be responsible for keeping the minutes and records of the Organization, insure that all notices are given in accordance with these By-Laws or as provided by law, keep the Seal of the Corporation and affix the same to corporate documents, and in general, perform all duties incidental to the office of Secretary and such other duties as may be assigned by the President or the Board. The Secretary should show excellent organizational skills, the ability to communicate clearly in the medium of writing, and should be able to keep complete, accurate and concise notes on all actions taken during meetings and other important events held by the Organization. Additionally, this person may be in charge of press releases and other informative media. Persons who hold this office are required to be a Ministerial member and may or may not also hold the position of Founder.

Section 5. Treasurer

The Treasurer shall be elected by the Board and shall be responsible to keep correct and complete records of account; accurately showing at all times the financial condition of the Organization. Subject to the direction of the Board, the Treasurer shall be the legal custodian of all funds of the Organization, shall keep a detailed account of its income and expenditures, and shall be responsible for payment of all expenditures of the Organization, including accounts payable and the preparation of tax documents and documentation. The Treasurer shall be responsible for the creation and filing of all corporate documents required by the local, state and federal governments. The Treasurer shall also provide an annual report on November 1st of each year on the current state of the Organization's funds. This person should show exceptional attention to detail, have a history of working with monetary distribution and tracking and have exceptional organizational skills. The Treasurer should be available for events and other organizational functions that require the dispersing and collection of funds or be able to designate someone to be in charge of these duties. Persons who hold this office are required to be a Ministerial member and may or may not also hold the position of Founder.

Section 6. Advisor to the Board

Advisory Director is elected by the Board and shall serve as an ambassador(s) of the Board to the Organization and to the general public when necessary. Their duties include advising the Board of the progress and any situations that may arise in the above mentioned committees or membership groups, overseeing committees and their functions, bringing ideas or suggestions from the above mentioned committees or membership groups to the Board for consideration, and in general, to advise the Board of Directors of the Organization's overall development. These advisors should show an ability to mediate, an enthusiasm for being active in their community as well as serving on the Board, and an ability to rationalize things from a multi-dimensional perspective. Persons who hold this office are required to be Ministerial members and may or may not also hold the position of Founder.

Article VII: Elections

Section 1. General

Elections will be held every other October (because the Board meeting and hand off is in November) after the established filing date of the Organization or every other consecutive year in order to nominate and establish a new Board of Directors. Officers will be notified five (5) days prior to the electoral meeting. At this time the nominating committee will present the candidates and a secret ballot vote will be taken to elect the new members of the Board by existing officers. This meeting will happen on or before October 31st of the election year.

Section 2. Nomination Committee

The nominating committee, consisting of no less than three Honored or Ministerial Members in good standing, will be chosen by the Board of Directors. The purpose of the nominating committee will be to locate, interview and nominate qualified candidates for the open positions on the Board of Directors on or before October of the election year. If a current member of the Board is running for re-election they too will be interviewed and reviewed by the nominating committee. The nominating committee shall then present the nominated individuals for election during the electoral meeting. The nominating committee may seek the advice and council of the Founders during their deliberation.

Section 3. Nominations for Election

Those wishing to be nominated for a seat on the Board must submit to the Nomination committee a list of qualifications, a letter of intent to serve on the Board, and 3 references. Members of the existing Board seeking re-election shall submit a letter to the nominating Board stating their intent. The nominating committee must then interview, review and qualify the candidates and pick the three best candidates for each seat on the Board. There may be no more than three (3) but no less than one (1) candidate(s) chosen for the election to each board seat during the electoral meeting.

Section 4. Electoral Meeting of the Membership

An electoral meeting shall be held every other October after the filing date of the Organization. During that meeting the nominating committee shall introduce the candidates to the Board of Directors and each nominated candidate shall give their qualifications and reason(s) for wanting to become a Officer to the Board of Directors. The Board will take a balloted vote to elect the new Officers. The nominating committee shall tally the votes and announce the final results of the election to the current Board of the Organization. The new Officers shall take office officially after the November 1st meeting of the Board in which they will be present to observe the Officer whose seat they will be taking. If there is only one qualifying candidate then the candidate with the best qualifications shall be automatically voted into office. If there is no qualifying candidate to fill the selected vacancy then the office shall remain vacant until such a time as a qualifying candidate can be elected into office. Officers vacating their seats after any election shall remain an advisor to the new Officer for the first eight (8) weeks after the November 1st meeting. They will serve to counsel and assist the new Officer in properly conducting themselves in the Office they have been elected to. If a Officer is re-elected during any election no changes will take place. If a seat is vacated during the course of a year the seat will remain vacant until the next election period, except in the case of a special electoral meeting or a lack of quorum being met.

Article VIII: General Provision

Section 1. Corporate Seal

The Board of Directors shall authorize the use of a corporate seal that shall have inscribed thereon the name of the Organization. The Seal of the Organization shall consist of a ten-pointed star consisting of two five pointed stars superimposed upon one another, with a triskelion representing the three rays of inspiration in the central decagram and surrounded by a circle with twelve points.

Section 2. Fiscal Year

The fiscal year of the Organization shall start on the first day of November and end on the last day of October in each calendar year unless otherwise determined by the Board.

Section 3. Indemnification

The Organization shall indemnify and hold harmless each of its Directors, founders, trustees, and officers, or former Directors, committee members, trustees, and officers or any person who may have served at the request of the Organization as a trustee or officer of another corporation, partnership, joint venture, trust, or other enterprise, to the fullest extent permitted by law.

Article IX: Amendments

These By-Laws may be altered, amended, or repealed, and new By-Laws may be adopted, by a majority vote of the Directors present at the annual meeting and with the unanimous approval of the Founders. However, in no event may any amendments be made which would violate state and federal law or affect the Organization's qualification as a tax-exempt Organization pursuant to Section 501 (c) (3) of the Code or corresponding section of any future federal tax code. No amendments may be made that would change the original intent or purpose of the Organization, including the removal of the founders and their positions within the Organization.

Article XI: Non-Discrimination

The Organization shall not discriminate on the basis of sex, sexual orientation, gender identity, race, age, religion, handicap, or ethnic origin.

The Organization reserves the right to grant membership (General, Honored or Ministerial) in accordance with its purpose, and to deny membership or service to anyone who is, in the sole discretion of the Board, not in accord with the Organization's nature, spirit, or purpose.

Article XII: Confidentiality

Every member shall keep confidential the names, numbers, and places of residency or occupational work of any other member within our Organization, with the exception of permission from that individual. This rule does not apply if someone is considered a public threat or a threat to the Organization and/or its Community. In this case the Organization will cooperate fully with the appropriate authorities releasing only necessary information for official business.

Article XII: Limitation of Liability

Unless otherwise expressly authorized by the Board, the Directors and officers shall serve without compensation and, pursuant to Section 508:16 of NH RSA, shall not be personally liable for bodily injury, personal injury, and property damage if the claim for such damages arises from an act committed in good faith and without willful or wanton negligence in the course of an activity carried on to accomplish the purposes of the Organization.

The Directors and officers of the Organization shall not be liable to the Organization or to its members for monetary damages for breach of their fiduciary duties to the full extent permitted by N.H. RSA Chap 292, unless they act in bad faith, intentionally violate the law, or derive improper personal benefits from the activities of the Organization.

Article XIII: Indemnification

The Organization shall indemnify and hold its Directors and officers, Founders, committee members, harmless from and against all suits, claims, injuries, or damages asserted against them, so long as the Director or officer to be indemnified has not acted in bad faith, or engaged in intentional misconduct, knowing violation of the law, or derived an improper personal benefit.

Article XIV: Conflicts of Interest

Any possible conflict of interest on the part of any Director, officer or employee of the Organization, shall be disclosed in writing to the Board and made a matter of record through an annual procedure and also when the interest involves a specific issue before the Board.

Where the transactions involving a Director, trustee or officer or in which a Director, trustee or officer has an interest exceeds five hundred dollars ($500) but is less than five thousand dollars ($5,000) in a fiscal year, a two-thirds (2/3) vote of the disinterested Directors is required. When the transaction involved exceeds five thousand dollars ($5,000) in a fiscal year, then a two-thirds vote of the disinterested Directors and publication in the required newspaper is required. These votes are subject to approval by a majority vote of the Founders. The minutes of the meeting shall reflect that a disclosure was made, the abstention from voting, and the actual vote itself.

Every new member of the Board will be advised of this policy upon entering the duties of his or her office, and shall sign a statement acknowledging, understanding of an agreement to this policy. The Board will comply with all requirements of New Hampshire law in this area and the New Hampshire requirements are incorporated into and made a part of this policy statement.

Article XV: Dissolution

Upon the dissolution of the Organization, the Board of Directors shall, after paying or making provision for or the payment of all liabilities of the Organization, distribute the assets for one or more exemption exclusively for the purpose of the Organization in such manner or to such organization or organizations organized and operated exclusively for charitable, educations, religious or scientific purposes as shall at any time qualify as an exempt organization or organizations under Section 501 (c)(3) of the Internal Revenue Code of 1986, or corresponding section of any future federal tax code, or shall be distributed to the federal government or to a state or local government, for a public purpose.

APPENDIX FOUR: TEMPLE POLICIES

Mystery School Confidentiality Policies

All Officers, Administrators, Staff and Mentors with access to applications, files and other confidential information submitted by applications, students and ministers are required to keep such information confidential. Such information is only to be shared or discussed as needed in the context of business administration privately.

Confidential information includes personal information such as mailing address and residence, financial information, account numbers, medical history and mental health history.

Sensitive information shall only be disclosed to parties deemed necessary on a case by case basis, to the appropriate individuals, as determined by the Instructor, Dean of Students, Registrar, Administrators, Council, Board Members, Founders or Mentors.

Those reviewing applications with questions or concerns regarding the physical and mental health of an applicant will bring such concerns to the applicant with appropriate sensitivity and direct communication.

Those instructing or mentoring a student will initially bring concerns directly to the student, and when situations are determined potentially hazardous, bring their concerns to their appropriate superior in the Temple. Whenever appropriate, concerned parties should encourage and if necessary, insist upon appropriate medical or psychological help for the individual.

Records of Applications and Class Information shall be kept for a minimum of five years, the general time of the full program of the Mystery School Seminary. Rejected Applications shall be kept on file for a minimum of five years, to be used when determining acceptance with a reapplying individual. After five years, records shall go into storage or destroyed at the discretion of the Sagittarius Lead Minister.

Animal Policy

It is the Temple's policy that animals are not allowed at meetings, classes, rituals or events at the office or rented establishments unless they are in an official helper capacity. Animals required for an event, lesson or class (animal healing, animal communication, etc) are there at the discretion and permission of the instructor or coordinator of the event. Students who feel it necessary to bring an animal to class must get the express permission of the instructor or coordinator, prior to the event. For the purposes of this policy, "animal" shall also include insects, arachnids, mollusks, and other invertebrates.

Conflict of Interest

See **Article XIV** of the By-Laws.

Appendix Five: Frequently Asked Questions

How do I become a member of the Temple of Witchcraft?

To become a General Member, simply attend three official events of the Temple of Witchcraft and make sure you check in at the start of the event so your attendance is logged. To become an Honored Member, enroll in the Mystery School through attending a course in person or online. To become a Ministerial Member, graduate from the Seminary and fulfill all requirements.

Do Temple members have to pay dues?

No. Membership is based upon your level of commitment to various organizations in the Ministerial Church, Mystery School and Seminary, with each having different classes of membership. To be a member you simply have to attend three official events, which may or may not have class fees or suggested donations, but there are no yearly membership dues to be a General Member of the Temple.

Do I have to be a Witch to be a member?

No, though the Temple's events and teachings focus on modern Witchcraft. Members who identify as Pagan, Neopagan, Heathen, Wiccan, Witch, Magician, Shaman or other Earth reverent identity will feel most at home. Those who identify as Spiritual, New Age, Non-Dogmatic, Gnostic, Theosophical, Interfaith, Healer, or Light Worker might find resonance with some of the teachings and events.

Are scholarships available for all events?

Yes, on a case-by-case basis, through arrangement with the specific instructor and/or institution or business hosting the event with the Temple. Please inquire.

Can anyone be a member of the Temple of Witchcraft?

Yes, if they are in harmony and alignment with our basic mission, purpose and beliefs. While we all learn from each other, potential members should not join with an agenda to radically change the mission or nature of the Temple. Only those who have had their membership revoked or have been banned by the Temple leadership due to behavioral issues are not welcome.

Do I have to be a member to volunteer?

Yes, though some projects might be in cooperation with other organizations of a similar nature and such events can be exceptions. Long term volunteer work should be done by full members of the Temple in any of the membership designations.

How long does it take to become a High Priest or Priestess of the Temple?

Generally the program is set for a five year minimum, though some trainings are accelerated and others are decelerated.

Do I have to start at Witchcraft I?

Generally those seeking ministerial accreditation are encouraged to start at the beginning of any program or tradition to fully understand the entire system. At times it is possible to "test out" of earlier levels, though a strict criteria will be followed and one may only test out with the full approval of the head of the Sagittarius Ministry and the Board of Directors recommendation. Advanced students can potentially test out of Witchcraft I and II, but are encouraged to take Witchcraft III and IV directly.

Now that I'm in the Temple, what do I call myself?

There is no -ism or -ian based upon names, personalities or founders within the Temple Tradition and organization. It is based upon sacred space, experience, and personal transformation. One is simply a Temple Witch. The tradition is simply the Temple of Witchcraft Tradition, or for short, the Temple Tradition.

How long does it take to become a Minister of the Temple?

Generally the program is set for a five-year minimum, though some trainings are accelerated and others are decelerated depending on the student and the instructor. Ordination is separate from ministerial membership.

What is required to become a Minister of the Temple?

One must graduate from all previous levels of Witchcraft I through IV and successfully complete the Seminary Training of Witchcraft V, requirements to become a Ministerial Member, to be considered a High Priest/High Priestesses of the Temple.

How do I volunteer?

Contact the Temple via the website or speak to a minister after an official event and inquire. Review the twelve Zodiac ministries, and keep in mind what areas you might be interested in serving and what you want to do. The Temple will put you in touch with the appropriate coordinator in that ministry.

How do I become ordained?

Fill out an Ordination Application once you graduate from the Seminary program.

How do I start an official group in the Temple?

Official groups are only to be started and administered by ordained ministers. Ordained ministers are welcome to submit an application for a new group to the Board of Directors.

How do I become a Deputy Minister?

First volunteer and be active in one of the twelve ministries. Speak to leaders within that ministry and either approach the Lead Minister of that sign or, for some, you may be approached directly about fulfilling such a role. All Deputy Ministers are appointed by the Lead Minister of said ministry, with final approval from the Board of Directors.

How do I become a Lead Minister?

Lead Ministers are chosen by the Board of Directors. If you have a desire to be a Lead Minister and fulfill all the requirements, please write to the Board via our website and inquire about any upcoming positions. All Lead Ministers must be approved by the Board of Directors.

How do I make donations?

Donations can be sent via Paypal through our website, or by check or money order mailed to: Temple of Witchcraft, 49 North Policy Street, Salem, NH 03079. If donating due to ministerial work, please make a note of the event/class/ritual when you send in your donation.

APPENDIX SIX: GLOSSARY OF TERMS

The following is a glossary of terms used in this book and within the Temple of Witchcraft. While many of them are standard terms in Paganism, Witchcraft, occultism, and Theosophy, their interpretations and descriptions are particular to the Temple of Witchcraft. Some of these particular interpretations are described in this book, others in the teachings and Book of Shadows of the Temple of Witchcraft.

A∴A∴: A magickal order created by Aleister Crowley in 1907. It operates as a system of tutorial, with members only knowing the person above and below them in the chain of education. The initials are often said to stand for *Argentium Astram*, or Silver Star, but that is not the sole meaning of the A∴ A∴.

Abramelin: A mythic figure who wrote the grimoire *The Sacred Magick of Abramelin the Mage*. The Abramelin Operation, to connect with your Holy Guardian Angel, was adopted by the Golden Dawn, Aleister Crowley, and through them, found its way into the modern eclectic occult movement, including the Temple of Witchcraft.

Abraxas: The name is a magickal formula, with each letter said to stand for one of the seven ancient planets, and an entity considered in various traditions as a demon, spirit, archon, or god. Carl Jung considered Abraxas as a high god who embodies opposites. He is depicted with a rooster's head and two snakes for legs, and appears in many charms and talismans. Similar in mystical form to Baphomet.

Aubrey, King: The Faery Lord and consort of Queen Aroxana in the Temple of Witchcraft tradition. Often envisioned with blue-green skin and stag or ram horns. He is both King and Priest, and often takes the role of healer and teacher with seekers.

Age of Aquarius: The coming zodiac age, after the Age of Pisces. Though many disagree with when it starts, with dates ranging wildly, the general thought is it will be an age of harmony and peace, technology, utopia, and unexpected events.

Age of Pisces: The previous age, characterized by sacrificial gods, hierarchical organizations and the rise of Christianity.

Age of the Great Blessing/Curse: The modern age where so much information, culture and religion, from many different times and places, is available all at once.

Air: One of the four classic elements. Associated with the mind, logic, memory, reason, thought, speaking, listening and communication. Its highest ideals are truth, and the breath of life.

Alchemy: The art, science and spiritual practice of transformation. Some forms deal with outer transformation through laboratory operations, while others deal with inner spiritual transformation. Alchemy has been practiced in both the East and the West for centuries, flowing with any of the religious systems its finds. Many modern Witches who are occultists are highly influenced by the practice of alchemy.

Alexandria: An ancient city in Egypt founded by Alexander the Great. It became a middle point between eastern and western cultures, and a repository for knowledge and wisdom on religion, philosophy, myth, mathematics, poetry and science. It's library was famous across the world until destroyed.

Alexandrian Wicca: The initiatory branch of British Traditional Wicca founded by Alex Sanders. Thought to be named after him, but usually Alexandria is considered the source of the name amongst Alexandrian Wiccans

Alpha: A brain wave state below normal waking state, or Beta, that is characterized by creative thought, intuition and psychic impressions.

Alphabet of Desire: A system of creating a personal sigil alphabet pioneered by Witch Austin Osman Spare, and adopted in the practice of Chaos Magick.

Ancestors: Those who were once physically incarnate who are now deceased, who have a connection to you. Ancestors can be of direct genetic lineage, or blood, but can also be spiritual ancestors from your tradition, adopted ancestors, ancestors of place, and those whom you feel a kinship to because of similar interests or backgrounds.

Anderson Feri Witchcraft: A branch of Witchcraft popularized by Victor and Cora Anderson, sometimes referred to as Feri Witchcraft or Anderson Feri Witchcraft.

Anglo-Saxon: An umbrella term for those of Germanic descent who invaded England, including the Angles, Saxons, and Jutes. Old English is the language of the Anglo Saxons. Their mythos and magick added to the cauldron of British occultism and religion.

Animist: A spiritual belief that everything is imbued with a spiritual essence and intelligence, including aspects of nature, such as plants, animals and stones, inanimate objects and unseen forces. Animistic religions involve communication and cooperation with these entities.

Aquarius: The eleventh sign of the Zodiac. Fixed air. Ruled by the planet Uranus and formerly Saturn. The sign associated with the New Age or New Aeon, the Age of Aquarius where brotherhood/sisterhood and community are balanced by the individual and technological innovation. The sign of the Rebel. Key phrase is I KNOW and key words include altruistic, unconventional, and erratic.

Aries: The first sign of the Zodiac. Cardinal fire. Ruled by the planet Mars. The sign whose cosmic age is associated most strongly with the rise of the Roman Empire. The sign of the Warrior. Key phrase is I AM and key words included leadership, courage, and headstrong.

Aroxana, Queen: The Faery Queen and leader of the sidhe host of New Hampshire, if not simply the Northeast, working in partnership with the Temple of Witchcraft. She is particularly honored near Midsummer's Eve.

Ascension: Usually a term indicating reaching the next level of human development through raising consciousness. Used by those inheriting the traditions of Theosophy, with its Ascended Masters, though the concept is not unlike the Mighty Dead of Witchcraft.

Ash: A sacred tree in the Northern European traditions. Considered the World Tree by the Norse. In the mythos of the Temple, it is considered the current World Tree of this creation. Ash is also an important tree in the Celtic Ogham system of magick and divination.

Assiah: The fourth and final of the Qabalistic Worlds, corresponding with the element of Earth and material reality.

Astral Body: In the system of the seven bodies, the third body. Literally translates as the "starry body" but in modern occultism refers to the energy body that encompasses your self image. The astral body can travel forth from the physical body in meditation, dreams and shamanic journey. Sometimes referred to as the lower emotional body. Associated with the solar plexus chakra.

Astral Plane: In the system of the seven planes, the third plane. Literally refers to the starry realm, but in modern occultism refers to an invisible level of reality where there is shape and energy with no physical form. Everything physical exists upon the astral plane simultaneously, but many things exist on the astral plane without a physical counterpart, such as ghosts. Sometimes referred to as the lower emotional plane.

Astrology: The study of the movements of the sky in relationship to the Earth, and how those movements correspond with events and experiences on Earth.

Atlantis: A mythic land referenced by Plato, Theosophists, and the modern metaphysical movement, believed to exist in the Atlantic Ocean in ancient times. A high civilization of magick and technology that fell due to hubris and misuse of power. In the Temple, we consider it a mandala of the ancient wisdom of the west, much like Shamballa holds in many eastern traditions.

Atziluth: The first of the four Qabalistic worlds, corresponding with the element of fire and the divine creator.

Autumn Equinox: A day of equal light and darkness as the balance is moving towards darkness. The transition of the Sun from the sign of Virgo to Libra and the start of the fall season. Also known as Mabon within the Wheel of the Year.

Avalon: The name of the otherworld in British traditions rooted in the myths of King Arthur. Apple Land and the realm of the Lady of the Lake. Sometimes depicted as a realm of faery women, other times, enlightened humans.

Babe of the Abyss: The Child of Light who, as an initiate, has crossed the abyss of Da'ath to be reborn again.

Banishing: Removal of unwanted forces or spirits.

Banishing Ritual of the Hexagram: A ceremonial magick rite to remove unwanted macrocosmic, or heavenly forces, particularly planetary energies.

Baphomet: The hermaphroditic lord of occultists, famously depicted by Eliphas Levi as a goat head upon a human body with female breasts, male phallus, goat hind quarters, wings and a pentagram and candle upon its brow, pointing both above and below. The name is also associated with the secret idol of the Knights Templar and, according to occultists, a code for the word Sophia, or Wisdom.

Bear: Animal totem of great strength and introspection, associated with shamans and healers. Potential totem for the Seventh Great Age.

Beltane: The spring fire festival when the Sun is in the zodiac sign of Taurus, popularly celebrated on May 1. Also known as May Day. In the ancient Celtic calendar it signaled the start of summer. Associated with vital life force, sexuality, dance and purifying fires.

Bent Line: The Second Ray or Blue Ray, associated with Love, Trust and the Faery Path.

Birch: A tree associated with success and fertility, despite the fact it does not produce a fruit. A potential vision of the World Tree in the Seventh Great Age.

Blackbird: A totem of wisdom and cunning that plays a role in the tale of Mabon and King Arthur. Also a guiding totem of the Fifth Great Age.

Blodeuwedd: Welsh goddess of flowers and owls. Created from flowers by the wizards Gwydion and Math, to marry Llew, whom she later betrays. As punishment, Gwydion turns her into an owl.

Blue Ray: the Second Ray or Bent Line, associated with Love, Trust and the Faery Path.

Blue Star Wicca: An American branch of Traditional Wicca descended from Alexandrian Wicca, emphasizes music and family connection with its members.

Book of Shadows: A book of rituals, spells and lore for a Witch. Traditions often have a specific book of rites copied from teacher to student, while individual Witches create their own unique Book of Shadows.

Bornless One: The Thelemic title for the Higher Self or Holy Guardian Angel, also known as the Bornless Self.

Briah: The second of the four Qabalistic Worlds, corresponding with the element of Water, form, and the realm of the archangels.

Brid: Also known as Bride, Bridget and later, St. Bridget, an Irish Celtic Goddess who is the daughter of the Dagda and celebrated at Imbolc/Candlemas.

British Traditional Wicca: An initiatory path of Wicca, most commonly divided into Alexandrian lines, for Alex Sanders and Gardnerian lines, for Gerald Gardner. One must be initiated by a valid, recognized teacher in the proper way to be considered a part of these traditions. They are the main root and source material of the modern eclectic Wicca movement.

Buddhism: The religion based upon the teachings of Siddhartha Gautama, started in India.

Bull Horned God: Manifestation of the animal side of the God at Litha, or the summer time, associated also with the sign of Taurus. Asterion, or the Minotaur, as well as some forms of Zeus, and the Babylonian Baal, are depictions of a bull god.

Cabot Tradition of Witchcraft: The tradition of Witchcraft founded by author, teacher, and activist, Laurie Cabot, and continued by the Cabot-Kent Hermetic Temple. The Cabot Tradition is the first tradition studied by Temple of Witchcraft founder Christopher Penczak, and many of his first teachings are heavily influenced by the Cabot Tradition.

Cabot, Laurie: The "Official Witch of Salem Massachusetts" and founder of the Cabot Tradition of Witchcraft. An avid activist for Witchcraft rights and a teacher of the science of the Craft, as well as the religion and art.

Calcination: The first alchemical operation, associated with the planet Saturn, the element of fire, the root chakra and the seventh gate of the Underworld.

Caldera: Crater opening compared to a cauldron. Also Kaldera.

Cancer: The fourth sign of the Zodiac. Cardinal water. Ruled by the Moon. The sign whose cosmic age is associated with our stone age ancestors as hunters and gatherers. The sign of the Mother. Key phrase is I FEEL and key words include maternal, psychic and moody.

Candlemas: See *Imbolc*.

Capricorn: The tenth sign of the Zodiac. Cardinal earth. Ruled by the planet Saturn. The sign of the Father. Key phrase is I USE and key words include responsible, disciplined, and conservative.

Cardinal: The energy of initiation, or new beginnings in the Zodiac. When the sun enters a cardinal sign, a season begins.

Celiced: (pronounced Kelly-Ked) The aspect of the Great Spirit associated with the Divine Heart. Based upon a Welsh term for the union of divinities Celi and Ced.

Celts: A large category of Indo-Europeans sharing similar language, beliefs and culture, who migrated across Europe. Today the Celts are strongly associated with Ireland, Scotland and Wales, and in the time of Caesar, Gaul (France).

Ceremonial Magick: The traditions of formal ceremony, often based in Hermeticism, Qabalah, alchemy, and grimoire techniques. Popularized by the Hermetic Order of the Golden Dawn, whose practices went on to influence Wicca.

Ceridwen: Welsh goddess of the cauldron, considered to be a master sorceress and mother of bards.

Cernunnos: Gaulish horned god figure, associated with animals and the forest.

Chakra: The spiritual organs within the body regulating the flow of energy and consciousness in harmony with the endocrine system. While we have many chakra points, traditional Vedic lore states we have seven main chakra points, from the base of the spine to the top of the head.

Chaldean Oracles: Fragmentary texts from the second century AD attributed to the Babylonians, with aspects of Hellenistic, Platonic, Persian, and Babylonian elements.

Chaos Magick: A modern outgrowth of Ceremonial Magick, where new paradigms are easily adopted and the traditional rigidity is discarded. While Peter Carroll is considered the father of Chaos Magick, Austin Osman Spare is often considered the grandfather, as it draws heavily on his sigilization method.

Child of Light: Refers to both the rebirth of the God at Yule as the Sun begins to wax in power again, and the alchemical experience of light, innocence and optimism that occurs while on the initiatory path. Both Tiphereth and crossing Da'ath can have associations with the Child of Light. In mythic ritual, Mabon is referred to as the Child of Light. Similar to Child of Hope and Child of Promise.

Christianity: The religion based upon the teachings associated with the figure Jesus of Nazareth. While exoteric Christianity has little to do with magickal practices, both esoteric forms of Christianity, and folk traditions can have quite a bit in common with magick and Witchcraft.

Coagulation: The seventh alchemical operation, associated with the Sun, the crown chakra and the first gate of the Underworld.

Conjunction: The fourth alchemical operation, associated with the planet Venus, the element of Earth, the heart chakra and the fourth gate of the Underworld. The completion of the alchemical operations at this stage is known as the Lesser Stone.

Core Shamanism: Central techniques and practices found in many different "shamanic" traditions across the world, stripped of their cultural associations.

Cow: Totem animal of great love and generosity. A totemic figure of the Sixth Great Age.

Cowan: Technically a mason who is not part of an initiated masonic order. A term used for non-Witches, or those who are not formally initiated into the Witch Cult, before the term Muggle became popular.

Craft: Short for Witchcraft, emphasizing the "work" and the art of our way. Craft refers to the tools and spells as well as the crafting of our souls.

Creatures of Flesh and Blood: Enfleshed spirits, and those formerly enfleshed, including fauna (animals), humans, totems, ancestors, and the Mighty Dead.

Crooked Line: The Third Ray or Yellow Ray, associated with Wisdom, Cunning, Knowledge and the creatures of flesh and blood. The Crooked Path or Crooked Road is also a term for the Witch's path in general.

Crown of Humility: The Fifth Hallow, forged internally by the initiate. The first tool relinquished in the descent of the Goddess. Associated with elemental spirit.

Cruthear: The aspect of the Great Spirit associated with the Divine Mind. Based upon a Scottish term for divinity as referenced as a shaper of form.

Cup of Compassion: One of the four hallows as viewed in the Temple of Witchcraft. Associated with Love and elemental water.

Current: A flow of magickal energy. Usually a current of energy flowing from the tradition's egregore is passed from initiator to initiate in ceremony, connecting the new member to the group consciousness of the tradition. Currents can also refer to the flow of energy in an Aeon or particular non-lineage initiatory model.

Dagda: The "good god" of the Irish tradition. He has a cauldron that no one goes away from hungry, a harp that changes the seasons when played, and a club that kills with one blow and restores life with the second. He is described a giant, but generally good natured. In occultism, he corresponds with the planet Jupiter.

Dance: A metaphor for the unfoldment of life and creation, as the God is the Singer and Song reverberating on the strings of the Goddess' Web. All creatures moves to this song as if in a complex dance.

Decan: A measurement of the Zodiac consisting of ten degrees. Each Zodiac sign has three decants.

Dedicant: One who had dedicated to the study and practice of the Craft, but has not been initiated.

Dedication: The ritual, often done solitary, performed to become a dedicant of a tradition.

Dissolution: The second alchemical operation, associated with the planet Jupiter, the element water, the belly chakra, and the sixth gate of the Underworld.

Distillation: The sixth alchemical operation, associated with the Moon, the brow chakra and the second gate of the Underworld.

Divination: The process or receiving information and guidance, often on the past, present or future, through some form of oracle system. Tarot, runes, tea-leaf reading, and scrying into a crystal ball are all considered methods of divination.

Divine Body: In the system of seven bodies, the seventh body, encompassing and interpenetrating all bodies, and connected to all other divine bodies. Considered the source of the Higher Self. Associated with the crown chakra.

Divine Heart: The aspect of the Great Spirit devoted to Love and the origin of the Second Ray. See also *Celiced*.

Divine Mind: The aspect of the Great Spirit devoted to Wisdom or Mind, and the origin of the Third Ray. See also *Cruthear*.

Divine Plane: In the system of seven planes, the seventh plane, the godhead or source, where the Divine Mind, Divine Heart and Divine Will are found.

Divine Will: The aspect of the Great Spirit devoted to Will or Purpose, and the origin of the First Ray. See also *Dryghten*.

Dolphin: A totem associated with breath and pleasure, also associated with the Sixth Great Age.

Dryghten: The aspect of the Great Spirit associated with Divine Will, based upon a supposedly non gender specific Saxon term roughly translating to "lord" or "ruler."

Dualism: Belief in the primary divine power of two aspects. Many consider Wicca, oriented on Goddess and God, as a dualistic religion.

Eagle: A totem whose teachings connect us to the heavens as a divine messenger. Considered the totem of the Second Great Age.

Earth: Earth refers to A) the element of Earth which embodies the principles of solidity, gravity and Law symbolized by the stone, coin, shield or pentacle, or B) the planet or planetary deity often called Mother Earth or Gaea/Gaia.

Earth Mother: The planetary being seen as a primal Goddess. An embodiment of Mother Nature.

Earth Religion: Religions that are Earth reverent and embrace nature. While many consider the term equivalent to Pagan, many religions that are Earth Reverent would not self-identify as Pagan, such as many Native American and tribal traditions.

Eclectic Wicca: A modern expression of Wicca drawing from British Traditional sources but not requiring a formal teacher to student initiation, and has an encouragement of additional information as the practitioner desires.

Ecstatic Mysteries: The mysteries of the third degree in the Temple of Witchcraft, involving shamanism and shadow work. The focus of this degree is journeying through drumming, sacred body posture, spirit medicine and soul healing. Ecstasy refers to being "beyond the flesh" in reference to exhibitory trance techniques to expand consciousness.

Egregore: The collective thought form of a group, tradition or order. Often personified as a magickal entity, shaped by the name, image and magick of the group.

Egypt: An ancient land in North Africa and the Middle East, known for a rich magickal and esoteric tradition, pyramids, and temples. Many modern occultist, magicians and Witches find inspiration in ancient Egypt.

Elder: Elder can refer to someone who is considered wise and experienced either in terms of age or years of practice. Elder also refers to a tree of the Celtic Ogham tradition, technically more of a bush, associated with faeries and the underworld. Considered the world tree of the coming Sixth Great Age.

Elemental Plane: Aspects of the Etheric Realm, or Plane of Forces, that are associated individually with the four elemental energies of fire, water, air and earth.

Elevation: An initiatory style ritual that follows the first initiation, often conferring a further rank or degree within a tradition. Many feel that initiation, or beginning, can only happen once, so each subsequent rank is an elevation to a new level.

Elm: The wisdom tree of the Fifth Great Age.

Emotional Body: In the system of seven bodies, the fourth body, often described initially as egg or sphere shaped, where emotions are generated, contained and exchanged. Sometimes referred to as the upper astral body. Associated with the heart chakra.

Emotional Plane: In the system of seven planes, the fourth plane where emotional exchanges and connections are made. Sometimes referred to as the Upper Astral, as it resides between the Astral Plane (Or Lower Astral) and the Mental Plane.

Enneagram: A nine pointed star. Can refer to a the traditional equilateral nine points, or the enneagram used in the Personality System of the Fourth Way founded by Gurdjieff.

Esbat: A lunar celebration, usually referring to a Full Moon Circle, but can also apply to the Dark Moon, New Moon or other lunar rites.

Esoteric: Referring to things designed for people with initiated knowledge. In Witchcraft, refers to wisdom teachings for those initiated upon the path, but in a strict sense, can refer to any body of specialized knowledge. The legal system is esoteric knowledge for lawyers and judges.

Eternal Sabbat: One depiction of the timeless union of past Witchcraft adepts, along with other other entities such as faeries, animal spirits and other imps. Akin to the Eastern expressions of Shamballa.

Etheric Body: In the system of seven subtle bodies occupying the seven levels of reality, the second body, closest to the physical level. The etheric body is the energetic pattern for the physical body. Associated with the belly chakra.

Etheric Plane: In the system of seven levels of reality, the second level of reality, energetically paralleling the physical world, manifesting the patterns that form the material universe.

Evocation: The formal process of calling or summoning a spirit to manifestation or appearance. In Witchcraft is simply refers to the calling of a spirit. In Ceremonial Magick, the spirit is usually evoked into a triangle structure.

Faeries: The elder race of spirit, predating humanity and entwined with the development of nature. The Fey Folk withdrew into the depths of the land after what is known as the Age of Lemuria by some, and continue to act as guides and patrons to Witches and seers. They are associated with the Blue Ray of Love and Trust, and the faerie blue fire.

Fall Equinox: See *Autumn Equinox*.

Fauna: Another term for the creatures of flesh and blood, animals including humans. Fauna are associated with the First Ray, the Red Ray of Will.

Feast of Hecate: A holy day associated with the Witch Goddess Hecate on August 13. Traditionally it was a ritual to appease her and prevent late summer storms from destroying the crops. In the Temple of Witchcraft, it has become our "ninth" sabbat.

Fermentation: The fifth alchemical operation, associated with the planet Mercury, the throat chakra and the third gate of the Underworld.

Fertility Mysteries: The mystery of the second degree in the Temple of Witchcraft, involving polarity, natural magick and creation through union. Focus of this degree is upon Goddess and God, Earth and Sky, Moon and Sun and the sacramental act of the Great Rite within. Many consider traditional Wicca a fertility cult.

Fire: An element that embodies the principles of energy, transformation, will, life force, and Light. Symbolized by the wand or torch.

First People: the First Humans, or the "other people" predating the concept of the "Fall" and separation.

First Ray: The Red Ray of Will and Power, linked with the Race of Angels, symbolized by the straight line and arrow or spear.

First Witch: Also known as the One Sorcerer, the consciousness of the Witch that is every Witch, from the First Witch in history to the last Witch in time. The most ancient ancestor and the most future incarnation of all Witches.

Five Gifts of the Sea People: A reference to both the myths of Atlantis and the Celtic Tuatha De Danann, who brought the hallows to Ireland. In the Temple they are simplified as the Stone, Sword, Cup, Spear/Wand, and Crown.

Fixed: The energy of sustainment in the Zodiac. When the Sun enters a fixed sign, the middle of the season occurs. Fixed can also refer to the stars of the heavens, fixed in constellations, differing from the planets, or wandering stars.

Flora: A term for the plants and plant spirits, associated with the Second Ray, the Blue Ray of Love.

Freemasonry: An often misunderstood secret initiatory group dedicated to public good. Freemasonry has influenced many of the founders and practitioners of modern Wicca, and many of the symbols found in Masonry share a common spiritual heritage with ancient Pagan Mystery Schools.

Frog: A totem of sensitivity, boundaries, transformation and voice or song. One of the totems possible to guide the Sixth Age.

Garden of the Gods: The Mythic image of the first time, the days before division and separation from nature. Parallels to it are found in other cultures, most famously in the Garden of Eden myth.

Gardnerian Wicca: The Branch of Wicca founded by Gerald Gardner, and greatly influenced by Doreen Valiente. Much of our modern practices of Wicca can be traced to the work of Gerald Gardner and Doreen Valiente.

Gaul: An ancient territory in Western Europe consisting of France, Belgium, Switzerland and parts of Italy and Germany, occupied by the Celtic people in the time of Caesar.

Gemini: The third sign of the Zodiac. Mutable air. Ruled by the planet Mercury. The sign whose cosmic age is associated with writing and language. The sign of the Trickster. Key phrase is I THINK and key words include communication, social, and flighty.

Giants: An ancient race, associated with the Theosophical myths of Hybornea. Primordial forces that shaped the continents and land masses, often considered the elder race to the faery folk. They are found in myth of both the northern and southern European traditions, as well as around the world.

Gnostic Mysteries: The mystery of the fourth degree in the Temple of Witchcraft, involving Qabalah and ceremonial magick. Focus of this degree is the study and experience of cosmology, creation of your own cosmological reality map and invocation of the Higher Self. Gnosis is usually translated as "knowledge" referring to knowledge received by direct experience.

Goat Horned God: Manifestation of the animal side of the God at Yule and through the sign of Capricorn. The depiction of the god as Pan, Baphomet, or the Sabbatic Goat God.

God: The male aspect of divinity, often depicted as a Father. The God can be divided as a God of Light and Life and God of Darkness and Death. In the Temple, the great God is known as the Singer and the Song.

Goddess: The female aspect of divinity, often depicted as a Mother. The Goddess is often seen as triune, as Goddess of the heavens, earth and underworld, or maiden, mother and crone. In the Temple the Goddess is seen as the Weaver and the Web.

Godhead: The divine creative source, beyond gender and division. Often equated with the Great Spirit, Kether in the Tree of Life, and beyond.

Golden Dawn: The Hermetic Order of the Golden Dawn is a ceremonial magician tradition highly influential in the modern occult movement and rise of Wicca.

Graeco-Egyptian Magickal Papyri: A collection of spell book fragments with rituals, hymns and charms, in a religious worldview that syncretized Greek, Roman, Egyptian, Babylonian, Jewish, and Christian religious figures, beliefs, and practices.

Great Above: A name for the Upper World, also known as the Overworld or Starry Heaven.

Great Below: A name for the Lower World, also known as the Underworld or the Deep.

Great Between: A name for the Middle World, also known as Middle Earth, or consensual reality.

Great Song: The Oran Mor, the song of creation resonating on the strings of the Web of Fate and the voice of the gods as the Singer, or Logos.

Great Spirit: Reference to the creative force beyond name and gender. All encompassing term for creator.

Great Work: The "Magnum Opus" of any Witch, Magician or Alchemist, referring to the process of enlightenment. The Western path is often described in terms of work, and craft, going back to the ancient craftsmen and temple builders, using skills in service to the divine, and the outer craft reflected an inner transformation.

Great Year: The cycle formed by the Precession of the Equinoxes, where a different zodiac sign influences consciousness for slightly longer than 2000 years, moving backwards through the Zodiac signs.

Greater Ritual of the Hexagram: Rituals to work with the planetary energies of the seven classical planets through the drawing of six lined star figures.

Greater Ritual of the Pentagram: Rituals to work with the elemental energies through the drawing of five lined star figures.

Greece: A region of southeastern Europe, on the Mediterranean Sea, where in ancient times, a classical Pagan civilization flourished. Many of our romantic notions of Paganism, accurate or not, are rooted in images, history, and mythology of Greece.

Grigori: See *Watchers*.

Halloween: See *Samhain*.

Hazel: A tree associated with wisdom, eloquence and magick in the Celtic traditions. Considered the wisdom tree of the First Great Age.

Hecate: Matron of Witches and Dark Goddess of magick, thresholds and torch bearing. In classical mythology, she is a titan predating the Olympic gods. Considered an ally and guide to modern

Witches, and honored in the Temple of Witchcraft as Mother of Witches, and Soul of the World.

Herbalism: The study and practice of plant based medicine.

Hermeticism: A series of philosophical, religious and magickal beliefs from writings and teachings attributed to Hermes Trismegistus ("The Thrice-Great Hermes"), who is considered to have connections to both the Greek god Hermes and the Egyptian god Thoth. Much of our standard magickal traditions such as the four elements and the seven planets, are a part of Hermetic thought, and Hermeticism has influenced much of the modern Western occult movement. It can be divided into the study of alchemy and nature, the study of the heavens through astrology and astronomy, and the study and use of theurgy, to commune with, and connect with divinity. Many consider the Hermetic philosophers to have a direct link to the development of modern science in the 17th century, and many notable scientists of the time also considered themselves Hermeticists, such as Isaac Newton.

Hesperides: A western paradise island in Greek myth, where a tree of golden apples is guarded by a serpent. Hercules visits Hesperides in his twelve labors.

Heuristic: From the Greek eureka, meaning "to find." Refers to experienced based techniques, and in the context of The Temple of Witchcraft, using mystical techniques to experience divinity and magick directly. Ritual, myth and poetry form a structure to experience, but eventually everyone must find their own way, and can add to the body of tradition.

Hexagram: A six pointed star. While the "Star of David" is the most well known configuration, there are several other versions of the hexagram used in ceremonial magick.

Hidden Company: The sanctified, or enlightened dead of the traditions of Witchcraft. Also known as the Mighty Dead, they are the allies and guides taking a role similar to the saints, bodhisattvas, and ascended masters of other traditions.

Higher Self: See *Watcher*.

Hinduism: A general term applied to a wide range of religious and cultural traditions native to India. Due to the Indo-European link, many modern European mystics and occultists look to India for inspiration and terminology.

Holly: A tree of protection and healing anger. The image of the dark side of the God, the Holly King, to match the Oak King of life and light. Considered the Wisdom Tree of the Fourth Great Age.

Holy Formless Fire: An expression of the Secret Fire that resides in the heart of all things and in the heart of the universe. An expression of divine light.

Holy Guardian Angel: See *Higher Self*.

Hybornea: The Theosophical homeland of the Second Great Age.

Imbolc: The winter Celtic fire festival when the Sun is in the sign of Aquarius. Translated to "ewe's milk" for it is marked by the herds of sheep lactating before giving birth to new lambs. Milk is often used in rituals for this reason. It is also sacred to the Celtic Goddess Bride, also known as Bridget, and celebrated with healing magick, poetry and crafting. Bride's cross and corn dollies are crafted and used in ritual. Like Yule, it is also a celebration of the returning light, and often candles are lit as the Sun god grows in power. Also known as Candlemas in Christian traditions. More correctly considered midwinter, being between the winter solstice and vernal equinox.

Initiate: One who has experienced initiation.

Initiation: "To begin." Initiation refers to a process, either conferred through an individual, group, life circumstances or through the spirits, that begins a new, usually magickal/spiritual/esoteric phase of life. Often it appears to be the end of a period of preparation and training, but in reality is just the start.

Invocation: The process of summoning a spirit within. In Witchcraft, invocation usually refers to bringing the spirit into the body of the priest/ess or practitioner to express itself, while in Ceremonial Magick, invocation simply means summoning a spirit into the magick circle.

Invoking Ritual of the Hexagram: A ceremonial magick tradition to invoke the power of one or more of the seven ancient planets into a ritual space.

Islam: A monotheistic, Abrahamic religion founded by the prophet Mohammed, considered the last prophet of God, or Allah, according to the faith. Like Judaism and Christianity, Islam also has a mystical side of teachings, Sufism, that is largely unknown by the modern populace.

Ivy: A plant associated with resurrection and climbing toward the heavens. It is one of two wisdom "trees" of the Second Great Age.

Jack of the Corn: Manifestation of the vegetal side of the God at Lammas, as the ripe golden grain. This is a manifestation of the Corn King or John Barleycorn, who is baked into bread and made into ale, the food and waters of life and resurrection.

Jack of the Frost: Manifestation of vegetal side of the God at Imbolc, as the frozen land and the spirit of ice, snow and cold. Akin to Jack Frost in folklore.

Jack of the Green: Manifestation of the vegetal side of the God at Beltane, as the green leaves and blooming flower. This is a manifestation of the Celtic Green Man, whose face can be seen carved into European Churches, and still seen in the leaves of the trees

Jack of the Lantern: Manifestation of the vegetative side of the God at Samhain, as the hollowed gourd, turnip and most popular, pumpkin, lanterns to ward off evil spirits and welcome good ones.

Judaism: The monotheistic religion of the Jewish people, originating in the Middle East and providing a framework for Christianity and Islam.

Jupiter: The planet of good luck, fortune and the higher self, associated with sky father gods and Chesed on the Tree of Life.

Knights Templar: See *Templars*.

Lammas: The summer fire festival when the Sun is in the zodiac sign of Leo, popularly celebrated on August 1. A celebration of the harvest, grains, bread and beer. In the Irish traditions, it is known as Lughnassadh, the "funeral feast of Lugh" though it technically refers to the funeral of Lugh's foster-mother, Taltiu, though the modern Neopagan Wheel of the Year sees it as the death or sacrifice of the Grain God. Often celebrated with games and competition, as well as feasting.

Lap of the Goddess: A wisdom saying "My fate is in the lap of the Goddess" meaning that I surrender and trust in the Goddess when I can no longer act on my own. Also the name of a former production company in the Boston area supporting metaphysical and Neopagan events, including sabbats and esbats.

Lapis: Reference to stone, and in the Temple to the Stone People, the consciousness within minerals and metals.

Lemuria: The third great land in the Theosophical myth cycle, where the elder race of Faeries ruled and guided the evolution of life upon the planet.

Leo: The fifth sign of the Zodiac. Fixed fire. Ruled by the Sun. The sign whose cosmic age is associated with the end of the Atlantean era. The sign of the Artisan. Key phrase is I CREATE and key words include artistic, entertaining and egotistical.

Lesser Banishing Ritual of the Pentagram: The basic banishing ritual of the microcosm in modern ceremonial magick.

Libation: A ritual offering of a sacred liquid, usually a drink such as wine, juice, tea, or water.

Libra: The seventh sign of the Zodiac. Cardinal air. Ruled by the planet Venus. The sign of the Judge. Key phrase is I BALANCE and key words include partnership, refinement and indecision.

Light: A conception of psychic energy as well as a symbol for consciousness, awareness, inspiration, evolution and "enlightenment."

Lightworker: A New Age term for an energy worker dedicated to the evolution of consciousness and the enlightenment of humanity, through the symbol and use of light.

Litha: The summer solar festival when the Sun transitions from the zodiac sign of Gemini into Cancer. Technically the start of Summer by modern calendars, but often called Midsummer or celebrated as Midsummer's Eve the night before. Associated with the Sun God, and the realm of the faeries, for twilight lasts longest on Midsummer, and twilight is considered a door to the faery realm.

Loom of Space and Time: The wheels of the weaver goddess, including the wheel of wyrd, justice and judgement.

Lorica: A "breastplate" but usually a charm or prayer of protection to be "worn" like armor.

Lower World: In shamanic cosmology, the underworld is viewed as in the roots of the world tree. The underworld is a place of both rest and challenges, associated with the dead, faeries and the dark goddesses and gods. Elementally it resonates with water and earth.

Lucifer: The archangel of light, appearing in many Gnostic traditions of Witchcraft. Due to the association as light bearer, as the name originally refers to both a Roman God of Light and a title for other deities who bear light, in angelic lore he can be linked to Uriel, the "light of God." Sometimes known as Lumiel.

Lughnassadh: See *Lammas*.

Lumiel: Another name for the Archangel of Light, sometimes known as Lucifer. See also *Prometheus*.

Mabinogion: A Welsh text of mythology, depicting the tales of characters believed to be gods and heroes from an earlier age, including information on King Arthur.

Mabon: The autumn solar festival when the Sun transitions from Virgo to Libra, starting the Fall season. Named after the Celtic child of light Mabon, who is often compared to the Greek goddess Persephone in modern Neopaganism, withdrawing to the darkness of the underworld and bringing with him the light and life of the world. Known as the fruit harvest, it is associated with apples and grapes. Some celebrate it as the Pagan "Thanksgiving" sabbat. Also known as the Autumn Equinox.

Macha: An Irish crow and horse goddess, who is part of the triplicy of the Morrighan.

Magician: One who practices magick, be it for personal gain, a profession, and/or a spiritual path.

Magick: There are as many definitions of magick as there are magicians, though a common starting place for it is the famous definition by Aleister Crowley, "the Science and Art of causing Change to occur in conformity with Will." Magick most often refers to ritual actions that create changes, both inner and outer, for the practitioner. The aim of spiritual magick is to eventually learn your True Will, and implement it in the world, though the exploration of needs and desires helps one discern what is and isn't True Will, when the magick is done in the spirit of 'harming none' and aligning with divine will.

Magick Circle: The primary ritual of modern Witchcraft, used to create sacred space.

Maqlu Rite: A Sumerian ritual performed by the ruler to protect the kingdom and king. In the Temple, a red ray ritual of protection and blessing.

Mars: The planet of will, action and energy, associated with warrior gods and Geburah on the Tree of Life.

Mental Body: In the system of seven bodies, the fifth body, where thought, language, abstract ideas, and intellectual memory reside. Associated with the throat chakra.

Mental Plane: In the system of seven planes, the fifth plane, where geometric structure, intellectual communication, and the creative impulse begin to take shape from impulse and image to intellectualized form.

Mercury: The alchemical principle of fluidity and absorption, in a triad with sulfur and salt. In the three soul model, Mercury can be associated with the Lower Self, the spirit and ancestral memory, though its associations change with your level of initiation.

Mercury: The planet of communication and learning, associated with psychopomps, messenger gods, healers, teacher and Hod on the Tree of Life.

Meritocracy: A leadership structure designed around the fusion of democracy by merit. One who contributes more to the overall organization and demonstrates an ability to handle responsibilities skillfully, gains more leadership roles.

Meruvia: The proposed Theosophical name of the homeland of the people of the Great Sixth Age. Some speculate it is one or both of the Americas.

Mesopotamia: The area of the Tigris and Euphrates rivers, considered the cradle of civilization as we know it, though many other ancient civilizations predating Mesopotamia have been discovered. The people known as the Sumerians, Babylonians, Akkadians and Assyrians have all ruled this area. Some consider their spiritual traditions, magick and culture the most ancient expressions of Paganism, "starting" some of the common images and archetypes we work with today.

Michael: The archangel of fire in the microcosm and of the Sun in the macrocosm. Depicted with a flaming spear or sword. Archangel of protection and light.

Middle World: In shamanic cosmology, the Middle World is depicted at the base of the World Tree. The Middle World is the physical, consensual reality, but also includes all of space and time, past and future. Elementally, the Middle World resonates with all four elements: earth, air, fire and water – as it stands between the Upper and Lower Worlds.

Midsummer: See *Litha*.

Mighty Dead: The sanctified, or enlightened dead, of the Witchcraft traditions, akin to the saints, bodhisattvas, or ascended masters. See also *Hidden Company*.

Mithras: The Greek version of the Persian god Mithra, who became the focus of a Mystery Tradition in Greece and Rome, popular with the Roman military and seen as a solar god. The Mithraic Cult influenced much of the symbolism of the emerging Christianity.

Modron: A Welsh Great Mother goddess. Mother of Mabon. Honored at the Autumn Equinox.

Monism: Theological concept stating that essentially all things are a manifestation of one thing. A guiding principle found in alchemy and Hermeticism.

Moon: The second of the ancient "planets" associated with the inner self, emotions, and karma, and with Yesod on the Tree of Life. Moon magick involves dreams, psychic abilities, and the astral tides to manifest or banish, and is considered the most important heavenly sphere in magick and Witchcraft, as it rules magick and links us to the other planets and stars.

Moon Goddess: In modern Witchcraft, the Moon is most often seen as an embodiment of the Goddess, representing her triple phase of maiden in the waxing Moon, Mother for the full Moon and crone for the waning Moon, regenerating in the darkness and becoming maiden again.

Morrighan: Also Morrigu, Morgan, Morrigan and Morhigan. An Irish goddess of battle, sorcery and sexuality, also associated with crows and horses. Seen as a triad along with the goddesses Anu, Badb and Macha or Badb, Macha and Nemain.

Mother Nature: An expression of the life force of Mother Earth.

Mu: See *Lemuria*.

Muggle: A modern term for one who is not magickally oriented.

Mutable: The energy of adaptability, change, or endings in the Zodiac. When the Sun enters a mutable sign, a season is about to end and change to the next.

Mystic: One who seeks to experience and eventually transcend different forms of divinity to achieve unity with the godhead without form.

Namer: A name in the Temple of Witchcraft for the Middle Self, akin to the personality. The part of consciousness that identifies with the "I" and likes to categorizes and name things.

Native American: A reference to the indigenous tribes of North America.

Neopagan: The "new pagans" or modern people reconstructing, reviving and reinterpreting the ancient European pre-Christian beliefs. See also *Pagan*.

Neptune: The planet of higher love, romanticism, art, and ecstasy, associated with both sea gods and with sacrificial gods such as Dionysus, and with Chokmah on the Tree of Life.

New Age: Reference to the coming, or new, aeon, associated with the sign of Aquarius, and predicted as a potential "golden age" of enlightenment and peace.

Nine Waves of Creation: In Temple mythos, the nine emanations creating the upper world deities, underworld deities and middle world deities, the angels, faeries and land spirits, the minerals, the plants and the animals.

Norse: The Scandinavian people before the Christianization of Scandinavia. The teachings and traditions of Norse Paganism are closely related to German and Saxon Paganism.

Oak: A tree of magick, power and leadership, associated with storm gods, lightning and mistletoe. An image of the world tree in the Fourth Great Age.

Occult: from the word ocular, meaning eye, and referring to things usually left unseen or hidden, such as esoteric wisdom.

Octagram: The eight pointed star. A symbol of Hod, Mercury and the Wheel of the Year.

Odin: The Norse all father god, who teaches the mysteries of the Runes and other forms of magick and inspiration.

Offering: The act of giving something of value or meaning for a higher cause. In the case of Witchcraft, often something given to a spirit or deity as an act of worship and love, and to strengthen the connection, communication, and reciprocity.

Omphalos: the "navel of the world" or sacred center. A concept often connected to the World Tree or World Mountain, and in ritual, used to denote the ritual space as the center of the world/cosmos.

One Sorcerer: See *First Witch*.

Oracular Mysteries: The mystery of the first degree in the Temple of Witchcraft, involving meditation, psychic development and awareness of inner consciousness. Focus of this degree is upon attaining inhibitory trance state, psychic defense, magickal theory, spirit contact and past lives. Oracular refers to the ancient oracles, those who gave psychic prophecy or prediction.

Oran Mor: The Great Song or Song of Creation. An expression of the Logos, or Word, in the Temple Tradition. The Great Song is both sung by the God, and is the God.

Ordination: The consecration of a High Priest/ess as a legal minister, with the same rights and responsibilities as other legal ministers. One who is ordained often takes Reverend, or Rev. as a title.

Orpheus: A mythic Greek figure known for his musical and poetic skills, whose teachings based on his experiences in the underworld became the basis of the Orphic Mystery Schools

Ostara: The spring solar festival when the Sun is transitioning from the sign of Pisces to Aries. Also known as the Vernal Equinox and considered the start of spring. Named after the little-known Teutonic deity Eostre, goddess of spring, regeneration, and resurrection. In the Wheel of the Year mythos, the Goddess arises from her underworld winter slumber and brings back the life force as the first flowers and greens. Eggs, as a symbol of life and regeneration, are traditionally decorated as mystical charms of blessing, healing and protection, and seeds are blessed and planted.

Other People: A reference to the people outside of the Biblical Garden of Eden, i.e. the Pagans. Also known as the People of Nod.

Overworld: See *Upper World*.

Owl: A bird totem of magick, mystery and hidden things, as well as the totem of the Third Great Age.

Pagan: From the Latin *paganus*, meaning "of the land", "country dweller" or "civilian." Grew to refer to Pre-Christian indigenous traditions of Europe and their reconstructions and reinterpretations. Sometimes used incorrectly to reference any non Abrahamic religion, including such wide traditions as Hinduism, Daoism, Buddhism, and Native American Spirituality, though such traditions usually do not refer to themselves as Pagan. See also *Neopagan* and *Heathen*.

Panentheism: Theological belief that divinity is simultaneously immanent and transcendent, encompassing all of nature and the universe, and all non physical or unproven dimensions of reality.

Pangaea: The land of the First Great Age. The name is a union of Pan, or All, and the Earth Mother Gaea.

Pantheism: Theological belief that everything in existence is divinity. All of nature, including all the universe, is "God." Divinity is immanent.

Paradise: Considered to be the original state of consciousness, but also the realm of return in the Seventh Great Age. See *Zep Tepi*.

Paradox: A statement or teaching usually with two opposing arguments that cannot be logically reconciled, yet can nonetheless be true. Paradox is the key to the mysteries.

Path of the Moon: The celebration of the lunar cycle through the practice of esbats, or Moon Circles. The Path of the Moon can celebrate the Full Moons, Dark Moons and/or New Moons, but usually consists of at least twelve to thirteen rituals a year, if not twenty six or more.

Pentacle: A five pointed star in a circle. Also a three dimensional object of the five pointed star, with or without the circle.

Pentagram: A five pointed star. Also a two dimensional drawing of the five pointed star, with or without a circle.

People of the Book: A reference to the prophetic traditions of the Abrahamic religions, based upon testaments and prophetic revelations over mystical technique.

Pine: A tree of leadership and an image of the World Tree in the Second Great Age.

Pisces: The twelfth sign of the Zodiac. Mutable water. Ruled by the planet Neptune and formerly Jupiter. The sign associated with the age of sacrificed gods and the rise of Christianity. The sign of the

Ecstatic. Key phrase is I BELIEVE and key words include empathic, mystical, and addictive.

Plane of Forces: A reference to the elemental energy planes of earth, air, fire and water. Can also refer in general to the seven (six plus the physical) subtle planes.

Pluto: The planet of higher will, transformation, and rebirth, associated with gods of the underworld and with Kether on the Tree of Life.

Polytheism: Religious belief in multiple gods.

Polytheism, Hard: Polytheism that believes individual gods are separate and distinct from one another.

Polytheism, Soft: Polytheistic philosophy stating that individual gods and goddess are linked to, or emanate from, a greater God and Goddess, who may in turn, emanate from a greater source. A concept popularized in modern occultism by Dion Fortune.

Precession of the Equinoxes: The cycle of the Great Year caused by a wobble in the Earth's axis, causing each great month to process backwards through the Zodiac signs for slightly more than 2000 years.

Prometheus: A Greek titan who steals fire from Zeus and brings it to humanity, seen both as technology and the desire to be illuminated and seek knowledge. He is punished and imprisoned by Zeus, but later freed by Hercules. Often compared to Lucifer.

Psychic Body: In the system of seven bodies, the sixth body, where psychic information is received and projected. Associated with the brow (third eye) chakra.

Psychic Plane: In the system of seven planes, the sixth plane, the connecting medium of psychic experiences.

Qabalah: Meaning "to receive" an esoteric system of cosmology and magick historically rooted in Jewish mysticism, though some believe it to also have links to Babylon and Egypt. Later fused with teachings on Christian mysticism, alchemy, Hermeticism, and other Pagan philosophies. Many variant spellings, though a loose guide is when spelled with a K, such as Kaballah, it refers to Jewish tradition, with a C, as in Cabala, it is Christian teachings and with a Q, Hermetic or magickal teachings.

Ram Horned God: Manifestation of the animal side of the God at Ostara, at the spring, through the sign of Aries. The depiction of the god as Amun Ra.

Reclaiming: A modern Witchcraft tradition started in California, drawing from the Feri Tradition, Dianic Witchcraft, and including environmentalism, political activism, feminism, and non-hierarchical structures. Author Starhawk is a founder of the Reclaiming tradition and one of its best known members.

Reconstructionism: The process of reconstructing a previous tradition out of the available lore, without other influences from different cultures or general occultism and metaphysics. There are many Pagan Reconstructionist movements and traditions, based in Celtic, Norse, and Egyptian religion, to name a few.

Red Ray: The First Ray or Straight Line, associated with Will, Power and the Angelic Path.

Resurrection Mysteries: The Mysteries of the Fifth degree in the Temple of Witchcraft, focusing on the rebirth that occurs from the creation of the Waters and Food of Life, alchemical allegories for the development of consciousness.

Retrograde: An astrological term for an optical illusion where a planet appears to be going backwards in its orbit, indicating that the areas of its rulership will seem to be disrupted, difficult, or moving backwards. Usually a great time for introspection and personal growth around that planet's area of rulership.

Rome: An ancient empire based on the Italian peninsula that expanded greatly, bringing many of its Pagan practices and philosophies across the western world. At various times in the Roman empire, magickal, religious and philosophical concepts from the Greek, Romans, Egyptians, Celts, Jews, and Christians mingled. Many people's modern concept of what it means to be Pagan is influenced by what we know of the Roman Empire.

Rosicrucianism: A series of organizations, groups and philosophies, some real and some mythic, associated with the adept Christian Rosenkreuz and using the rose cross as a symbol. The teachings are both on the mysteries of nature and the mysteries of the spirit worlds, drawing from ancient wisdom. They have influenced Freemasonry and Hermetic teachings, and their influence can be felt in modern Wicca today.

Sabbat: One of the eight Wheel of the Year holidays in modern Paganism and Witchcraft.

Sacred Space: Ritual space. An area that has been blessed, consecrated or hallowed for the purpose of ritual, magick and/or worship. While most Pagans believe all space is sacred, the act of declaring it so through ritual prepares one for deeper communion.

Sacrifice: A ritual or action "to make sacred" or "holy," usually an offering that implies giving up something for the sake of another. In the context of Witchcraft and Paganism, a special offering. Most modern Witches today have nothing to do with any type of blood or animal sacrifice, though we respect the rights of our fellow magickal practitioners in the traditions of African Diasporic religion, to do so. In such cases, sacrifices were and are often part of communal meals, where the meal is shared with the spirits and the people. It is a difficult concept for those disconnected from their own food source and the reality of death in the chain of life.

Sagittarius: The ninth sign of the Zodiac. Mutable fire. Ruled by the planet Jupiter The sign of the Teacher. Key phrase is I UNDERSTAND and key words include education, philosophy, and tolerant.

Salmon: A totem in the Celtic traditions associated with Wisdom, eating the hazelnuts of wisdom. A totem of the First Great Age.

Salt: Sodium chloride, a mineral used for purification and protection. The alchemical principle of solidness, also that which unites sulfur and mercury. In the three soul model, salt can be associated with the Middle Self, or personality identifying with the body, though its associations change with your level of initiation.

Samhain: The fall Celtic fire festival when the Sun is in the zodiac sign of Scorpio, popularly celebrated on October 31. Known as the meat harvest, it is a celebration of the ancestors, when contact with the realm of the dead is easiest due to the life force withdrawing to the underworld as the foliage withers and traditionally herds were slaughtered for the meat to be salted or smoked as food in the winter. Celebrated through divination, communing with the spirits, and veneration of the gods and goddesses of the underworld. The popular holiday of Halloween is based upon this holiday.

Saturn: The planet of karma, manifestation, and binding, associated with gods and goddesses of time, death, and the eternal, and with Binah on the Tree of Life.

Scorpio: The eighth sign of the Zodiac. Fixed water. Ruled by the planet Scorpio and formerly by Mars. The sign of the Guardian. Key phrase is I DESIRE or I TRANSFORM, and key words include powerful, mysterious, and obsession.

Sea People: A mythic name to the people of Atlantis, considered to be great sailors. There is evidence of an ancient, globe-faring civilization, of which the Atlanteans may be a memory.

Second Ray: The Blue Ray of Love and Trust, linked with nature and the Faery Races, symbolized by the Bent Line and Bending Branch.

Second Road, The: The astral plane, the psychic medium through which many Witches and magicians travel. Also the title of a newsletter produced in the 1990s by Temple founders Christopher Penczak and Steve Kenson.

Secret Fire: The divine spark found in all things and in the godhead and center of the cosmos.

Self Initiation: An initiation performed by oneself onto oneself, considered controversial by many if considered a true initiation, and not a dedication. Differentiated from the Solitary Initiation.

Separation: The third alchemical operation, associated with the planet Mars, the element Air, the solar plexus chakra, and the fifth gate of the Underworld.

Septagram: A seven pointed star, sometimes known as a faery star. Also associated with the seven gates of the Underworld and all the related teachings.

Serpent: While the snake is the Western Water guardian in the Temple's totem scheme, indicating the medicine of change and transformation, the Serpent is a manifestation of the Child of Light, Child of the Goddess and God, embodying Wisdom, and the union of the three rays.

Servitor Spirit: A purposely created thoughtform for a specific function. Also known as an artificial elemental or construct.

Shadow: A natural part of the self that simply dwells in darkness, but can have imprinted upon it all the feelings, thoughts and memories we seek to discard without integration. Soon it can act as an independent entity, often sabotaging our conscious efforts. The third degree of the Temple is designed to build a relationship with the shadow.

Shaman: A practitioner of shamanism, though some distinguish a shaman who holds the function of a recognized spirit worker, ceremonial leader, and healer in their community from a shamanic practitioner, an individual who practices the techniques of shamanism for personal self-development outside of a larger community or cultural context.

Shamballa: The eastern name for the city of enlightened masters and immortals. It is often described as part of the mountains of Tibet, or hidden in the Gobi desert.

Shaper: A name in the Temple of Witchcraft for the Lower Self, akin to the child self or animal self, being pre-verbal and requiring ritual play for clear communication.

Shrine: An altar where the focus is to honor one or more spirits or deities, where offerings can be made.

Singer: An image of the God of Creation and the Word, or Logos.

Sky Father: Manifestation of the God as the Sky sheltering the Earth, associated with the winds, clouds, storms and sometimes the Sun and stars.

Smudge: To spiritually cleanse using the smoke of purifying herbs and resins, such as sage or frankincense.

Solitary Initiation: An initiation not done through the agency of human hands, but directly from the spirits. Distinguished from Self Initiation.

Solitary Wicca: Modern Wicca practiced outside of a traditional coven structure, as popularized by Scott Cunningham.

Song: See *Oran Mor*.

Sorcery: The practice of magick, specifically one who influences fate or fortune. Linked to the practice of sortilege, or divination by lots predicting the future. Some use sorcery to distinguish magick, often for personal gain, from the religion of Witchcraft. Others include sorcery as a part of Witchcraft.

Soul: The divine or essential self. In the Temple, using the three soul model, when used singularly, soul most often refers to the highest self.

Source: The Godhead, Divine Plane, and Divine Mind.

Spear of Victory: One of the four hallows as viewed in the Temple of Witchcraft. Associated with Light and elemental fire.

Spring Equinox: See *Vernal Equinox*.

Stag: Animal totem of protection, perception and the forest, the traditional earth element animal totem of the Temple and the totem of the Fourth Great Age.

Stag Horned God: Manifestation of the animal side of the God at Mabon and in the autumn. Cernunnos and Herne are manifestations of the stag god.

Star Goddess: The Goddess as embodied by the entire universe. In the Charge of the Goddess poetry, the Goddess is dual, microcosm of the Earth and macrocosm of the Stars.

Stone of Sovereignty: One of the four hallows as viewed in the Temple of Witchcraft. Associated with Law and elemental earth.

Straight Line: The First Ray or Red Ray, associated with Will, Power and the Angelic Realm.

Sufi: Considered to be a mystical branch of Islam, focusing on meditative techniques to experience divinity directly. The famous Whirling Dervishes are a branch of Sufism. While many consider it the most pure form of Islam, others believe its practices predate Islam and simply took on Islamic terminology and images when Islam became the dominant religion. British occultists such as Doreen Valiente, speculated on the influence of Sufic cults on the Witchcraft teachings of Europe.

Sulfur: The alchemical principle of individuality and light, in a triad with mercury and salt. In the three soul model, Sulfur can be associated with the Higher Self and the individual soul, though its associations change with your level of initiation.

Summer Solstice: The longest day of the year, when the Sun is transitioning from the sign of Gemini to Cancer, and officially the start of the summer season in the modern calendar, despite also being known as Midsummer, as well as Litha in the Wheel of the Year.

Sun: The first of the ancient "planets" associated with the self, and personality, and Tiphereth on the Tree of Life. Sun magick involves health, wealth and success.

Sun God: In modern Witchcraft, the Sun is most associated with the God and life force. While we know the true Sun is eternal to us, it waxes and wanes over the course of the year, creating the image of the God of Life and the God of Death.

Supreme Ritual of the Pentagram: The most complex pentagram ritual of modern Hermetic magick.

Swan: A totem that guides souls, associated with the constellation Cygnus and myths of bird people. One of the potential totems of the Seventh Great Age.

Sword of Truth: One of the four hallows as viewed in the Temple of Witchcraft. Associated with Life and elemental air.

Tantra: A term for eastern traditions that are more mystical and esoteric, usually involving ritual, mantra, visualization, mandalas, meditation and sometimes, ritual sex. It often translates as "text" or "to weave" but implies esoteric associations of those terms.

Tara: The center of Ireland and the home of the Tuatha de Danann, or Children of the Goddess Danu.

Taurus: The second sign of the Zodiac. Fixed earth. Ruled by the planet Venus. The sign whose cosmic age is associated with the building of ancient temples and bull sacrifices. The sign of Steward. Key phrases is I HAVE and key words include stability, sensuality, and stubborn.

Templar: The Knights Templar were a Christian order associated with the crusades and the Temple of Solomon, existing during the

Middle Ages. They were deemed heretical by Pope Clement V and accused of practicing blasphemy, homosexuality, Witchcraft, and worshiping an idol or head named Baphomet. Theories abound that it was simply a political hunt as the order became more wealthy than most monarchs by introducing the first international banking system, while others believe they were truly an occult order with teachings far beyond the Church. The mystery of the Order of the Templars continues to inspire occultists, magicians, and Witches today.

TempleFest: The Temple of Witchcraft's annual summer festival, started in 2010.

Teutons: Reference to the Germanic tribes or people. The Norse and Anglo-Saxons were both branches of the German people, it is sometimes used in reference to all Germanic branches collectively.

Thelema: Greek for "will." The religion proposed by Aleister Crowley, as outlined in *The Book of the Law* text.

Third Ray: The Yellow Ray of Wisdom and Cunning, linked with the Creatures of Flesh and Blood, and symbolized by the serpent or the lightning strike.

Thorn: References Hawthorn, also known as Whitethorn, Blackthorn, and Rose thorn bushes, all powerful plants with associations to the Faery Realm. One of the wisdom trees in the mythology of the Third Great Age.

Thoughtform: Also known as an artificial elemental or construct, a semi-permanent magical energy capable of performing a series of simple magickal commands over an extended period of time. Some thoughtforms are unintentionally created constructs that become unconsciously trapped in the energy body and must be removed for optimum health and energy.

Three Souls: Reference to the multiple soul theory found in ancient mysticism, stating that we have at least three souls, or soul parts. Today, the most basic description is the Higher Self, the Middle Self and the Lower Self.

Towathan: The collective spirit of the Temple of Witchcraft.

True Will: The true purpose or soul's desire of any individual. Considered to be a part of the Holy Guardian Angel or Higher Self, known in the Temple as the Watcher. Magick is the quest to discover and implement the True Will.

Tzadkiel: An archangel whose name translates to "mercy of God." Tzadkiel is the archangel of Jupiter and Chesed.

Underworld: See *Lower World*.

Upper World: In shamanic cosmology, the upper world is envisioned in the branches of the world tree, among the clouds, sky, planets and stars. The Upper World is a place of timeless perfection and detached knowledge. Elementally, it resonates with air and fire.

Uranus: The planet of the higher mind, innovation and inspiration, associated with both sky gods and rebellious figures such as Prometheus and Lucifer, and with Da'ath on the Tree of Life.

Uriel: An Archangel whose name usually translates to "light of God" or "brightness of God." Uriel is the archangel of Earth in the microcosm, usually called upon in the North of ceremonial magick circles, and the archangel of Da'ath and Uranus in the Macrocosm of the Tree of Life, being the archangel of hidden knowledge.

Venus: The planet of love, romance, friends and attractions, associated with goddesses of love and sex, enchantresses, faery queens, and Netzach on the Tree of Life.

Vernal Equinox: Also known as the Spring Equinox. A day of equal light and darkness as the balance is moving towards the light. The transition of the Sun from the sign of Pisces to Aries, starting the Zodiacal new year and the spring season. Also known as Ostara in the Wheel of the Year tradition.

Vine: A sacred plant associated with death and resurrection gods, and often considered a "tree" in the Celtic Ogham tree systems. One of the wisdom trees in the mythology of the Second Great Age.

Virgo: The sixth sign of the Zodiac. Mutable earth. Ruled by the planet Mercury, though some associated the asteroids or Chiron with it. The sign of the Healer or Servant. Key phrase is I ANALYZE and key words include service, discernment, and perfectionism.

Voodoo: Voodoo (also Vodou and Voudoun, among other spellings), is an African Diasporic religion where native African beliefs and practices were syncretized with Catholicism. Two of the more well known, and different, strains are associated with Haiti and New Orleans. Due to the convergence of occult practices in small shops in America, Voodoo has been an influence upon the modern American Witchcraft movement.

Wandering Stars: The seven classical planets of Mercury, Venus, Mars, Jupiter, Saturn and the two luminaries of the Sun and the Moon.

Watcher: A name in the Temple of Witchcraft for the Higher Self, akin to the Holy Guardian Angel or Bornless One.

Watchers: A race of angels said to have "fallen" from heaven and taught humanity the customs of civilization, including art, science, agriculture, writing, and Witchcraft. Many believe the first Witches were descended from these fallen spirits.

Water: An element that embodies the principles of flow, emotion, astral tides, and love. Symbolized by the cup, chalice, or bowl.

Way of Wyrd: Following the path of fate, and learning to weave your own fate, through magick, through bending and shaping the pattern of the tapestry.

Weaver: An image of the Goddess of Creation and Fate.

Web: The tapestry of fate woven by the Goddess. The interconnections of all things, seen and unseen.

Well of Fate: The Well of Wyrd, that feeds the World Tree and helps grow out our "fate" in the world, or the course of all our lives.

Well of Healing: See *Well of Life*.

Well of Inspiration: See *Well of Memories*.

Well of Life: Also known as the Well of Healing, a repository of life force.

Well of Memories: The Well of Inspiration, where all knowledge, magick and lore resides.

Well of Wyrd: See *Well of Fate*.

Wheel of Fate: The lowest of the three wheels, Qabalistically consisting of Malkuth, Hod, Tiphereth, Netzach and Yesod in the center. Its sacred sound is Awen.

Wheel of Judgement: The highest of the three wheels, Qabalistically consisting of Tiphereth, Geburah, Binah, Kether, Chokmah, Chesed with Da'ath in the center. Its sacred sound is Aum.

Wheel of Justice: The middle of the three wheels, Qabalistically consisting of Yesod, Hod, Geburah, Da'ath, Chesed, Netzach, Yesod and Tiphereth in the center. Its sacred sound is IAO.

Wheel of the Year: The modern calendar of Pagan celebrations, uniting practices and traditions from several different Pagan cultures. Most notably it unites the solar festivals (solstices and equinoxes) with the agricultural fire festivals of the Celts.

Wheel of Wyrd: See *Wheel of Fate*.

Wicca: One form of the modern revival of the religion of Witchcraft. Today, Wicca is often divided into more organized forms of British Traditional Wicca (See *Gardnerian* and *Alexandrian*) and more personal forms of self initiatory Eclectic and Solitary Wicca, as popularized by Raymond Buckland and Scott Cunningham.

Willow: A tree associated with faeries and the Moon. An image of the world tree in the Third Great Age.

Winter Solstice: The longest night of the year, when the Sun is transitioning from the sign of Sagittarius to Capricorn, and the official start of the winter season in the modern calendar, despite being known as Midwinter, as well as Yule.

Witch: A practitioner of Witchcraft. One who feels they are inherently oriented to being a Witch spiritually or genetically, or one who has been initiated into a Witchcraft tradition.

Witchblood: A controversial teaching involving either a genetic factor to Witchcraft or a spiritual factor within the blood. Some see it as exclusionary, while others believe we all have Pagan ancestors eventually, and are all therefore, "of the blood." The Witchblood needs to be awakened or catalyzed in some way, and training and initiation in Witchcraft often does just that.

Witchcraft: A science, art, and religion of magickal spirituality and philosophy. Witchcraft is considered both a mystery tradition, for the evolution of the soul, and a vocation, for practitioners to serve the greater community of people, planet, and spirits.

Witchdom: Both a term for the invisible paradise of "enlightened" or "realized" Witches, different from the Summerlands, and a term for the sovereign space upon which all Witches stand, live and serve.

Witching Hour: A liminal time for magick, usually referring to midnight or just before dawn, but also the time beyond time that all Witches step into to perform magick, regardless of the physical time.

Wolf: Animal spirit of protection, family and teaching. Potential totem of the Seventh Great Age.

World Tree: The axis mundi, or world axis that is the center of the world/universe, envisioned as a great tree. The most well known World Tree in myth is the Norse tree Yggdrasil. Other depictions of the axis mundi is a mountain or ladder.

Wotan: A variant name of the god Odin/Woden.

Yellow Ray: the Third Ray or Crooked Line, associated with Wisdom, Cunning and the Witch.

Yetzirah: The third of the four Qabalistic Worlds, corresponding with the element of air and the realm of the angels.

Yew: A magickal tree associated with ancient wisdom, death and the ancestors. Sometimes known as the "needle ash." The image of the World Tree in the First Great Age.

Yoga: Usually translated as "yoke" or "union" referring to unite oneself with the divine through its practice. While most commonly thought of as a physical exercise system, there are many ways to practice yoga and yogic philosophy

Yuga: A Cosmic cycle in the Vedic, or Hindu, system of calculating the Great Ages. Creation is divided into four descending and four ascending Yugas, though there is disagreement on the actual time span of each yuga. Akin but not synonymous to an Aeon or Age in the Western system of cosmic ages.

Yule: The winter solar festival when the Sun is transitioning from the sign of Sagittarius to the sign of Capricorn, starting the winter season. Celebrated as the return of the light and the birth of the god as the sun child. Yule logs, mistletoe, decoration of evergreens and lighting candles are traditional parts of this celebration. Also known as the Winter Solstice.

Zep Tepi: In Egyptian myth, the time before time where the gods, humans and all of creation were in harmony upon the Earth.

Zodiac: The twelve signs appearing around the Earth. The sidereal zodiac is the actual stellar constellations named after the signs, while the tropical zodiac is the measurement of the space around the Earth, associated with the seasons. At one time, both were in alignment, but they now create two complimentary, but different systems of astrology. Zodiac is sometimes translated as "wheel of animals" even though many of the signs are not animals.

The Temple of Witchcraft
MYSTERY SCHOOL AND SEMINARY

Witchcraft is a tradition of experience, and the best way to experience the path of the Witch is to actively train in its magickal and spiritual lessons. The Temple of Witchcraft provides a complete system of training and tradition, with four degrees found in the Mystery School for personal and magickal development and a fifth degree in the Seminary for the training of High Priestesses and High Priests interested in serving the gods, spirits, and community as ministers. Teachings are divided by degree into the Oracular, Fertility, Ecstatic, Gnostic, and Resurrection Mysteries. Training emphasizes the ability to look within, awaken your own gifts and abilities, and perform both lesser and greater magicks for your own evolution and the betterment of the world around you. The Temple of Witchcraft offers both in-person and online courses with direct teaching and mentorship. Classes use the *Temple of Witchcraft* series of books and CD Companions as primary texts, supplemented monthly with information from the Temple's Book of Shadows, MP3 recordings of lectures and meditations from our founders, social support through group discussion with classmates, and direct individual feedback from a mentor.

For more information and current schedules, please visit: *www.templeofwitchcraft.org*.

www.ingramcontent.com/pod-product-compliance
Lightning Source LLC
Chambersburg PA
CBHW050551170426
43201CB00011B/1647